Growing the Virtual Workplace

The Integrative Value Proposition for Telework

Alain Verbeke

Robert Schulz

Nathan Greidanus

Laura Hambley

Edward Elgar
Cheltenham, UK • Northampton, MA, USA

Published by
Edward Elgar Publishing Limited
Glensanda House
Montpellier Parade
Cheltenham
Glos GL50 1UA
UK

Edward Elgar Publishing, Inc.
William Pratt House
9 Dewey Court
Northampton
Massachusetts 01060
USA

A catalogue record for this book
is available from the British Library

Library of Congress Cataloguing in Publication Data
Growing the virtual workplace : the integrative value proposition for telework /
Alain Verbeke . . . [et al.].
    p.   cm.
Includes bibliographical references and index.
1. Telecommuting.   I. Verbeke, Alain.
HD2336.3.G76   2007
331.25—dc22

2007030268

ISBN 978 1 84720 389 2

Printed and bound in Great Britain by MPG Books Ltd, Bodmin, Cornwall

Contents

Acknowledgements   vi
Foreword by Scott McNealy   vii
Summary   ix

1   Introduction   1

PART I   TELEWORK IMPACTS   13

2   Telework impacts: the employee perspective   15
3   Telework impacts: the organizational perspective   36
4   Telework impacts: the societal perspective   53

PART II   TELEWORK TRACKING   73

5   Telework tracking: the employee perspective   77
6   Telework tracking: the organizational perspective   89
7   Telework tracking: the societal perspective   102

PART III   TELEWORK IMPLEMENTATION   135

8   Telework implementation: the employee perspective   137
9   Telework implementation: the organizational perspective   151
10   Telework implementation: the societal perspective   168

PART IV   TELEWORK ADOPTION   189

11   Telework adoption: an employee perspective   191
12   Telework adoption: an organizational perspective   215
13   Telework adoption: a societal perspective   229

References   242
Index   255

Acknowledgements

The research reported in this book was supported by the McCaig Chair in Management, Haskayne School of Business – University of Calgary, Transport Canada's Moving on Sustainable Transportation (MOST) project, and Teletrips Inc., Calgary.

We should like to thank Dr Viviane Illegems, Vrije Universiteit Brussel, Belgium, for her contribution to Chapter 7. Dr Illegems' work was supported by a grant from the Onderzoeksraad, Vrije Universiteit Brussel. The authors are indebted to Ian van de Burgt, Vas Taras, Jack Maslen and Charles Backman of the University of Calgary as well as Paul Brugman and Sarah Vanden Bussche from the Vrije Universiteit Brussels for their contributions, which included data analysis and editorial feedback.

We also gratefully acknowledge the important contribution of Dr Brad Abernathy (PhD, Princeton), who carefully edited the entire draft manuscript and made numerous substantive and style changes, thereby greatly improving the quality of the book.

Finally, we should like to thank all the firms, managers, and employees who provided most of the new data presented in this research volume. Teletrips Inc. provided critical information surrounding telework tracking. Human resource managers and over 280 employees from several organizations dedicated their valuable time to complete telework-related questionnaires and provided useful input at numerous information sessions. Their views were instrumental in improving our understanding of the adoption challenges and perceived impacts of telework and the growth of the virtual workplace.

Foreword

Sun Microsystems has been committed to virtual work teams and teleworking for more than a decade. This book from the Haskayne School of Business at the University of Calgary soundly articulates the concept and implementation of telework. The book also highlights our belief and the industry's realization that The Network is the Computer, a concept Sun has been driving since the 1990s and something that has helped teleworking become a reality.

In 2001, a number of drivers came together to move telework implementation from an interesting idea to a practical and necessary reality. First, access and use of broadband technology became widespread and more comfortable to many in both the workplace and the home setting. Next, the events of 11 September delivered a sobering realization of the corporate risks of business interruptions.

In addition, shareholder and management pressures to get a handle on real estate costs grow by the day. Also, the sheer volume of traffic (and therefore commute times) has increased in many urban areas around the world. This has led to much discussion about the rising level and impact of carbon emissions and the toll this takes on infrastructure such as highways and public transportation.

In December 2001, Sun provided home-based broadband connections to any employee who wanted to work from home or a decentralized office at least some of the time. More than 50 per cent of Sun employees now participate in our telework program, officially called Open Work. As a result, we have saved about $400 million on real estate costs over the past five years and reduced CO_2 emissions by about 30 000 metric tons each year. And, our employees are happy (we probably get more work out of them too).

We 'walk the talk' at Sun. We are further ahead than most companies in this area. Over the past three years, Sun has received many awards for our Open Work program, including:

- 2006 Best Workplaces for Commuters by the US Environmental Protection Agency (EPA) and the US Department of Transportation (DOT)
- 2006 AWLP Work–Life Innovative Excellence Award
- 2005 Optimas Award presented by *Workforce Management*
- CoreNet Global Innovators Award.

In the spirit of our strategy to share or open source our technology, we share our Open Work best practices with customers and partners around the world. Our Open Work unit, under the leadership of Ian Gover, has helped customers increase productivity, morale and employee retention and save money. Many of these principles are highlighted in this book.

And, furthering our claim as the most partnered company on the planet, Sun plans to partner with Professors Verbeke and Schulz at the Haskayne School of Business in the integration of our individual capabilities. Specifically, we will publish the results of telework and virtual work teams for at least 38 000 people in our internal database.

At Sun, we like to fly our own airplanes. Using our technology to drive telework and virtual teams is a natural fit for us. Teleworking is here and The Network is the Computer.

Scott McNealy, Chairman
Sun Microsystems, Inc.
November 2007

Summary

Telework is the substitution of communication technology for work-related travel. A teleworker typically commutes a few days a week into a central office and works at a 'virtual' workplace (usually his or her home) for the remainder of the week. In this book, we argue in favour of increasing present levels of telework or, as we like to put it, growing the virtual workplace. The case for growing the virtual workplace is compelling: we provide an analysis of the integrative value proposition for telework and also develop the EOS integrative framework as a tool to understand and promote the practice.

When we use the concept of value proposition, we mean a concise and specific description of the benefits (value) of a particular course of action to a target audience or stakeholder. For example, a value proposition might describe to a customer why one company's services are superior to those of its competitors and should therefore be selected by the customer. In this particular case, there are three target audiences: employees, organizations and society at large. We talk about an *integrative value proposition* to make the point that, on the telework issue, the interests of the three stakeholders above are aligned. We therefore believe it would be a mistake to suggest a separate value proposition for each stakeholder.

Accordingly, we choose to formulate the single, unified, integrative value proposition as follows: employees, organizations and society alike should grow the virtual workplace, as the multiple, tangible benefits of telework for each of these three stakeholders greatly outweigh its costs.

The book unpacks, analyses and defends this integrative value proposition. We conclude that, if telework is implemented effectively and where appropriate, then for each stakeholder the benefits of telework will greatly outweigh the costs. A few examples will suffice here to clarify our thesis that the interests of the three stakeholders are aligned.

Employees, especially highly skilled ones, usually value flexibility and autonomy when performing their jobs. However, they also care about their organizations' costs and productivity, if for no other reason than to increase the likelihood of their continued employment. Furthermore, employees are often concerned about societal-level challenges such as the impact of business on air pollution and greenhouse gas (GHG) emissions, as they are also citizens affected by such impacts.

Organizations (meaning manager-owners or senior management representing the employer) know that employee recruitment and retention are key to their own survival and performance, and they realize that providing telework options can contribute to these organizational objectives. However, they often also genuinely care about employee job flexibility and satisfaction per se. Furthermore, they realize that the organization's environmental and social responsibility objectives can be served by telework. In this case, therefore, organizational objectives overlap to a large extent with societal objectives.

Societal decision-makers (such as politicians and public administrators) face challenges in the realms of competitiveness, community health and ecological footprint per capita. Often these decision-makers realize that performance at the national, regional or municipal level ultimately results from micro-level parameters, including organizational costs and productivity, as well as employee job flexibility and satisfaction, all of which can be served by increased telework adoption.

Thus, each of the three stakeholders not only derives net benefits from the practice of telework but also cares about the perspectives of – and outcomes for – the other two.

In order to understand how stakeholders derive these benefits and can contribute to growing the virtual workplace as efficiently as possible, we borrow from classic strategic management frameworks and categorize the telework process into four broad constructs: telework adoption (strategy formulation), implementation (strategy implementation), tracking (measurement/feedback) and impacts (performance). Using those four constructs and the three stakeholders – employees (E), organizations (O) and societal decision-makers (S for society) – we develop the *EOS integrative framework* to examine not only the interaction among employees, organizations and society, but also the interaction among telework impacts, tracking, implementation and adoption.

As an example of the first interaction, the organization's adoption of – and support for – telework may have a profound effect on the employee's decision to telework. This book discusses how actions of each of the three stakeholders affect the actions of the others. As an example of the second interaction, proper telework tracking will provide feedback that will influence the details of future telework implementation. The book discusses how actions in each of the four construct areas affect actions in the others.

Thus, the integrative value proposition and the EOS integrative framework are integrative in complementary ways. The integrative value proposition is integrative in the sense that the stakeholders' goals are aligned. The EOS integrative framework, on the other hand, is integrative in the sense that what one stakeholder does will affect what another stakeholder does, and also in the sense that actions in one construct area (such as tracking) will affect actions in other construct areas. With integration so central to the book, we clearly take a holistic approach to the phenomenon of telework.

However, we also pragmatically acknowledge the need to examine the phenomenon's constituent parts. Because each of the four constructs can be examined from each of the three stakeholder perspectives, we present a 3 × 4 matrix into which telework research can be organized. After an initial, introductory chapter, the book therefore contains 12 more chapters, one for each construct/stakeholder combination. As a consequence of this organization, readers can, if they wish, read only the chapters they consider most directly relevant to them. For example, managers could choose to read only the chapters about the organization's perspective (Chapters 3, 6, 9 and 12), while those interested in the employee's perspective may want to focus their attention on Chapters 2, 5, 8 and 11. Finally, those interested in the societal perspective will find Chapters 4, 7, 10 and 13 of particular interest. It should be noted that Chapter 7 is rather technical and geared primarily to transport economists and analysts.

We place more emphasis than other authors on telework tracking because, beyond identifying and quantifying telework impacts, tracking also provides feedback to influence future telework implementation programs. Importantly, it can change the mindset of decision-makers about the value proposition of telework.

The book contains numerous practical tips – specific to each stakeholder – on how best to implement telework. For example, for the employee, there are self-assessment, home office design and best-practice telework guidelines. For the organization, there are guidelines for telework job and employee selection, telework program design, and the management of virtual teams. For the societal decision-maker, there is a frank assessment of the real effectiveness of the six major proposed telework-enabling policies: providing moral support, disseminating information, leading by example, creating an enabling infrastructure, instituting tax and regulatory policies, and creating incentives and disincentives.

This book is written for managers, employees, policymakers and academic experts on telecommuting and the virtual workplace. Technical sections are identified as such and can be safely skipped without affecting the reader's understanding of the book as a whole.

To Our Parents and Families,
Whose Unconditional Love Transcends all Distance

It is an inconvenient truth that many people in advanced economies currently spend most of their professional lives in unfortunate office towers and inefficiently consume time, energy, and public infrastructure during their lengthy commutes to and from work.
Their lives could be so different . . .

1. Introduction

Technology is becoming increasingly sophisticated, with the speed of information exchange enabling many more options for how, when, and where work is conducted (Manoochehri and Pinkerton, 2003). Such changes have resulted in increasingly virtual organizations which are geographically distributed, electronically linked, and functionally/culturally diverse (DeSanctis and Monge, 1999). The impact of technology on individuals and organizations is widespread, and has resulted in the ability to do many jobs from anywhere at any time (Cascio and Shurygailo, 2003). One type of work arrangement that technological advancement has enabled is telework, which is the substitution of communication technology for work-related travel. The importance of studying telework is suggested by its increasing prevalence, its potential economic, environmental and social benefits, and the new set of advantages and challenges that such a work arrangement poses to both organizations and employees.

In an effort to grow the virtual workplace, this book analyses telework from an integrative perspective. An integrative view not only captures the phenomenon from societal, organizational and employee perspectives but also describes how these three levels interact with four identifiable constructs that compose telework. These constructs are derived by unbundling the process into the following four categories: impacts, tracking, implementation, and adoption. Utilizing both the current literature and results from our extensive telework case studies, we explore each of these categories using employee, organizational and societal levels of analysis.

DEFINING TELEWORK AND THE VIRTUAL WORKPLACE

The virtual workplace is a workplace unfettered by traditional limits of time and space, where employees can work from geographically dispersed areas, both within and outside standard business hours. Virtual work is largely synonymous with the concept of telework, and we use these terms interchangeably throughout this book.

Although research on teleworkers[1] is increasing, there is not yet a single agreed-upon definition of telework. One suggested definition is that

1

telework entails working away from the office one or more days per week, using a computer and/or other communication technologies (Belanger, 1999). Another definition, suggested by a leading telework information website, is: 'telework, often referred to as telecommuting, occurs when paid workers reduce their commute by carrying out all, or part of, their work away from their normal places of business, usually from home' (InnoVisions, 2004).

For the purposes of this book, telework will be defined as 'the substitution of communication technology for work-related travel, which may take place from home, a satellite office, a telework centre, or any other workstation outside of the main office' (Illegems and Verbeke, 2003). Teleworkers are usually home-based, but may also work from the aforementioned locations (Potter, 2003). This kind of virtual work may range from occasional to full-time, and is typically done on a part-time basis (for example, one or two days per week). It excludes doing extra work, above and beyond a full-time work day, from home during the evenings or weekends. An employee's telework arrangement may be formal (that is, the employer has a formal telework policy) or informal (that is, arranged on an informal or ad hoc basis with the employee's supervisor).

Telework is often mistakenly treated as being 'all or nothing', thereby comparing teleworkers with non-teleworkers (that is, office workers). The belief that telework needs to be a full-time work arrangement is a common misconception. Many teleworkers remotely participate in their workplace on a part-time basis, spending the rest of their time at the office. This provides an effective balance between time in the office to collaborate with colleagues and attend meetings and time teleworking to complete more focused tasks that do not require face-to-face (FTF) contact. Therefore, telework should be conceived on a continuum ranging from occasional to full-time.

Our definition of telework includes 'peak shifting', in which the employee alters her commuting schedule to avoid peak traffic times, teleworking before or after going into the office. Thus, a part of the employee's regular work is done from home in order to decrease commute time. Although this has been excluded from most definitions of telework, we believe it is an increasing phenomenon that warrants inclusion.

HOW PEOPLE TELEWORK

Teleworkers are able to work virtually by using various information and communication technologies (ICT). These include advanced information technologies such as e-mail, videoconferencing, teleconferencing, discussion groups, chat rooms, project management software, collaborative design tools, knowledge management systems, and message boards. Along with these more advanced technologies, ICT includes less sophisticated but widely used communication technologies such as the telephone and fax machine (Bell and Kozlowski, 2002). Note that, on our definition of 'telework', such technologies need not involve continuous, online communications (Illegems and Verbeke, 2003).

RATIONALE FOR STUDYING TELEWORK

Telework's employee, organizational, and societal-level impacts justify further study on this phenomenon. Telework affects multiple stakeholders, including the teleworkers themselves, their families, their organizations, various levels of government, and society at large (Illegems and Verbeke, 2003).

Figure 1.1 displays some of the many stakeholders that are influenced to varying degrees by telework. This is not an exhaustive list of all stakeholders, but identifies those frequently discussed in the literature. As shown in the figure, telework affects individuals (for example, employees and contract workers), small and large groups (for example, families, organizations, cities), and various levels of government. In this book we analyse the telework process from three broad perspectives: societal, organizational, and employee.

The virtual work arrangement has potential economic and non-economic cost savings and can increase efficiencies and productivity. At the same time, telework has potential negative impacts, and many challenges impede telework's full potential. Further study will measure telework impacts and offer a guide to achieving the optimal benefits of this type of work arrangement.

Beyond the above rationale, the continuing increase of telework adoption highlights the importance of further study into this phenomenon. The Gartner Group predicts that by 2008 there will be over 100 million people worldwide who telework more than eight hours per month (Gartner, 2005). In Canada, approximately 1 million people teleworked at least eight hours per week in 2006, and 1.65 million at least eight hours per month (Gartner, 2005). In the US, the Department of Labor found in 2001 that 19.8 million persons did some work from home as part of their primary job (US Department of Labor, 2001), and by 2004 the Association for Advancing Work from Anywhere reported that 24.1 million US workers teleworked (from home) at least one day per month (ITAC, 2004). In Europe, there are around 20 million teleworkers (Gareis, 2002).

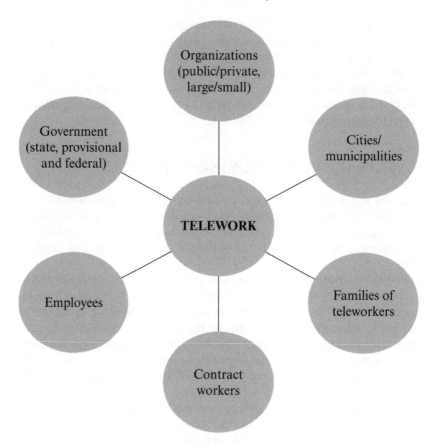

Figure 1.1   Telework stakeholders

The growth of telework coincides with and is enabled by the growth of technology. Technology has been a major driver of telework, making it possible for many employees to do some or all of their work from outside of the office, typically from home. In particular, the Internet has played an important enabling role; a recent survey found that in 2003 6.7 million Canadian households had Internet access, a 5 per cent increase from 2002 (InnoVisions, 2004). Of these, 4.4 million, or 65 per cent, had a high-speed cable or telephone-line connection, up from 56 per cent a year earlier.

Another recent driver of telework is the increasing awareness and acceptance of such work arrangements. The US Employment Policy Foundation, a non-profit, public policy research and educational foundation based in Washington, DC, that focuses on workplace trends and policies, suggested that roughly 65 per cent of jobs are amenable to teleworking, at least on a part-time basis (EPF, 2001). At the same time, people seem to desire the flexibility that telework offers; for example, a survey of both New York and London commuters reported that 77 per cent of respondents would telework if their employer offered that option (Netilla Networks, 2004). The increasing rates of telework, the increased openness of employees toward it, and the many potential local and global impacts of its adoption provide a solid rationale for further study on this type of flexible work arrangement.

THE INTEGRATIVE VALUE PROPOSITION FOR TELEWORK

When we use the concept of value proposition, we mean a concise and specific description of the benefits (value) of a particular course of action to a target audience or stakeholder. For example, a value proposition might describe to a customer why one company's services are superior to those of its competitors and should therefore be selected by the customer. In this particular case, there are three target audiences: employees, organizations and society at large. We talk about an *integrative value proposition* to make the point that, on the telework issue, the interests of the three stakeholders above are aligned. We therefore believe it would be a mistake to suggest a separate value proposition for each stakeholder.

Accordingly, we choose to formulate the single, unified, integrative value proposition as follows: employees, organizations and society alike should grow the virtual workplace, as the multiple, tangible benefits of telework for each of these three stakeholders greatly outweigh its costs.

The book unpacks, analyses and defends this integrative value proposition. We conclude that, if telework is implemented properly and where appropriate, then for each stakeholder the benefits of telework will greatly outweigh the costs. A few examples will suffice here to clarify our thesis that the interests of the three stakeholders are aligned.

Employees, especially highly skilled ones, usually value flexibility and autonomy when performing their jobs. However, they also care about their organizations' costs and productivity, if for no other reason than to increase the likelihood of their continued employment. Furthermore, employees are often concerned about societal-level challenges such as the impact of business on air pollution and greenhouse gas (GHG) emissions, as they are also citizens affected by such impacts.

Organizations (meaning manager-owners or senior management representing the employer) know that employee recruitment and retention are key to their own survival and performance, and they realize that providing telework options can contribute to these organizational objectives.

However, they often also genuinely care about employee job flexibility and satisfaction per se. Furthermore, they realize that the organization's environmental and social responsibility objectives can be served by telework. In this case, therefore, organizational objectives overlap to a large extent with societal objectives.

Societal decision-makers (such as politicians and public administrators) face challenges in the realms of competitiveness, community health and ecological footprint per capita. Often these decision-makers realize that performance at the national, regional or municipal level ultimately results from micro-level parameters, including organizational costs and productivity, as well as employee job flexibility and satisfaction, all of which can be served by increased telework adoption.

Thus, each of the three stakeholders not only derives net benefits from the practice of telework but also cares about the perspectives of – and outcomes for – the other two.

THE EOS INTEGRATIVE TELEWORK FRAMEWORK

The potential and realized impacts of telework suggest the need for a conceptual framework that offers an integrative and robust method for both analysing and conveying current information on the telework phenomenon. Thus, in this book we develop a conceptual framework that encompasses multiple components of the telework implementation process, while also analysing these from various perspectives. Borrowing from classic strategic management frameworks, we categorize the process into four broad constructs: telework adoption, implementation, tracking and impacts. Figure 1.2 incorporates these constructs into a generalized strategic management process framework (note that the strategic management constructs are included in parentheses).

In the traditional model, the telework adoption construct centres on the decision to adopt or not adopt telework with particular attention paid to the characteristics that predict the direction of this decision. In classical strategic process models, the adoption (strategy formulation) construct is influenced by goals, internal resources, and the external environment.

The telework implementation construct revolves around the activities that move the decision to adopt telework to a realized process. Implementation, by its very nature, is usually process driven and often suggests operational or functional protocols to achieve the successful realization of a strategic choice.

The telework tracking construct centres on the process of capturing, analysing and providing feedback on the consequences or impacts stemming

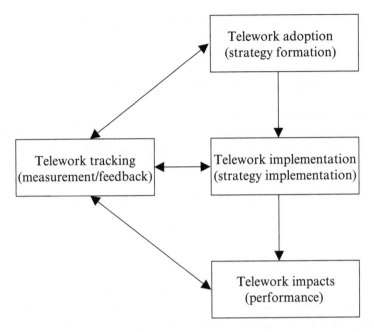

Figure 1.2 Traditional telework strategic management model

from telework adoption and implementation. As depicted in Figure 1.2, there is a feedback loop in the model. All the constructs are linked together through this loop by the telework tracking construct. Thus, telework tracking acts as the linchpin for the telework process model, providing bidirectional connections between telework adoption, implementation and impacts. While often neglected by academia and practitioners alike, tracking is integral to telework adoption and implementation as it provides a mechanism for ongoing feedback to the various stakeholders. Tracking is also critical in providing an objective measure of impacts or consequences. Telework impacts do not directly come from telework tracking, but the ability to quantify such impacts through tracking may influence subsequent telework adoption and implementation, thus further influencing telework impacts.

The impact construct, much like the performance variable in strategic management models, captures the consequences of increases or decreases in telework adoption, as well as the effectiveness of the telework implementation.

While the above traditional model adequately captures the constructs involved in the telework process, an attempt to grow the virtual workplace requires a new model with a different focus. In the traditional model described above, telework impact is the final objective or dependent measure in the telework process. It is our contention, however, that to grow the virtual workplace the traditional model must be inverted in order to shift the focus toward increasing telework adoption. Thus, represented linearly, the **old** model took the form:

Adoption → Implementation → Tracking → Impact

The new model, however, shifts the focus to growing the virtual workplace and focuses on the influence that each construct has on increasing or decreasing telework adoption. Thus, represented linearly the **new** model takes the form:

Impact → Tracking → Implementation → Adoption

While the newly conceived framework shifts the focus to the growth of the virtual workplace, we also contend that a truly integrative framework must also incorporate the perspectives of key telework stakeholders. As previously described, these stakeholders can be categorized into three broad groups or levels: employee, organizational, and societal. Incorporating these three stakeholders and the four constructs from the telework process framework produces the EOS integrative telework framework, depicted graphically in Figure 1.3.

The EOS integrative framework places telework adoption at the centre of the figure with subsequent concentric rings representing each of the other constructs. Telework adoption is the central ring not only because it is the focus of the new framework (used to grow the virtual workplace) but also because it is the decision (to telework or not to telework) that ripples out through implementation, tracking, and ultimately telework impacts.

While telework adoption is the centre of the EOS integrative framework, the framework is unified: each ring or construct relies on and influences the other rings or constructs within the framework. Finally, the integrative telework framework includes employee, organizational, and societal perspectives. As depicted in Figure 1.3, these three perspectives intersect all four constructs of the telework process, indicating that each construct can be viewed from each stakeholder perspective. The three perspectives are also given equal weighting in the integrative framework, as each perspective interacts with, affects, and relies on the other two stakeholder perspectives.

OVERVIEW OF THE BOOK

While the EOS integrative telework framework provides a holistic view of the telework phenomenon, it also provides a mechanism to unbundle

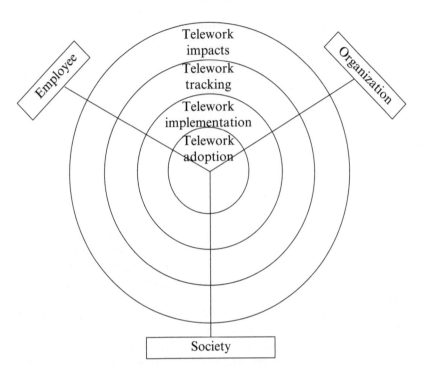

Figure 1.3 EOS integrative telework framework

telework research into a number of manageable categories. Essentially the framework's three stakeholder levels and four process constructs produce a 3 × 4 matrix (12 components) into which telework research can be organized. The framework matrix is displayed in Table 1.1, which indicates the chapter in this book that covers each topic.

As depicted in the table, this book is divided into four parts that align with the four constructs from the telework process model. Following the EOS integrative framework, the first part of the book focuses on telework impacts from the three stakeholder perspectives. Thus, in Chapter 2 we review the impacts of telework from the employee's perspective by grouping positive, negative, and neutral impacts into the following five categories: telework's impacts on (1) the organization, (2) operations, (3) organizational efficiency, (4) external stakeholders and (5) other aspects of employees' lives.

In Chapter 3 we review the organizational level telework impacts and group these impacts into the following four categories: impacts on (1) strategic human resource (HR) issues, (2) operational HR issues, (3) organizational efficiency, and (4) external stakeholders. Finally, in Chapter 4 we explore societal-level telework impacts. These impacts largely come from

Table 1.1   The EOS integrative telework framework

	Telework impacts (Part I)	Telework tracking (Part II)	Telework implementation (Part III)	Telework adoption (Part IV)
The employee perspective	Ch. 2	Ch. 5	Ch. 8	Ch. 11
The organizational perspective	Ch. 3	Ch. 6	Ch. 9	Ch. 12
The societal perspective	Ch. 4	Ch. 7	Ch. 10	Ch. 13

telework-induced commute reductions, which can in turn influence air pollution, road congestion, noise pollution, road accidents, energy consumption, road maintenance, new road construction and usage of mass transit. Beyond commute trip reductions, cities and regions are also affected by non-commute-related telework impacts such as economic impacts, new job opportunities, community development and safety, environmental impacts beyond emission reductions, and operational continuity.

Part II of the book transitions from telework impacts to telework tracking. In this part we note that, while often neglected, the tracking of this workplace trend is integral to telework adoption and implementation as it provides a mechanism for ongoing feedback to the teleworker, the organization, and government policymakers. Essentially we argue that one cannot quantify these impacts or grow the virtual workplace without a mechanism for tracking and measuring telework adoption. Although there are many tracking options at the employee, organizational, and societal levels, they are rarely used. In Chapters 5 and 6 we review a number of telework tracking options for employees and organizations, respectively. For illustrative purposes we then provide a more detailed description of the Teletrips tracking tool. In Chapter 7 we provide societal-level tools, in the form of economic models and standard coefficients, to assist in quantifying telework penetration and the associated spillover effects.

In Part III of this book we turn our focus to telework implementation. We note that the discussion surrounding implementation becomes progressively more complex as one moves from the employee level to the organizational level and finally to the societal perspective. Thus, Chapter 8 of this book reviews basic employee-level guidelines. These fall into the categories of self-assessment, home office design, and telework policies and procedures (for example, time management, work/life balance, communication and socialization). In Chapter 9, the discussion shifts to organizational implementation of telework. Implementation procedures at this level fall within the categories of telework job selection, telework employee selection, the design of the telework program, evaluation concerns, and the management of virtual teams.

In Chapter 10 we cover telework implementation at the societal level, which is highly complex owing to the numerous stakeholders, objectives, and intervening variables inherent to this level of analysis. In this chapter we equate much of societal telework implementation with public policy, and within the telework context we review the influence of the following six policies: moral support, disseminating information, leading by example, supporting enabling infrastructure, regulations and tax codes, and incentives and disincentives.

The final part of this book, Part IV, focuses on the telework adoption decision that lies at the core of the telework process. At the employee and organizational levels we rely heavily on our primary data (employee and organization survey results) to explore the telework adoption decision. In Chapter 11 we analyse our employee-level data, which suggest that employees with more 'experience' (be it age, organization tenure, or work experience) or more children at home are more likely to adopt telework. Telework adopters also rated potential telework impacts significantly higher (more positive) than non-telework adopters. Not surprisingly, one of the most salient predictors of employee telework adoption was support for telework from the employee's organization.

Acknowledging that organizational perceptions of telework greatly influence employee-level adoption decisions, we turn our attention to the organizational telework adoption decision in Chapter 12. At the organizational level strategic HR factors were perceived as the most positive telework impact, while operational HR issues were the most negatively rated impacts. This suggests that managers believe that, while telework may have positive impacts on retaining, developing and attracting employees, it makes the operational functioning of employees less effective.

Finally, in Chapter 13 we turn our attention to societal-level telework adoption, which is simply the aggregation of the data from all of a society's teleworkers and organizations engaged in telework. These adoption rates vary across cultures and countries. At the societal level we also offer our analysis of the future of telework, including the saturation point and future drivers of growing the virtual workplace. We believe that, with advances in ICT, the virtual workplace will continue to grow, and we forecast an increasing societal awareness and acceptance of telework. In this chapter we also identify five significant factors that will continue to encourage future virtual workplace growth. We categorize these into the five 'C's of climate change mitigation, continuity planning, congestion avoidance, competing for employees, and communication advances. We conclude Chapter 13, and the book, with a summary of the overall findings from the four parts of the book, particularly focusing on the relationship between these findings and growing the virtual workplace.

READERSHIP OF THIS BOOK

This book will be of interest to several groups either directly or indirectly impacted by telework. While we build an integrative framework that will be of interest in its entirety to most audiences, the organization of the book around the components of the EOS integrative framework allows for quick reference to chapters of particular interest to different stakeholders. These include:

1. Senior and mid-level managers/HR managers of small to large organizations in both the private and public sectors who may currently have teleworkers or be considering telework as an option. In particular, these managers will be interested in the organizational perspective on telework as outlined in Chapters 3, 6, 9 and 12.
2. Employees of small to large, public or private organizations who currently telework or may be considering telework as an option. Employees will be particularly interested in the analysis from the employee's perspective found in Chapters 2, 5, 8 and 11.
3. Policymakers such as mayors, city councillors and municipal administrators who may be interested in assessing telework's impacts (as telework may influence regional development policy, transport policy, environmental policy, urban planning policy and labour policy (Huws et al., 1999)). These policymakers will find the chapters from the societal perspective (4, 7, 10 and 13) most applicable to their interests.
4. Academic experts on telecommuting and the virtual workplace, such as transport economists and management scholars. This audience will be particularly interested in the societal-level telework tracking templates overviewed in Chapter 7 and the primary data analysis of employee- and organizational-level telework adoption found in Chapters 11 and 12.

NOTE

1. Teleworkers are also referred to as 'telecommuters' in the literature. 'Telecommuter' refers specifically to substituting only the daily commute to and from work, whereas 'telework' is a broader term encompassing the substitution of communication technology for any work-related travel (Illegems and Verbeke, 2003).

PART I

TELEWORK IMPACTS

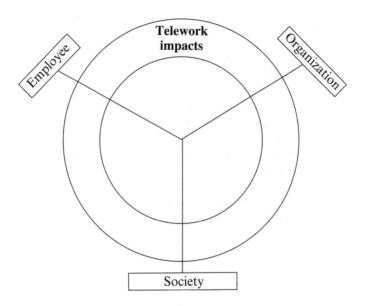

In this first part of the book we explore telework impacts from employee, organizational and societal perspectives. The impacts, or consequences, of telework take many forms: positive, negative or neutral; direct or indirect; short-term, medium-term or long-term. Exploring such impacts is important as they often constitute the end-goal or performance metric of adopting and implementing telework behaviour. For many stakeholders, it is the consequences of telework that will influence future adoption decisions.

The following three chapters use the extant literature on telework impacts, presenting the impacts from each of the employee, organizational, and societal perspectives.

In Chapter 2 we assess the impacts of telework from the employee's perspective. We group them into the following five categories: impacts on (1)
the organization, (2) operations, (3) organizational efficiency, (4) external
stakeholders and (5) other aspects of employees' lives.

In Chapter 3 we review the impacts of telework from the organizational
perspective. Organizations implement telework for a variety of reasons, but
most importantly because it can reduce costs and increase productivity,
and because employees view it as a benefit (Illegems and Verbeke, 2003).
Telework becomes a possibility only if management perceives that the
benefits associated with telework outweigh its costs (Illegems and Verbeke,
2003). The organizational effects of telework may be grouped into the following four categories: impacts on (1) strategic HR issues, (2) operational
HR issues, (3) the organization's efficiency and (4) external stakeholders.

In Chapter 4, the final chapter of this section, we explore the impacts of
telework from a societal perspective. We divide these impacts into two
broad categories; the first revolves around the impacts of commuter trip
reductions, thereby reducing road transport externalities; the second captures social, ecological, and economic telework impacts not directly related
to commute trip reductions. The first category, telework-induced commute
trip reductions, can influence air pollution, road congestion, noise pollution, road accidents, energy consumption, road maintenance, new road
construction and usage of mass transit. The second category, non-
commute-related telework impacts, includes economic impacts, new job
opportunities, community development and safety, environmental impacts
beyond emission reductions, and operational continuity.

2. Telework impacts: the employee perspective

The growth of the virtual workplace will ultimately be dictated by the adoption of telework at the employee level. There are many reasons why employees decide to adopt or not adopt telework. In most cases the employee must decide that the personal benefits of telework outweigh the costs in order to consider this work arrangement (Illegems and Verbeke, 2003). The employee's personality and life situation will affect the relative weights assigned to these advantages and disadvantages (Illegems and Verbeke, 2003).

This chapter describes the positive and negative impacts of telework as identified by researchers and practitioners. These may be grouped into the following five categories, all viewed from the employee's perspective: impacts on (1) the organization, (2) operations, (3) organizational efficiency, (4) external stakeholders and (5) other aspects of employees' lives. We will discuss the positive, neutral, and negative impacts in each of these categories in the following sections. Telework impacts are classified as neutral if research findings are mixed (that is, some research has found it to be a positive impact, while other research treats it as a negative impact). It is also important to note that, while we classify telework impacts as positive or negative according to current research, the impacts experienced by one employee may not apply to another, but we have classified these according to what research has generally found for the groups of people studied.

IMPACTS ON THE ORGANIZATION

As we have claimed with our concept of an integrative value proposition, employees have a vested interest in how telework affects their organization, and in turn themselves as employees. Telework can positively influence employees' commitment and loyalty to their organization, their commitment to excellence, their job satisfaction, and their decision to join an organization. In these areas, the employee's interests and the organization's interests overlap. Potential neutral or ambiguous telework impacts include employment contract flexibility. Also, teleworkers may or may not feel part

Table 2.1   Telework's organizational impacts

Positive impacts	Neutral impacts	Negative impacts
Joining the organization	Flexibility of employment contract	Knowledge sharing with other employees
Commitment and loyalty to the organization	Feeling part of the organization's culture	
Commitment to excellence	Design and structure of employee's job	
Job satisfaction	Status/promotion in the organization	

of their organization's culture, depending on the specifics of that culture. Telework can also positively, neutrally, or negatively influence the design and structure of an employee's job, depending on the job in question. A common fear about telework is that it will negatively affect one's status within an organization. Teleworkers may feel they are a new class of workers that is 'out of site, and therefore out of mind' (Illegems and Verbeke, 2004). Further, they may feel that physical isolation from the office will decrease promotional opportunities (Kurland and Egan, 1999). However, in organizations that value flexibility and are output-oriented, telework could have a positive impact on teleworkers' status and promotion. The nature of this effect (negative or positive) is thus very much dependent on the organization considered. Furthermore, empirical research indicates that these employee status/promotion fears are generally unfounded.

Teleworking can negatively affect employees' ability to share knowledge within the group. This is particularly true in the sharing of tacit knowledge, which is often shared by FTF interaction in the office, such as through spontaneous, informal, water cooler-type meetings. A summary of organizational impacts from the employee perspective is presented in Table 2.1, followed by a more detailed discussion of each of these impacts.

Positive Telework Impacts

Joining the organization
Telework can positively influence an individual's decision to join an organization. Research has found that recruiting potential is a positive impact of telework. For example, in a survey of large and small US organizations 50 per cent of employees stated that having the option to telework was a 'very attractive' incentive to join a company (Ceridian, 1999). Also, an

April 2005 Ipsos-Reid poll indicated that 42 per cent of Canadians said they could be retained at one job or lured into another by the option to telework from home at least one day a week (InnoVisions, 2004). Thus, the incentive of telework is definitely considered a perk or benefit by many individuals, and may positively influence their decision to join a company. It may also help employees narrow down choices between potential employers, as those that offer flexible work arrangements such as telework may be favoured in job decisions.

In particular, telework can increase work opportunities for persons with disabilities (Illegems and Verbeke, 2003). It allows these individuals to work from their homes, thereby better accommodating their personal needs than would a centralized office. This opens up work and career possibilities for people who may otherwise be 'sidelined', such as persons with physical disabilities who need special accommodations (Raghuram et al., 2003).

Commitment and loyalty to the organization
Telework has been found to positively impact employees' commitment and loyalty to their organization. For instance, a survey of 665 American workers found that 78 per cent of teleworkers called themselves 'very committed' to their company, compared with only 53 per cent of non-teleworkers (Wirthlin Worldwide, 1999). Similarly, another US survey found that 66 per cent of employees rated the option to telework as an 'excellent' reason to stay with an organization (Ceridian, 1999). According to these studies, if the company is willing to accommodate the employees' situation by allowing telework, then the employees feel more valued and see this willingness as a demonstration of their company's commitment to them.

Furthermore, telework facilitates an employee staying with an organization in cases of employee or employer relocation (Illegems and Verbeke, 2003). Thus, if the organization relocates, the teleworkers are more independent of location and thus may be able to retain their jobs even when moving is not an option. Likewise, if an employee needs to relocate, the option of telework provides a means of staying with the organization.

Commitment to excellence
Telework has been found to increase employees' commitment to excellence. The previously mentioned survey of 665 American workers found that, compared with non-teleworkers, teleworkers were significantly more positive in their attitudes about working (Wirthlin Worldwide, 1999). Satisfied teleworkers tend to be more productive and demonstrate better teamwork (Manoochehri and Pinkerton, 2003). Virtual work can therefore lead employees to be more positive and committed to achieve excellence in their work. This is considered a positive impact of telework from the employee's

perspective, as it is likely to lead to increased satisfaction and more rewards and recognition for high performance and commitment.

Job satisfaction

Telework has generally been found to positively impact employees' job satisfaction (Illegems and Verbeke, 2004). A survey of AT&T teleworkers found that 66 per cent were more satisfied with their jobs since beginning a telework arrangement (with only 1 per cent reporting that they were less satisfied (Roitz et al., 2004)). The Wirthlin survey of 665 American workers has already been mentioned (Wirthlin Worldwide, 1999); further support can be gleaned from a survey of 5000 teleworkers of BT, one of Europe's leading telecommunication companies, that found 90 per cent of them satisfied or very satisfied with teleworking (Hopkinson et al., 2002).

Neutral Telework Impacts

Flexibility of employment contract

Telework may offer organizations greater employment contract flexibility, as it enables the organization to offer less costly work arrangements that may be on a part-time or contract basis (Illegems and Verbeke, 2003). Such flexibility may or may not be positive from the employee's perspective, depending on career goals and work arrangement preferences. For example, one employee may want the security and stability of a full-time employee contract and will view any changes to this arrangement negatively. Another may enjoy the greater flexibility that comes with doing part-time or contract work as a teleworker, thus viewing this as a positive change. We have classified this as a neutral telework impact owing to the potentially differing views of employees.

Feeling part of the organization's culture

Teleworkers may or may not feel part of their organization's culture, depending on the specifics of that culture. Some organizational cultures support telework, while others do not (for example, they are suspicious that teleworkers are not 'pulling their weight' or are 'slacking off'). Thus, an organization's culture is an important determinant of whether teleworkers feel isolated or connected, supported or shunned (Ellison, 2004). Teleworkers who feel isolated and shunned are more likely to be dissatisfied, less productive, and leave the organization. In contrast, those who feel connected and supported are likely to be more satisfied, productive, and committed. Because the organization's culture can either positively or negatively affect the teleworker's feelings of inclusion in that culture, this impact is also categorized as neutral.

Design and structure of employee's job

Telework may positively, neutrally, or negatively impact the design and structure of an employee's job, depending on the job in question, making this impact neutral as far as the employee is concerned. A job may be suitable for telework, with only small adjustments required to its design and structure. The design and structure of an employee's job is negatively affected by telework only if extensive changes are required to adapt it to telework, making it less challenging or interesting. Such major changes to the core functions and tasks of a job may lead the employee to experience increased frustration and stress (Smith et al., 2003). When only minor changes to a job are required (for example, changes in how information is transmitted and communication takes place), its design and structure would be affected neither positively nor negatively.

Telework can also have a positive effect on job design and structure. A pharmaceutical company, for example, gave researchers home-based offices to replace their company-based offices, which enabled them to radically change the way they performed research (Helms and Raiszadeh, 2002). These employees could write up experiments and conduct much of their writing and administrative work from home, while continuing to access the lab when needed. These jobs were therefore positively affected by telework, as they were carried out in a more efficient way that better matched the nature of the work and the employees' personal styles. Thus, whether the design and structure of a job is positively or negatively affected by telework depends on the nature of and changes to the job in question.

Status/promotion in the organization

A common fear for employees is that telework will negatively affect their status within an organization. Teleworkers can feel like a lower class of worker that is, as quoted in the introduction to this section, 'out of site, and therefore out of mind' (Illegems and Verbeke, 2004). Physical isolation from the office can lead to the impression that promotional opportunities will pass them by (Kurland and Egan, 1999). However, in organizations that value flexibility and are output-oriented, telework could have a positive impact on teleworkers' status and promotion. The nature of this effect (negative or positive) is thus very much dependent on the organization considered.

Furthermore, research indicates that these employee fears are unfounded, thus leading us to classify employee status/promotion as neutral in this regard. For example, over 90 per cent of teleworkers at AT&T state that teleworking has not had a negative impact on their career (Roitz et al., 2004). In fact, 38 per cent say that teleworking has helped their career advancement. It is suggested that employees maintain their status and advance by staying in regular contact with influential people, and by making periodic (for example, weekly) visits to the office to balance FTF with virtual work.

Research on teleworkers in Europe found that employees who were already teleworking, or positively inclined to telework in the near future (adopters), did not see telework as influencing their promotion possibilities (Illegems and Verbeke, 2004). In contrast, non-teleworkers with negative views toward telework (non-adopters) viewed telework as more negatively influencing promotion possibilities. Researchers recommend that, in order to avoid negative effects on promotion, teleworkers should keep themselves visible by teleworking only part-time (Illegems and Verbeke, 2004). Further, through their actions, organizations can show employees that telework will not adversely impact their career paths. For example, organizations can implement processes to ensure non-discrimination in performance evaluations between teleworkers and non-teleworkers (Kurland and Egan, 1999).

Negative Telework Impacts

Knowledge sharing with other employees
Organizational knowledge can be either explicit (easy to codify) or tacit (difficult to codify) (Nonaka, 1994). Telework can negatively affect employees' ability to share intra-group knowledge. More specifically, telework seems to negatively affect the exchange of tacit knowledge more than the exchange of explicit knowledge (Ellison, 2004). Tacit knowledge is often shared by FTF interaction in the office, such as through informal conversations, mentoring, and spontaneous contact between employees (for example, over coffee or at the water cooler). Although it can take place through other communication media, such as by telephone or videoconference, these methods do not allow for the same level of spontaneity as FTF interactions do. Although recent research indicates that, owing to advanced technologies, telework does not appear to negatively affect knowledge sharing between employees (Belanger, 1999), it is still thought by some employees and researchers to be a negative telework impact for employees, especially when it comes to tacit knowledge exchange. For example, teleworkers may not obtain crucial information that they can use to enhance their performance.

IMPACTS ON OPERATIONS

Another key consideration from the employee's perspective is the impact on operational HR issues. Employees experience these impacts directly, because they affect their job and work. It is important to note that the employee's perspective on these issues may differ from the organization's viewpoint.

From the employee perspective, positive impacts of telework include the ability to structure workdays and work from home when inconvenienced, thus increasing autonomy and flexibility, and reducing absenteeism. Neutral impacts of telework include effects on the employee's motivation, relationship and communication with her manager, ability to give input into work processes, and communication with other employees.

From the employee's perspective, a negative impact of telework is that she may feel that her performance is unfairly appraised, owing to being out of sight (and off-site). Telework has also been found to negatively affect informal training opportunities, such as mentoring and spontaneous learning (for example, by the water cooler, over lunch or in the hallways (Kurland and Bailey, 1999)). Virtual work can also negatively affect an employee's access to formal training opportunities (such as courses, seminars, workshops). Other potentially negative impacts are reduced availability and access to ICT, fewer relationships with other employees who do not telework, and reduced access to information needed to work effectively. Based on the literature surrounding the employee perspective, Table 2.2 offers a summary of the positive, neutral, and negative impacts that telework has on operational HR issues, followed by a more detailed description of each impact.

Table 2.2   Telework impacts on operations

Positive impacts	Neutral impacts	Negative impacts
Autonomy, flexibility and ability to structure one's workday	Employee motivation to perform specific jobs	Informal training possibilities
Reducing absenteeism	Relationship and communication with manager	Accessing formal training
	Opportunity to give input into processes	Availability of and access to ICT
	Communication with other employees in the organization	Relationships with other employees who do not telework
	Performance appraisal and manager's ability to supervise employees	Access to information needed to work effectively

Positive Telework Impacts

Autonomy, flexibility and ability to structure one's workday
Another positive impact of telework is that it increases employees' autonomy, flexibility, and ability to structure their workdays. High on the list of
telework benefits for employees is autonomy, which is defined as the degree
of discretion that the worker has in selecting appropriate work behaviours,
deciding the order and pace of job tasks, and coordinating these activities
with others (Barrick and Mount, 1993). Flexibility is also one of the most
important perceived telework benefits for the employee (Perez et al., 2002).
Compared with office work, telework has clearly been associated with
employees perceiving greater flexibility in the timing and location of their
work (Hill et al., 1998). For example, teleworkers have stated that they have
greater flexibility to work wherever and whenever makes sense, and that in
particular the flexibility to work at peak personal times (such as early
morning or late at night) is much valued. Both greater autonomy and
flexibility of work time give the employee more ability to structure her
workday.

Reducing absenteeism
One positive consequence of this increased flexibility deserves special
mention: telework reduces absenteeism. Telework enables employees to
work from their homes when they are ill (Illegems and Verbeke, 2003). Even
when employees are too sick to come into the office (for example, not
feeling well enough to commute, or contagious), working from home may
still allow them to complete some work. Further, teleworkers are less likely
to miss work for other reasons, including sick children and personal
appointments. Teleworkers can take care of personal and family needs,
and still complete the remainder of their workday from home. From an
employee's perspective this may mean higher job performance, lower stress
and potentially a reduction in lost wages. (As we will discuss in the next
chapter, reduced absenteeism is also a positive impact from the organization's perspective – yet another example of how stakeholders' interests
align, motivating an integrative value proposition.)

Neutral Telework Impacts

Employee motivation to perform specific jobs
The effects on an employee's motivation to perform specific jobs are here
classified as neutral telework impacts because it can be either positively or
negatively affected. The effects on motivation largely depend on the individual teleworker's skills and experience working virtually, as well as per-

sonality characteristics. An important key to staying motivated is avoiding procrastination, which is particularly challenging when teleworking (Dinnocenzo, 1999). For example, there are many potential distractions in the home environment, including household chores, family interruptions, personal tasks and television. To avoid these, teleworkers need to keep focused by outlining major goals and daily to-do lists, organizing their work into chunks, setting deadlines, and taking breaks or switching activities periodically (Dinnocenzo, 1999). With experience, most teleworkers should be able to develop these skills and remain motivated when working from home.

Relationship and communication with manager

Likewise, the manager–employee relationship and communications can be either positively or negatively affected. Whether managers have confidence in employees influences whether an organization adopts telework and which employees are permitted to telework (Harrington and Ruppel, 1999). The level of managerial confidence in employees is also likely to affect the relationship between managers and teleworkers.

Research has found that certain managerial styles can positively affect communications and the relationship between managers and teleworkers. Specifically, teleworkers who characterized their managers as relating to them casually and informally perceived themselves as being treated more fairly and justly than those who perceived a more formal relationship (Kurland and Egan, 1999). Further, research on European teleworkers found that they perceived telework as leading to no additional problems with a direct supervisor, and therefore having no effect on overall job satisfaction (Illegems and Verbeke, 2004).

Opportunity to give input into processes

Virtual worksites can either positively or negatively affect employees' ability to give input into the processes that affect them. If supervisors use various forms of communication (for example, FTF, e-mail, telephone) to ensure that teleworkers have a voice in the processes that affect them, then the potentially negative effects of telework are likely to be mitigated (Kurland and Egan, 1999). Teleworkers should also be proactive in giving input into processes that affect them. For example, staying visible and keeping in touch with colleagues and finding opportunities to be involved in projects, special assignments and task teams are methods of ensuring one's voice is being heard (Dinnocenzo, 1999).

Communication with other employees in the organization

In the past, telework has been thought to negatively affect a teleworker's communication with other employees in the organization. This is due to the greater perceived challenges of communicating virtually as compared with FTF in the traditional office (Belanger et al., 2001). For example, researchers found that individuals in communication-intensive jobs needed to expend more effort to adapt and structure their communications, and thus they felt less productive teleworking than in office environments (Belanger et al., 2001).

Related to decreased communication with other employees is the problem of social isolation. The previously mentioned survey of 5000 tele-workers at BT found that 19 per cent of respondents felt that one of the most significant drawbacks of telework is lack of social interaction, which can be demotivating and depressing (Hopkinson et al., 2002). These researchers give some suggestions to overcome social isolation, such as having at least one telephone call per day with another team member, even just to say 'hello'.

As with knowledge sharing, communicating virtually is becoming easier owing to enhanced communication technologies, and because many com-munications in the office now take place electronically anyway (for example, it is not uncommon to e-mail co-workers on the same floor as opposed to walking to their offices to ask questions).

A seldom recognized benefit of telework in terms of communication with colleagues is that interactions with individuals considered difficult, unpleasant or ineffective can now be reduced in number and scope, thereby eliminating the stress or emotional upset characterizing continuous, infor-mal interaction with such individuals. For these reasons, communication with other employees will be treated as a neutral telework impact.

Performance appraisal and manager's ability to supervise employees
Sometimes, employees may feel that their performance is being unfairly appraised because they are out of sight. Further, they may feel their man-agers are not providing the same level of supervision as non-teleworkers receive. However, the nature of this effect (negative or positive) depends on the management style used: if management uses a well-designed, outcome-based performance appraisal system (such as, management by objectives), the shift to telework may lead to better job performance and also better per-formance appraisals.

Managers and employees should work together to define performance goals and provide regular feedback to each other. Further, both parties should give and welcome feedback at any time; during performance reviews, the employee's performance both as a worker and as a teleworker should be discussed (Zbar, 2002). The manager should set a timetable to periodically reassess the telework program and the worker's achieve-ments, and stick to this schedule (Zbar, 2002). In sum, a well-designed and well-implemented performance appraisal system is important to ensure that teleworkers perceive that they are being fairly evaluated.

Negative Telework Impacts

Informal training possibilities

Telework has been found to negatively affect informal training opportunities, such as mentoring and spontaneous learning (for example, by the water cooler, over lunch or in the hallways; Kurland and Bailey, 1999). Employees who telework, even if only part of the time, perceived themselves as having less access to informal training/learning opportunities compared with their office-based co-workers (Cooper and Kurland, 2002). In particular, research has found that teleworkers miss three types of development activities that frequently occur in the conventional office: (1) interpersonal networking with others in the organization, (2) informal learning that enhances work-related skills and information distribution, and (3) mentoring from colleagues and superiors (Cooper and Kurland, 2002). This form of 'professional isolation' can undermine their professional development, and represents a potentially negative impact of telework for employees.

Accessing formal training

Telework can negatively affect an employee's access to formal training opportunities. For instance, workshops, courses, or seminars may be scheduled on telework days, forcing the employee to miss them. To mitigate this negative impact, teleworkers need to make a special effort to be available for formal training by coming into the office or training location as needed. Part-time telework enables employees to spend part of their workweek in the office, making them less likely to miss formal training opportunities. Full-time teleworkers, in contrast, would need to arrange their schedule to accommodate formal training opportunities that they cannot complete virtually.

Teleworkers need to be proactive in obtaining the skill development they need to perform their jobs and work virtually. In general, there is an increasing expectation that workers will take responsibility for developing their own skills and managing their own careers, rather than relying on their organizations to do this for them (Dinnocenzo, 1999). This is due to the increased rate at which people change jobs, employers, and careers, and get caught in merger/acquisition situations. Teleworkers should periodically review their development needs and actively locate resources, both within and outside their organization, to help them develop the skills necessary for their career advancement (Dinnocenzo, 1999). These actions can help mitigate the negative impact of remote work on access to formal training opportunities.

Availability of and access to ICT
Another potentially negative impact of telework is reduced availability of and access to information and communication technologies (ICT). To do their jobs efficiently and effectively, teleworkers need certain ICT, which may include fast communication links, and hardware that can handle the company's software (Manoochehri and Pinkerton, 2003). Having the necessary ICT increases teleworker productivity, performance, and satisfaction (Belanger et al., 2001). Many employees will not have the necessary ICT at home (for example, fast Internet access), and if the organization fails to supply the necessary technologies or technical support, teleworkers are likely to become frustrated and dissatisfied.

Relationships with other employees who do not telework
Another potentially negative impact of telework concerns the teleworker's relationships with employees who do not telework. This issue largely stems from resentment and distrust of teleworkers by non-teleworkers. Non-teleworkers may have misperceptions about what telework arrangements involve, and may equate being off-site with being unproductive or less accessible (Dinnocenzo, 1999). Depending on the status of these individuals, 'their [non-teleworkers] impact can range from mild annoyance to a serious undermining of [the teleworker's] credibility and effectiveness' (Dinnocenzo, 1999, p. 109).

Recommendations for teleworkers to strengthen relationships with non-teleworkers include: (1) being highly responsive to voice mail, e-mail, and other communications so that non-teleworkers view them as accessible, (2) confronting any negative comments or resentment head-on by discussing it with co-worker(s), and (3) making the time to stay connected with office co-workers through regular communication that will show a virtual presence (Dinnocenzo, 1999).

Access to information needed to work effectively
Telework may negatively affect access to the information needed to do a job effectively. The extent of this impact will probably depend on whether the information is electronic or non-electronic.

If the information needed to do one's job is largely electronic, then access to it will depend on the ICT available from a remote location, which can significantly impact productivity, performance, and satisfaction (Belanger et al., 2001). Thus, if ICT accommodates the virtual worker in getting the information she needs, she will probably be more productive and satisfied. In contrast, if technological resources are unavailable or suboptimal, completing tasks via telework may be more difficult and will lead to decreased productivity and satisfaction.

In some cases an employee may rely on non-electronic information to do her job. Whether this is the case will depend on the nature of the job and industry. For example, some companies have policies around non-electronic information that can only be accessed at the office, such as oil/gas well maps that cannot be taken home for security purposes. In these cases, teleworkers need to plan for certain days in the office to access this information. The extra time required to coordinate one's schedule around accessing non-electronic information represents a potentially negative impact of telework.

IMPACTS ON ORGANIZATIONAL EFFICIENCY

Impacts of telework on an organization's efficiency include effects on the employee's ability to get work done, as well as the employee's personal financial costs/savings.

Efficiency impacts that are positive from the employee perspective include increased productivity and reduced expenses related to coming into the office. Another positive impact is the ability to work when the office shuts down owing to natural or man-made catastrophes (such as extreme weather or bombings). Neutral impacts of telework from the employee's perspective include the reduction in office space, and the impact on teamwork. Negative impacts of telework include difficulty in scheduling meetings, and risks to the security of company data. Another negative impact of telework is the personal ICT expenditures that may be required. The telework impacts on organizational efficiency from the employee's perspective are listed in Table 2.3, and there follows a more detailed discussion of each impact.

Positive Telework Impacts

Productivity

Telework is thought to increase the amount of time spent working for employees through saved commute time, more focused time, lack of interruptions, and greater flexibility about when and where to work. By avoiding interruptions, teleworkers can more easily complete tasks that require considerable thought (Bailey and Kurland, 2002). Teleworkers who are more productive are more likely to perform well and achieve recognition and rewards. Thus, productivity is frequently cited as a positive impact of telework.

AT&T has consistently found over the past few years that increased productivity is the most significant benefit of telework (Roitz et al., 2004), with

Table 2.3   Telework impacts on organizational efficiency

Positive impacts	Neutral impacts	Negative impacts
Productivity	Availability of space in office when needed	Scheduling meetings
Expenses related to coming to the office	Teamwork	Security of company data
Capability to continue work when working in the office is impossible		Personal expenditures on ICT in home office

teleworkers reporting about one additional productive hour per workday (equating to a 12.5 per cent increase in productivity). In a survey of 2000 teleworkers at BT, 78 per cent considered themselves more productive, and 69 per cent stated that their working hours increased because of telework (Hopkinson et al., 2002). In particular, 45 per cent of respondents reported an increase of more than nine hours per week, which is a fairly large increase in working time. Interestingly, some participants noted that one reason they produce more when teleworking is in order to show non-teleworkers that they are being productive and not simply taking time off when teleworking.

Although seen as a benefit of telework through the eyes of the organization, the increase in working time due to telework may be viewed negatively by employees if it takes time away from their non-work lives. The constant availability of their computer and work may blur the distinctions between work and home and lead to overwork (Ellison, 2004). Thus, teleworkers need to set reasonable limits to their work hours to avoid taking on even more work than they did at the office (Dinnocenzo, 1999).

Expenses related to coming into the office
Telework reduces an employee's expenses related to coming into the office, clearly a positive impact of telework from the employee's perspective. By not commuting, employees can save on the costs of driving (for example, gas, vehicle maintenance, parking) or transit fare. Additional cost savings may be corporate clothing (less required as there is no need to dress up from home), dry-cleaning, food (less money spent on eating out) and other incidental expenses that would decline when away from the office (Kurland and Bailey, 1999).

Capability to continue work when working in the office is impossible
The ability to continue working when the office shuts down owing to natural or man-made catastrophes (such as extreme weather or bombings

(Daniels et al., 2001)) is another positive impact of telework. Although operational continuity is more beneficial to organizations than employees, employee benefits include continuity in employee work, and in some cases their earnings, which might be stopped if they relied on coming into the office to work. Further, teleworking during these catastrophes undoubtedly results in less stress for employees than if they had to evacuate the office.

Neutral Telework Impacts

Availability of space in office when needed
A major benefit of telework for organizations that we discuss in the next chapter is the reduction in office space costs, since work can be carried out in people's homes or less costly facilities (such as telework centres (Illegems and Verbeke, 2003)). This means that when an employee opts to telework full-time, she will no longer have a dedicated space in the office. Similarly, part-time teleworkers may also lose their dedicated space, but may end up having a shared office. Also, 'hotelling' is an option organizations some-times implement for full- or part-time teleworkers, which involves booking temporary office spaces or cubicles for a specific day or period of time. Responses to hotelling have been mixed, as employees who come in part-time tend to prefer a specific space as opposed to moving around (Ellison, 2004). Organizations such as Deloitte & Touche, however, have successfully implemented a form of hotelling, called SmartSpace, which allows profes-sionals to book various types of space as needed (Froggatt, 2001). Deloitte & Touche believes this concept has increased employee productivity, provided greater flexibility, and assisted in breaking down the typical hierarchical office environment. In sum, whether the availability of office space when employees need it is a positive or negative impact of telework seems to depend on the organization and type of workspace arrangement implemented.

Teamwork
One potential positive impact of telework on teamwork is that individuals who have difficulty getting along with others socially can now focus entirely on their work and bring only their professional skills to a team, rather than less functional inputs that may stress and upset intra-team relationships.

That being said, though, telework can easily degrade teamwork, and efforts must be made to establish and maintain effective virtual teams. Establishing shared values and trust between employees both in and out of the office is critical to success (Dinnocenzo, 1999). The key components to establishing shared values and trust in working relationships are reliability, consistency and integrity. Another key to effective virtual teamwork is establishing effective virtual meetings. This will probably involve using a combination of different technologies tailored to the nature of the meeting (for example, teleconference, videoconference, document-sharing programs), and making sure participants are trained in the use and etiquette of such technologies (Dinnocenzo, 1999).

Importantly, as will be discussed in more detail in Chapter 3, virtual communication should not replace all FTF team interaction. Thus, teleworkers are likely to perceive teamwork as more positive if they have at least periodic FTF communication with their team-mates (for example, project kick-off meetings, periodic team meetings).

Negative Telework Impacts

Scheduling meetings

Telework can make scheduling meetings more difficult for employees, so this impact is categorized as negative. Meetings involving teleworkers require greater coordination, especially FTF meetings that need to be booked for times when teleworkers are in the office. Employees may be affected by this telework impact if it causes them to spend more time and resources to schedule meetings compared with their office counterparts. We note that scheduling meetings with teleworkers is becoming easier as a result of improved ICT (for example, online scheduling programs, team collaboration tools, e-rooms, project forums).

Security of company data

As discussed in more depth in Chapter 3, an increased risk to the security of company data represents a potentially negative organizational impact of telework (Illegems and Verbeke, 2003). To mitigate this, organizations use many methods, which are continually improving with advanced security technologies. From the employee's perspective, these security measures may negatively affect their view of virtual work. Although there does not seem to be research to support this, it is likely that the added security measures (such as firewalls and extra layers of data security) present time-consuming obstacles and hassles for teleworkers. This may be especially true if adequate technical support and high-speed Internet connections are at times unavailable.

Furthermore, additional security policies for teleworkers may also cause inconvenience. For example, a policy might require teleworkers to use their computer solely for business and to access only certain information from home (Manoochehri and Pinkerton, 2003). Overall, security of company data seems to be a negative impact of telework from the perspective of employees.

Personal expenditures on IC Technologies in home office
Personal expenditures on ICT may be required by teleworkers. Depending on the organization, these expenses may or may not be reimbursed. If an organization does not supply home office technology, employees may be less interested and willing to telework (Illegems and Verbeke, 2003). AT&T, a world leader in telework programs, does not typically pay for home office equipment unless the employees have released their AT&T dedicated office space (Roitz et al., 2004). Employees who telework part-time may not want to give up their office space (for example, for a shared or hotelling situation), so may end up incurring their own personal home office expenses.

Researchers recommend that companies create policies clearly outlining which home office expenses they will and will not reimburse (Manoochehri and Pinkerton, 2003). These policies should be consistently applied across teleworkers and periodically reviewed and updated. Organizations should carefully consider which technologies or minimum equipment configurations are necessary for teleworkers to successfully carry out their work (Belanger et al., 2001).

WHAT TELEWORK MEANS FOR EXTERNAL STAKEHOLDERS

The impacts of telework on external stakeholders go beyond the organization and its employees to those affected externally, such as customers, families, and the public. It is important to consider how employees view these impacts.

Telework can potentially enhance an organization's image (Illegems and Verbeke, 2003). From the employee's perspective, this is considered positive, as employees will appreciate working for organizations that are viewed as more progressive and environmentally friendly. (As we will discuss in the next chapter, this is a positive impact for organizations as well, and thus yet another example of stakeholder interests aligning in a single integrative value proposition.) Finally, telework also opens up additional possibilities for childcare and eldercare (Illegems and Verbeke, 2003). This too we consider a positive impact of telework from the perspective of employees, as it affords them more flexibility to accommodate their families' needs (Whitehouse et al., 2002). A summary of these impacts is presented in Table 2.4.

Positive Telework Impacts

Image of organization
Telework can potentially enhance an organization's image (Illegems and Verbeke, 2003). If knowledgeable about the environmental and social

Table 2.4   Telework impacts on external stakeholders

Positive impacts	Neutral impacts	Negative impacts
Image of organization		
Possibilities for child- and eldercare		

benefits of telework, the public will view organizations offering such programs more positively (that is, as more progressive and environmentally friendly (Harpaz, 2002)). From the employee's perspective, this is considered positive, as employees will appreciate working for organizations that are viewed as more progressive and environmentally friendly.

Possibilities for childcare and eldercare
Examples of how telework provides childcare advantages for workers include giving them the flexibility to drop off and pick up children from school, and enabling them to care for sick children without having to miss work. Parents can also more easily attend school functions and after-school activities, while dealing with day care arrangements and problems more readily (Froggatt, 2001).

In the case of eldercare, teleworkers can more easily assist elderly dependents, including driving them to medical appointments, and dealing with illnesses and emergencies (Froggatt, 2001). In sum, teleworkers benefit from knowing that their dependents, such as children and the elderly, are being cared for.

OTHER IMPACTS OF TELEWORK ON EMPLOYEES' LIVES

Telework not only affects employees' work, the organization, and external stakeholders; it also has various impacts on employees' personal lives. As telework often takes place at home, it inevitably affects employees' non-work lives, positively, negatively, or both (neutrally). Overall, telework has been found to positively influence employees' work/life balance. A related positive impact is that telework contributes to a higher quality of life for employees. Neutral impacts of telework include effects on separating work and non-work life and on job stress. Table 2.5 summarizes telework's impacts on these other factors in the employee's life.

Table 2.5   Other impacts of telework on employees' lives

Positive impacts	Neutral impacts	Negative impacts
Balancing work and non-work life	Separating work and non-work life	
Overall quality of employee's life	Job stress	

Positive Telework Impacts

Balancing work and non-work life
Overall, telework has been found to positively impact employees' work/life balance. Here are some sample comments about telework's positive effects on work/life balance:

> Every morning, rather than suffering the frustrations of a morning commute, I have breakfast with my sons. (Carroll, 2004)

> Even when I am extremely busy I have time for my children in the evenings and we always cook and eat our evening meal together. I know this would be impossible with a storefront. (British Columbia teleworker quoted in InnoVisions, 2004)

> I like the fact that after my shift is over, it's over . . . no travel time, no rush hour, no added stress, and because I work mostly early morning shifts I am able to pick my daughter up from school and spend a few hours just her and I before dad gets home. I find I am less irritable and much happier since I started this job. (Alberta teleworker quoted in InnoVisions, 2004)

Research has corroborated this positive telework impact. For instance, the survey mentioned above of 5000 teleworkers at BT found that 73 per cent of its teleworkers felt that their work/life balance was good or very good (Hopkinson et al., 2002). Further, in a study examining the effects of telework on perceptions of three types of conflict (time-based, strain-based, and behaviour-based), research found that teleworkers who worked from home at least two to three days per week reported lower levels of work/family conflict in all areas (Madsen, 2003). Greater work/life balance can partly be attributed to saved commute time. The 2000 American Community Survey found that the average commute time to and from work is nearly an hour. Thus, by eliminating commuting time, telework alleviates some work/family time pressures (Potter, 2003). Telework can also help reduce conflict between work and family responsibilities by allowing for the possibility of simultaneous domestic work (for example, doing a load of laundry during a work break) (Whitehouse et al., 2002).

The improved work/life balance leads to many additional positive benefits for teleworkers. For instance, such workers are better able to take care of sick children, be available for important family commitments, and take care of personal needs (Hill et al., 1998). Personal needs can include routine doctor or dental appointments, letting tradespeople into the house, and dealing with car repairs (Froggatt, 2001). Also, the flexible scheduling of telework can assist women in balancing the dual roles of mother and worker, thereby reducing stress from potential role overload (Smith et al., 2003).

Overall quality of employees' life
Telework has generally been found to contribute to a higher quality of life for employees, owing to the many positive impacts that have been discussed in this chapter. For instance, the previously mentioned survey of 5000 BT teleworkers found that 85 per cent of them feel their quality of life is good or very good (Hopkinson et al., 2002), and 82 per cent feel that telework-ing is important or very important to their quality of life.

Neutral Telework Impacts

Separating work and non-work life
Home-based telework may result in a lack of psychological separation, making it difficult for some workers to dismiss work stressors after working hours, and also to filter out home-related stressors during work hours (Smith et al., 2003). A new teleworker must learn how to continu-ously juggle work and home pressures throughout the workday (Smith et al., 2003). A commute may serve as a useful 'interlude' between the office and home, and missing out the commute may blur this boundary (Ellison, 1999). Because their office is usually in their home, teleworkers may find it challenging to 'switch off' from work (Whitehouse et al., 2002) and may be prone to continue working when they should be finished for the day.

Teleworkers who wish to separate work from non-work must make a con-scious effort. Researchers recommend that these remote workers establish cues to let them know when it is time to leave off (Hill et al., 1998). They should also establish rituals to end their telework day, such as turning off computers and ringers on business phone lines, as well as shutting office doors.

Of course, some teleworkers enjoy the variety that comes with this lack of work/non-work separation, so we have classified this impact as neutral.

Job stress

Telework can either positively or negatively affect an employee's job stress. This largely depends on the telework arrangement and the employee's ability to separate work from non-work life. Stress may result from having to deal with work intruding on home life and vice versa (Smith et al., 2003). Telework may disrupt family relationships and cause new roles to be adopted, which can be experienced as stressful (Ellison, 1999).

Conversely, telework can reduce work stress owing to the previously discussed benefits of increased work/life balance and flexibility, and other positive telework impacts. Indeed, researchers have generally found that teleworkers believe that their work arrangements do not promote stress (Hill et al., 1998). Findings regarding job stress and teleworkers are mixed, so this impact is categorized as neutral.

CONCLUSION

Growing the virtual workplace will require highlighting for the employee telework's positive impacts while also addressing its potential negative impacts. Some impacts have been classified as 'mixed' because they may be positive, neutral, or negative, depending on the individual, the organization, and other factors. In general, many of the negative impacts of telework can be mitigated by properly implemented and managed telework programs and by employees learning how to more effectively deal with the challenges of telework. In Chapters 8 and 9 of this book we address these issues by offering telework implementation guidelines for employees and organizations. It should also be noted that in Chapter 11 of this book we explore the telework adoption decision from the employee's perspective, and there we rely heavily on the potential impacts of telework discussed above. We now turn our attention from the impacts of telework from the employee's perspective to explore potential impacts from the organizational perspective.

3. Telework impacts: the organizational perspective

Organizations implement telework for a variety of reasons, but most importantly because it can reduce costs, increase productivity, and appeal to employees (Illegems and Verbeke, 2003). However, there are also negative or neutral impacts to consider when examining the merits of telework in a workplace. Telework becomes a possibility only if management perceives that the benefits outweigh the costs (Illegems and Verbeke, 2003). This chapter provides an overview of the positive, neutral and negative organizational impacts identified in the literature. These are grouped into four categories: impacts on (1) strategic HR issues, (2) operational HR issues, (3) organizational efficiency and (4) external stakeholders. We will repeatedly observe that many of the benefits to the organization are also benefits to employees and to society at large, further justifying our decision to adopt a single integrative value proposition for telework.

As identified in the literature, each category contains a mix of positive, neutral and negative impacts, the impacts being classified as neutral if some research findings are positive and others negative. It is important to note (as we did with employee impacts) that a positive impact experienced by one organization may be a negative one for another. We have simplified this by classifying the impacts according to what research has found to be generally the case.

STRATEGIC HR ISSUES

Impacts on strategic HR issues include the long-term impacts of telework on the organization's human capital resource base (Illegems and Verbeke, 2003). These impacts cannot easily be captured in monetary terms, are often qualitative in nature, and are the broader, longer-term effects on the organization's competencies (Illegems and Verbeke, 2004). These impacts are summarized in Table 3.1 and described in more detail in the following section.

Table 3.1 Telework impacts on strategic HR issues

Positive impacts	Neutral impacts	Negative impacts
Recruiting potential	Organizational culture	Knowledge sharing between employees
Employee contract flexibility	Design and structure of jobs	
Employee commitment to excellence		
Employee retention/loyalty		

Positive Telework Impacts

Recruiting potential
Recruiting potential is an organization's ability to recruit talent from either the immediate area or other regions, and increased recruiting potential has been found to be a positive impact of telework. This opens up new labour markets such as individuals with disabilities and those who are unable to work full-time in an office (for example, because of young children or elderly dependents) (Illegems and Verbeke, 2003). Without the option of telework, these sources of labour can go unutilized.

Research findings have supported recruiting potential as being a positive impact of telework. For example, research by Ceridian Employer Services, a Minneapolis-based provider of outsourced payroll and employer services, found that 50 per cent of employees polled at large and small US companies said the ability to telework was a 'very attractive' incentive to join a company (Ceridian, 1999).

Employee contract flexibility
Telework may offer organizations greater flexibility in dealing with the labour force (Illegems and Verbeke, 2003). From the organization's perspective, this is a positive impact. For example, during periods of workload or market fluctuation, telework offers employers the option of retaining part-time or contract employees, thus meeting HR requirements during peak periods while providing cost savings, both in terms of full-time salaries and office space costs, during low-demand periods. Companies such as IBM have adopted telework programs as an alternative to layoffs (Helms and Raiszadeh, 2002). This gives some employees the option to telework rather than be laid off, and has been a successful program overall. Another form of employee contract flexibility is that non-strategic employees can be retained as contractors, thereby reducing the costs incurred by organizations (Illegems and Verbeke, 2003). The added contract flexibility

and associated cost savings offered by telework may not always be viewed positively by employees or unions, but are nonetheless considered a telework benefit from the organization's perspective.

Employee commitment to excellence

Another positive impact of telework is increasing employees' commitment to excellence. The previously cited survey of 665 American workers demonstrated that teleworkers were significantly more positive in their attitudes about working than non-teleworkers (Wirthlin Worldwide, 1999). Further, teleworkers rated their company more positively than non-teleworkers on almost all corporate performance attributes. Satisfied teleworkers have been found to demonstrate increased productivity and teamwork (Manoochehri and Pinkerton, 2003). Thus, telework can lead employees to be more positive and satisfied, and hence more committed to excellence in their jobs. From the organization's perspective, this increased commitment to excellence is a positive impact of telework as it results in higher performance and commitment, as well as lower turnover.

Employee retention/loyalty

Employee loyalty and retention is another positive impact of telework. According to the survey of 665 American workers (Wirthlin Worldwide, 1999), teleworkers were much more likely to call themselves 'very committed' to their company than non-teleworkers (78 per cent versus 53 per cent). The survey of large and small US companies by Ceridian Employer Services also found that telework increases employee retention/loyalty, with 66 per cent of employees surveyed stating that having telework as an option is an 'excellent' reason to stay with a company (Ceridian, 1999).

Neutral Telework Impacts

Organizational culture

An organization's culture provides members with shared norms, values and expectations to help them survive uncertainties they regularly encounter (Kurland and Egan, 1999). The impact of telework on an organization's culture may be positive or negative, and the direction of these impacts is greatly affected by the culture's openness to telework. Strong assumptions about management and work make some organizations less open to telework than others (for example, when work is performed strictly between 9 a.m. and 5 p.m. or when subordinates must be seen and directly controlled) (Standen, 2000). Thus, whether telework negatively or positively affects an organization's culture depends on the specific culture in question and the proportion of employees who telework.

Telework may positively affect culture through 'liberalizing' it, or engendering greater shared values and trust across the organization (Standen, 2000). Other authors conclude that telework is more likely to negatively affect an organization's culture, as teleworkers may be less socialized in the culture (Kurland and Egan, 1999). In particular, teleworkers may be excluded from the informal network and the organization's socialization process, and therefore feel less a part of the corporate culture. This may especially be the case for new employees who start teleworking without adequate socialization in the office. It is suggested that problems around socialization can be mitigated by implementing part-time telework (Illegems and Verbeke, 2003). Another potential negative impact of telework is that poorly implemented telework programs will dilute an organization's culture as teleworkers will drift away from the organization's values (Standen, 2000).

Overall, an organization needs to encourage and support telework initiatives in order for telework to positively affect its culture. Further, leaders need to work at building trust and sharing information across virtual and office workers, so that organizational culture can be positively influenced by telework.

Design and structure of jobs

Not all jobs are suitable for telework. Organizations must identify which types of jobs are best suited for telework by analysing job characteristics (Manoochehri and Pinkerton, 2003). Some jobs may be suitable for telework with only minor adjustments to their design and structure. The design and structure of jobs is negatively impacted by telework only if extreme changes are required to adapt the job to telework, such as when the core functions and tasks need to be completely revamped. For example, if the job is redesigned and consequently becomes less challenging and interesting, telework would be considered as negatively affecting job design and structure (Smith et al., 2003). In most cases, however, only minor changes are required (for example, changes in how information is transmitted and communication takes place). Whether the effect on the design and structure of jobs is a positive or negative impact of telework remains to be researched.

Negative Telework Impacts

Knowledge sharing between employees

Telework is often thought to decrease or negatively impact the sharing of tacit knowledge between employees, which in turn negatively affects the organization as a whole. This is due to the perception that teleworkers are 'left out of the loop' and excluded from relevant meetings or information exchanges. Although ICT can help organizations distribute explicit knowledge, it is much less useful for transferring tacit knowledge (Ellison, 2004).

In contrast to the above negative impact, recent research indicates that telework may not negatively affect knowledge sharing between employees. Research that analysed communication patterns in distributed work groups found that teleworking seems to have no impact on communication structure (Belanger, 1999). In other words, teleworkers seem to be included in the office network, and are involved in knowledge sharing at an equal level to their office counterparts. This is probably due to the enhanced communication technologies available to both office and teleworkers and the fact that a significant amount of communication in the office is now conducted electronically. More research is needed, however, to determine whether knowledge sharing is no longer a negative impact of telework.

OPERATIONAL HR ISSUES

Impacts on operational HR issues encompass the impacts of telework on the day-to-day operations of the organization. These impacts tend to be shorter-term than the previously mentioned strategic HR impacts, and include the positive and negative impacts of telework on absenteeism, work time (that is, number of work hours per day), social contact, promotion opportunities, training possibilities (such as mentoring), training costs, employee performance appraisals, and the manager's ability to supervise employees. These are summarized in Table 3.2.

Positive Telework Impacts

Reducing Absenteeism
A positive impact of telework is that it may reduce absenteeism by allowing employees to work from their homes when they are feeling unwell (Illegems and Verbeke, 2003). In other words, telework may lead to a redefinition of 'too sick to work' because, without having to commute or meet FTF with co-workers, one's level of illness may still allow for some level of productivity (Illegems and Verbeke, 2004). Further, employees who can telework are less likely to miss work owing to other reasons, such as sick children and personal appointments. Indeed, in the 1999 America National Telework Survey, Joanne H. Pratt Associates found that, if workers were unable to telecommute while managing personal and family needs, they would be absent from work on an average of 45.3 additional occasions, representing a total of 22 workdays (Potter, 2003). Telework enables workers to take care of personal family needs (most occasions only requiring two to

Table 3.2   Telework impacts on operational HR issues

Positive imapcts	Neutral impacts	Negative imapcts

Reducing absenteeism
Working time
		Social contact
		Promotion opportunities
		Training possibilities
		Training costs
		Appraising employee
		  performance
		Manager's ability to
		  supervise employees

four hours of their time) and complete the remainder of their workday in their home office. Further support comes from a study of European HR managers from organizations already implementing telework, who rated reduction in absenteeism as a positive impact of telework (Illegems and Verbeke, 2004). On this issue, the interests of the employee, the organization and society align.

For organizations in particular, decreased absenteeism can translate into large financial savings. For example, results from the 1999 Telework America National Telework survey found that employers can save $10 000 per teleworker per year from decreased costs of employee absenteeism and retention when employees telework (Pratt, 1999).

Working time
Another positive impact of telework for the organization is increasing employees' working time, or the number of hours they work each day. This is thought to be due to teleworkers having fewer interruptions, social interactions, and breaks than their office counterparts. Teleworkers may also increase their work time by applying the saved commute time to their workday (Illegems and Verbeke, 2003). Increased working time may not always be viewed as a positive impact by employees, but it offers potential productivity advantages from the organization's perspective.

Negative Telework Impacts

Social contact
A lack of social contact, or social isolation, is commonly cited as a negative impact of telework (Smith et al., 2003). Socially isolated employees are a risk for organizations as they are more likely to be dissatisfied, to be less productive, and to leave. Social isolation is particularly problematic for

those who telework full-time and are rarely in the office. For part-time tele-workers who may spend a considerable amount of time at the office, social isolation is less of an issue (Smith et al., 2003). Also, if telework takes place at a satellite office or telework centre, its negative effects on social isolation may be greatly decreased (Illegems and Verbeke, 2003). Interestingly, a study of 83 HR managers in Brussels found that managers who had already implemented telework viewed social isolation as less serious than those for whom the problem was theoretical (Illegems and Verbeke, 2003). In other words, some of the problems related to telework implementation as per-ceived by organizations not engaged in telework, such as social isolation, turn out to be less serious than expected.

Promotion opportunities

Telework is often thought to negatively affect an individual's promotion opportunities, especially if the organization uses subjective as opposed to objective performance evaluations (Illegems and Verbeke, 2003). Researchers have found that virtual workers often equate being out of sight with being out of mind for promotions and other organizational rewards (Kurland and Egan, 1999). This effect, discussed in more detail in the pre-vious chapter, affects organizations in that it may result in turnover of employees who feel they are being given less than fair consideration for pro-motions. Applying consistent, objective performance measures across tele-workers and office workers is thought to significantly decrease the risk of excluding teleworkers from promotions (Illegems and Verbeke, 2003).

Training possibilities

It is generally thought that telework negatively affects training opportun-ities, especially informal training such as mentoring and spontaneous learning that takes place by the water cooler, over lunch, or in the hallways (Kurland and Bailey, 1999). Research has found that employees who tele-work, even if only part of the time, perceived that they had less access to informal development opportunities than their on-site colleagues did (Cooper and Kurland, 2002). Further, teleworkers indicated that when they are out of the office they risk missing information that could support their work and professional development. This study also found that managers felt they were less able to coach and mentor teleworkers owing to fewer opportunities to observe them in action. Indeed, the spatial distance between team members and the use of non-FTF communication can impede the leader's ability to mentor and develop followers (Bell and Kozlowski, 2002).

Managers and leaders need to consciously make an effort to ensure that they provide teleworkers with informal learning and mentoring opportunities. Research shows the importance of the leader building strong relationships with followers by conducting regular one-on-one meetings, investing time getting to know followers, and periodically visiting followers in their own environments if at all possible (Hambley et al., 2005).

Training costs
The costs of training teleworkers represent another potentially negative impact of telework for organizations. Training may be needed to (1) assist the teleworker in setting up a home office, (2) plan for security, safety, and ergonomics in the home office, (3) set up optimal schedules and work plans, (4) learn to deal with family, friends and neighbours, (5) provide strategies for staying focused on work, (6) offer suggestions for staying in touch with colleagues and clients, and (7) help employees learn to manage their careers as teleworkers (Illegems and Verbeke, 2003).

Managers may also need training on how to effectively supervise teleworkers. Such training might include (1) implementing outcome-based performance management, (2) giving ongoing performance feedback, (3) keeping teleworkers connected with office-related social and information networks, and (4) detecting problems early (for example, a person ill-suited to telework) (Illegems and Verbeke, 2003). Of course, some organizations will fail to make this important training available, but those that do provide it will incur the associated costs.

Appraising employee performance
Another negative impact of telework is that it may be more difficult for managers to appraise teleworker performance. Managers often feel that employees who are out of sight are more challenging to appraise than those in the office. Using a well-designed, outcome-based performance appraisal system, however, is thought to alleviate this potential problem. For example, researchers have examined the use of management by objectives (MBO) as a method to manage the performance of off-site employees (Konradt et al., 2003). Using this approach, both superiors and subordinates jointly define performance goals, coordinate their efforts toward attaining those goals, and provide regular feedback. These researchers found that the quality of MBO both reduced stress and increased job satisfaction for teleworkers. Such objective performance appraisal processes give teleworkers a clearer understanding of their tasks and individual work roles, and ease the performance appraisal process for managers.

Manager's ability to supervise employees
Telework tends to be viewed as negatively affecting a manager's ability to supervise employees. Managers often express concerns about controlling

employees who work away from the office (Bailey and Kurland, 2002). As discussed in regard to performance appraisal, supervising out-of-sight employees requires managers to rely on measures other than physical observation to control and monitor employee performance (Kurland and Egan, 1999). New processes for controlling, measuring and evaluating will be needed, as not all of the systems used in the traditional office apply virtually (Helms and Raiszadeh, 2002).

ORGANIZATIONAL EFFICIENCY

Telework's impact on organizational efficiency includes the employees' ability to get work done, as well as the associated financial implications. The pros and cons as they affect employees' work include such factors as schedules for meetings, productivity changes, office space requirements, overhead costs (for example, support staff, parking), adjustment capability when catastrophes occur, teamwork, security of company data and the costs of ICT. These are summarized in Table 3.3.

Positive Telework Impacts

Productivity

One of telework's most cited positive impacts is increasing worker productivity. Telework is thought to enhance productivity by reducing interruptions, allowing employees to work at their 'peak' or most effective times, reducing commute time, and reducing incidental absence (Illegems and Verbeke, 2003).

A survey of 83 HR managers in Brussels found that organizations that had already implemented telework rated productivity advantages even more positively than those that had not (Illegems and Verbeke, 2003). Also, a study of 157 teleworkers and 89 office workers at IBM found that teleworkers perceived themselves to be more productive than office workers did (Hill et al., 1998). They cited the following reasons for their increased

Table 3.3   Telework impacts on organizational efficiency

Positive impacts	Neutral impacts	Negative impacts
Productivity	Teamwork	Scheduling meetings
Office space and overhead costs		Security of company data
Adjustment capability when catastrophes occur		Costs of ICT

productivity: less commute time, fewer distractions, greater flexibility to work at peak times, more comfortable work environment and the ability to work outside standard office hours. Another study of 175 HR managers in Spain found that increased productivity was rated as the most important benefit of telework (Perez et al., 2002).

The productivity increase may also be due to teleworkers' tendency to work extra hours. A qualitative study of eight Australian organizations found that virtual staff tended to undertake additional work outside normal work hours (Whitehouse et al., 2002). This additional effort may be unsustainable over the long term, however, and could lead to higher stress and decreased work/life balance.

This increased productivity can translate into substantial financial gains for organizations. For instance, AT&T has been studying and quantifying telework benefits and barriers since 1992. Of their management employees, 30 per cent telework full-time, and another 41 per cent telework one to two days per week (Roitz et al., 2004). AT&T has consistently found that tele-workers report efficiency gains of an extra hour's worth of work each day.

Increased productivity is yet another issue on which the interests of the employee, the organization and society at large generally align, further jus-tifying our decision to analyse the case for telework in terms of a single inte-grative value proposition.

Office space and overhead costs

Another positive impact of telework is cost savings due to decreased need for office space and overhead expenses. Telework allows organizations to reduce office costs, as work can be carried out at less costly facilities or in employees' homes (Illegems and Verbeke, 2003). Part-time teleworkers can share offices, thereby reducing the overall amount of centralized office space required. Reduction of fixed costs, including office space, was reported as the second most important benefit of telework in a study of 175 Spanish companies (Perez et al., 2002). In addition to saving the costs of office space, telework can lead to additional cost savings for organizations, reducing the need for parking (Harpaz, 2002) and clerical/support staff (Manoochehri and Pinkerton, 2003).

There are many examples of organizations that have saved considerable office space costs through telework. The annual real estate cost savings due to telework can be significant, as evidenced by IBM 's reported savings of $75 million (Kurland and Bailey, 1999), AT&T 's reported savings of $34 million (AT&T, 2003) and Nortel 's reported savings of $22 million (Nortel, 2004). Nortel has calculated savings of approximately $9000 in facility costs for each full-time teleworker. For its part-time and full-time teleworkers, Nortel has implemented less costly drop-in desks and collaborative work areas. Another organization reporting major cost savings from telework is Sun Microsystems, with nearly 50 per cent of 38000 employees participating to some extent in its telework program. It reports annual savings due to telework of $15 million in administrative costs, $2.8 million in power costs, $6.5 million on desktop updates and $68.9 million in reduced real estate costs (Bednarz, 2005).

Adjustment capability when catastrophes occur
Another positive impact of telework is that it allows organizations to more easily adjust to catastrophes, such as extreme weather or earthquakes (Daniels et al., 2001), as well as bombings or bomb scares. While the centralized office is evacuated, teleworkers can continue working. The more employees who are equipped to telework, the more continuity of critical work functions the organization can achieve during these natural and man-made catastrophes. Indeed, home-based telework proved extremely effective in maintaining business functions and alleviating traffic congestion following the 1994 Northridge Earthquake in Greater Los Angeles (Sato and Spinks, 1998). Likewise, when the events of 11 September 2001 destroyed millions of square feet of office space in Lower Manhattan, companies and their workers were left to find alternative workspace; for many, home became – and remains – the answer (Zbar, 2002). Further, AT&T reported that employees in Florida were able to telework through the hurricanes in the late summer of 2004, which forced traditional offices to close (Roitz et al., 2004). Telework boosted productivity, saved time, and maintained revenue that would otherwise have been lost.

The private sector seems better equipped to deal with disasters through telework than the public sector. According to an American government reform committee that is examining telework within the federal workforce, many federal departments and agencies are unprepared to operate in the event of a catastrophe (Crockett, 2004). These departments and agencies realize that telework allows organizations to continue to function through natural or terrorist incidents that disrupt business or force an extended evacuation of buildings, as was the case with numerous government buildings following the 11 September 2001 attacks and the anthrax disruptions later that same year. Despite these substantial benefits, the number of teleworkers in the federal government is still far below the legal requirements set by Congress in 2000 (Crockett, 2004). These legal requirements are represented by Section 359 of Public Law 106-346, which requires each executive branch agency to establish a telework policy 'under which eligible employees of the agency may participate in telecommuting to the maximum extent possible without diminished employee performance' (Crockett, 2004, p. 2). The rationale for this law is that allowing federal employees to telework can potentially save US taxpayers a substantial amount of money in real estate costs for the federal government. This law has fallen far short of its initial objective of 100 per cent participation within the federal workforce by the end of 2004.

Neutral Telework Impacts

Teamwork

Previously, it was thought that telework necessarily had a negative effect on teamwork. This is clearly no longer the case, as successful virtual teams are prevalent (Kirkman et al., 2002). The number of virtual teams is increasing, owing to increased inter-organizational alliances, globalization, outsourcing, and alternative work arrangements, such as telework (Staples and Webster, 2003). Virtual teams have the advantage that they can be configured and reconfigured rapidly, drawing on a wide geographical area, to adapt to changes in incoming work (Roitz et al., 2004).

Many of telework's negative effects on teamwork are overstated. In one study, HR managers who had not implemented telework were far more concerned about its impact on teamwork than those who had already implemented it (Illegems and Verbeke, 2003). Further, a study conducted with teleworkers and office workers at IBM found that telework did not seem to negatively affect teamwork at all (Hill et al., 1998). Teleworkers reported the same types of challenges with teams as did office workers. Thus, the impact of telework on teamwork seems to be neutral.

As will be discussed further in Chapter 9, difficulties surrounding teamwork in a telework environment can often be mitigated with such tools as team collaboration software, also known as 'groupware', which can help individuals to work together using ICT (Illegems and Verbeke, 2003). It is also important that virtual communication does not replace all FTF interaction. Research supports the importance of FTF work in building familiarity among team members (Wiggins and Horn, 2005). In particular, teams communicating through computerized media perform better if team members are more familiar with each other (for example, have been introduced FTF prior to beginning virtual teamwork). Familiarity seems to greatly improve coordination on complex, interdependent tasks, which are the types that virtual teams frequently face.

Negative Telework Impacts

Scheduling meetings

Telework can make scheduling meetings more difficult, so this impact is categorized as negative. Meetings involving teleworkers require greater coordination, especially FTF meetings that need to be booked for times when teleworkers are in the office. Having regular virtual or FTF meetings may be particularly necessary if teleworkers' jobs require a high level of coordination and idea generation with colleagues (Kurland and Egan, 1999).

However, these concerns around scheduling meetings with teleworkers are diminishing owing to the improved ICT available to today's organizations. For example, team collaboration tools allow virtual teams to schedule and plan for meetings (for example, E-Rooms, SharePoint, Lotus Notes, project forums, collaborative space). Traditional documents such as meeting agendas can be distributed via everyday communication technologies, such as e-mail (Dinnocenzo, 1999).

Security of company data

A potential negative organizational impact of telework is the risks it might pose to the security of company data (Illegems and Verbeke, 2003). Giving employees access to company servers and databases from outside the office increases the risks of unauthorized access and theft of confidential information. To safeguard against these risks, organizations can use many means, which continue to improve with increasingly sophisticated technologies. In a study of 83 organizations in Brussels, HR managers from organizations which had not yet implemented telework were more convinced that data security was a problem than those already implementing telework (Illegems and Verbeke, 2003).

Researchers recommend that organizations create telework policies that address how and when equipment and information should be used (Manoochehri and Pinkerton, 2003). For example, the policy might require teleworkers to log off whenever they leave their computer unattended, to use their computer only for business, and to access only certain information from home.

Costs of ICT

Another negative impact of telework is the ICT costs that organizations may need to incur. To do their jobs efficiently and effectively, teleworkers need certain ICT, which may include fast communication links, and hardware that can handle the company's software (Manoochehri and Pinkerton, 2003). These technologies require additional outlays for such items as computer hardware, software and telecommunication devices. Such costs can be especially prohibitive for smaller firms (Bailey and Kurland, 2002). Costs of providing technical support for the home office may also need to be incurred (Harpaz, 2002). Although in certain cases employees may supply their own home office technology, this may decrease employees' interest and willingness to telework (Illegems and Verbeke, 2003). Organizations should formulate policies that clearly outline which home office expenses will and will not be reimbursed (Manoochehri and Pinkerton, 2003).

EXTERNAL STAKEHOLDERS

The final category of organizational telework impact involves external stakeholders such as customers, families and the public. These benefits or costs are not fully internalized by the organization, but can still be viewed as critical to its competencies (Illegems and Verbeke, 2004). Customer service (for example, extended hours of service), the image of the organization (such as an image of environmental responsibility), the ability to respond to environmental regulations/concerns, the interpretation of relevant labour legislation (for example, insurance issues), ease of meeting health and safety standards, and relations with trade unions all come into play. These are summarized in Table 3.4.

Positive Telework Impacts

Customer service
A potentially positive impact of telework is that it allows organizations to offer extended customer service by remaining open for longer hours. For example, organizations may more easily staff 24-hour call centres by allowing teleworkers to work from home during night shifts. On the other hand, research suggests that telework does not always lead to improved customer service (Illegems and Verbeke, 2003). Thus, the positive effects of telework on customer service are likely to depend on the type of services offered by the organization, and may apply only in particular cases.

Table 3.4   Telework impacts on external stakeholders

Positive impacts	Neutral impacts	Negative impacts
Customer service		Interpretation of relevant labour legislation
Image of the organization		Ease of meeting health and safety standards
Ability to respond to environmental regulations/concerns		Relations with trade unions

Image of the organization
Furthermore, telework can potentially enhance an organization's image
(Illegems and Verbeke, 2003). If the public know about the environmental
and social benefits of telework, they are likely to perceive organizations
offering these types of flexible work arrangements more positively (for
example, as more progressive and environmentally friendly (Harpaz, 2002)).

Ability to respond to environmental regulations/concerns
Increasing attention to environmental management has raised many new
dilemmas for firms (Kolk, 2000). Organizations are facing increasing obligations to comply with environmental regulations, through such instruments
as the Kyoto Accord (in Europe) and the Clean Air Act (in the United
States). Another positive impact of telework is that it lowers emissions
because it decreases the number of commuting vehicles (Illegems and
Verbeke, 2003). As more governments start to regulate emissions credits,
more companies may opt to implement and track telework. An innovative
tool for undertaking such tracking is described in Chapter 5. As we will
discuss more in the next chapter, an increased ability to meet environmental regulations and concerns is yet another area where organizations' and
society's interests largely align, justifying our decision to adopt a single
integrative value proposition.

Negative Telework Impacts

Interpretation of relevant labour legislation
The role of telework in current labour legislation is somewhat problematic as
neither Canada nor the US has incorporated telework into labour legislation.
For example, the US federal labour and employment policy is currently tailored to employees who work in a central office location (Potter, 2003).
Similarly, Canada's employment and labour standards have not yet incorporated telework. We consider the absence of applicable labour legislation as a
negative impact for organizations. For example, companies' obligations in
setting up employees' home offices are unclear, as are the associated taxation
and insurance issues. This lack of teleworker-specific labour legislation can
create uncertainty, and even the danger of labour disputes and lawsuits
(Illegems and Verbeke, 2003). New labour and employment policies need to
be created that apply to telework, as the current level of ambiguity reinforces
managerial resistance to this work arrangement (Potter, 2003).

Ease of meeting health and safety standards
Telework may pose challenges to meeting health and safety standards.
When employees work from home, it is more difficult for the employer to

ensure that health and safety standards are met (Illegems and Verbeke, 2003). Furthermore, the employer's obligation to ensure a safe workplace becomes unclear. For example, are injuries to teleworkers or business visitors at a telework site (such as the home) during working hours compensable? The answer is unclear (Potter, 2003). Also, in the case of US employees, if there is a workplace safety problem in the home office the teleworker may be unable to anonymously report it to the Occupational Safety and Health Administration (OSHA), as would be possible if working in the office (Kistner, 2002). It is suggested that organizations perform the initial setups and conduct periodic checks of the employee's home office to ensure conditions meet appropriate standards (Manoochehri and Pinkerton, 2003), even though this may impinge on employee privacy.

Relations with trade unions

Telework can be viewed negatively by trade unions, who may see such arrangements as leading to increased part-time and contract work, resulting in employees losing the protections of collective work legislation (Illegems and Verbeke, 2003). A union representative in the US, Patrick Hunt, cautions employers that telework could potentially exploit low wage earners (Kistner, 2002). He believes telework can lead to abuses such as unforeseen costs for low earners (for example, phone lines and computers) pushing their pay below the legal minimum. He states that

> we've spent 70 years passing labour laws that protect people: the eight-hour day, paid overtime, workplace safety standards. They've been enforceable because you've had a concentration of workers in one place. You could see the abuses. If we start telecommuting, abuses can occur away from public sight. (Kistner, 2002, p. 1)

Because of these types of concerns, organizations may view telework as negatively affecting relations with trade unions. Some organizations, however, have had some success working with unions to consider telework programs. For example, AT&T made an agreement with two labour unions to consider launching a telework pilot (Kistner, 2002). Overall, until unions are more familiar with the benefits of telework and this work arrangement becomes more mainstream, their suspicions and resistance are likely to continue.

CONCLUSION

The virtual workplace offers many positive impacts at an organizational level. That said, there are also negative impacts that organizations must assess. Many of these potentially negative results, however, can be avoided or minimized by implementing telework programs properly, a topic covered in Chapter 9 of this book.

In this chapter, we have seen that many of the positive impacts at the organizational level are also positive impacts for employees and society at large, justifying our decision to present the case for telework in terms of a single integrative value proposition. In the next chapter we move the telework impact discussion up one level from that of the organization to that of a society.

4. Telework impacts: the societal perspective

Beyond impacts on employees and organizations, telework adoption also has broader, macro-level, societal effects. Societal-level impacts are important as they influence public policy and regulations that set the framework for potential telework adoption at all three levels of analysis (employee, organizational and societal). It is also at the societal level that telework's environmental impacts are best assessed, as such impacts are felt on a regional and even global scale. Compared with other transportation policy tools, telework has many advantages for cities and municipalities (Illegems and Verbeke, 2003). For one, telework requires relatively modest public expenditures, as the available ICT typically already accommodates telework.

From a societal perspective telework benefits cities by decreasing the number of vehicles using the roads. Telework's influence on commute trip reductions will have long-, medium- and short-term impacts. These impacts include effects on residential relocation, car ownership, modal splits, non-commute trips and latent demand. Telework-induced commute trip reductions can impact air pollution, road congestion, noise pollution, road accidents, energy consumption, road maintenance, new road construction and the usage of mass transit. Beyond commute trip reductions, cities and regions are also affected by non-commute-related telework impacts: economic impacts, new job opportunities, community development and safety, environmental impacts beyond emission reductions, and operational continuity.

The short-term, medium-term, and long-term commute-related impacts of large-scale telework adoption are depicted in Figure 4.1. These impacts are briefly outlined in the following sections; further elaboration and quantification of these impacts are provided in Chapter 7, which focuses on tracking telework at the societal level.

TELEWORK'S INFLUENCE ON VEHICLE TRIPS

As shown in Figure 4.1, many societal-level telework impacts are derived from the assumption that telework reduces total vehicle trips and

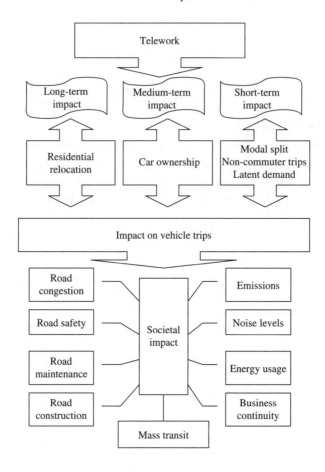

Source: adapted from Illegems and Verbeke, 2004.

*Figure 4.1   Societal impacts from telework-related commute trip
            reductions*

vehicle-kilometres. Thus, in this section of the chapter we argue for (and
attempt to quantify) this crucial premise and provide a detailed analysis of
telework's influence on vehicle trips. While telework offers the potential to
reduce work-related commute trips, we acknowledge that teleworkers tend
to have longer commute distances, so on non-telework days these employees actually increase societal-level vehicle trip times and distances. We
also acknowledge that telework will influence non-commute-related business trips and non-business trips for both the teleworker and members of
his or her household. Finally, we must also consider latent demand when

assessing telework-induced trip reductions, as less congested roads will increase the demand for commuting on those roads.

The Transportation Problem

Many current transportation problems result from the fact that cities usually consist of a number of concentric zones. In the centre of the city is the central business district with retail stores and offices. The next concentric zone often contains deteriorating older manufacturing plants and warehouses. This is then followed by a zone of older, high-density residential areas that are often declining into slums. Finally, the outermost zone consists of newer housing developments. In these newer developments, there is a 'jobs–housing imbalance' (Nilles, 1977, 1991; Gordon et al., 1991) and, as a result of the concentric zone layout, the distance between these homes and the central workplaces is often long.

Simultaneously, at the inter-city level, there is a trend away from the dominant traditional commuting patterns of 'centre-to-centre' and 'periphery-to-centre' toward a new pattern of 'suburban zone to suburban zone'. This trend also contributes to transportation problems, since urban mass transit systems are designed primarily to transport people to the city centre (Nilles, 1988). In some cases, this 'suburban zone to suburban zone' trend also occurs at the intra-city level; while this alleviates commuting to the city centre, it aggravates congestion on the ring roads around the city, as individuals commute between (often distant) suburban areas of the same city.

The effect of ICT on travel is complex. ICT has two types of effects on travel: substitution effects and complementarity effects. With a substitution effect, one system replaces particular functions of another system. In the case of telework, a particular use of ICT will sometimes replace a particular trip. There are two types of complementarity effects. In the first, one system causes an increase in the efficiency of another system. For example, the use of ICT will lead to better organizational coordination, which will make some travel unnecessary. In the second type of complementarity, increased use of one system causes increased use of the complementary system. Instead of simply reducing trips, ICT use can also generate trips (Salomon, 1985, 1986; Mokhtarian, 1990; La Bella et al., 1990).

Parameters Influencing the Number and Distance of Vehicle Trips

When the purpose of a trip is merely to exchange information, ICT can often substitute for the trip (Lyons et al., 1998; Kraemer, 1982). Two prime candidates for substitution are commuting and work-related travel other than commuting. In urban areas, 30 per cent to 40 per cent of all vehicle-kilometres travelled are commuting trips (Gray et al., 1994; Mannering and Mokhtarian, 1995; Salomon, 1984, 1990; Nilles, 1991; Ritter and Thompson, 1994; Mokhtarian, 1998). One would therefore expect that telework would alleviate congestion (Salomon, 1984). However, experience shows that the initial congestion relief is only temporary (Salomon, 1984). Latent demand (that is, new demand resulting from telework adoption) arises and moderates the achieved reductions in congestion levels. In other words, as teleworkers leave the roads, other workers will, to some extent, take their place. We will address latent demand below; for the moment we will ignore it.

Ignoring latent demand, then, the reduction in teleworkers' commuting trips will decrease the total number of teleworker trips. Consequently, road congestion during peak hours will be alleviated. During peak hours, even a small reduction in traffic can reduce congestion significantly. For instance, during the 1984 Olympic Games in Los Angeles, a 7 per cent reduction in traffic decreased congestion by 60 per cent (Ritter and Thompson, 1994).

The effect on passenger traffic flows is different if, instead of staying at home, the teleworker commutes to a telework centre or a satellite office. In these cases, the commuting trip becomes shorter and at least some commuting trips move out of the busiest road sections during peak times. Furthermore, non-motorized modes of travel (such as bicycling or walking) become more realistic options, owing to the shorter commuting distances involved (Sampath et al., 1991; Nilles, 1988).

Estimates and empirical data are available to quantify how much telework reduces teleworkers' commuting trips. For instance, an analysis of telework adoption in the Bergen and Oslo areas revealed a potential regional travel reduction of between 3 per cent and 6 per cent, assuming a 20 per cent telework penetration level[1] (Lie and Yttri, 1999). An analysis for the United States predicted a reduction in vehicle trips of 5.4 per cent during peak hours if 32 per cent of the workforce were to telework 1.8 days per workweek (Rathbone, 1992). Although not based on surveys, these estimates are in line with the empirical findings of two Dutch experiments. In the first experiment, a sample of workers started teleworking approximately once a workweek, and their number of trips decreased by 19 per cent during peak hours. A second Dutch experiment found a decrease of 11 per cent (Hamer et al., 1991, 1992). These results are presented in Table 4.1.

Table 4.2 summarizes several studies that analysed the reduction in commuter vehicle-kilometres per telework occasion. The data from these studies must be analysed carefully in order to be properly understood. For instance, the ENTRANCE (ENergy savings in TRANsport through innovation in the Cities of Europe) Southampton study found that, even before the introduction of telework, the average number of commuting trips

Table 4.1   *Impact of telework implementation (1.2 days per workweek) on number of trips made by teleworkers in the Netherlands study*

Day/time	Experiment 1 (%)	Experiment 2 (%)
General	−17	−10
Peak hours	−19	−11
Off-peak hours	−15	−10
Weekday	−18	−13
Weekend	−13	0

Source: Hamer et al., 1991 (experiment 1) and Hamer et al., 1992 (experiment 1 and experiment 2).

Table 4.2   *Savings in commuter vehicle-kilometres per telework occasion*

Study	Average distance of round-trip commute (kilometres)	Percentage drive-alone	Commuter vehicle-kilometres saved per telework occasion
State of California Pilot Study (USA)	62.4	81	50.54
Puget Sound Study (USA) ENTRANCE	57.6	63	36.29
Southampton study (UK)	48	95.8	45.98
Arizona AT&T (USA)	49.76	74	36.82
Bell Atlantic studies (USA)	64	n.a.	n.a.
San Diego studies (USA)	62.08	79	49.04
Southern California Association Governments (SCAG) (USA)	67.2	67	45.02
VUB-Brussels study (Belgium) – current teleworkers	85.6	59	50.5
VUB-Brussels study (Belgium) – potential regular teleworkers	82	52	42.64

Source: adapted from Mokhtarian et al., 1995 and Lyons et al., 1998.

per day was only 1.5, while one would expect this number to be 2. This seemingly odd result can be explained by the fact that, if part of the commuting trip was used to attend a meeting or to take care of a personal matter, the trip was no longer classified as 'commuting'.

Another seemingly odd result from the ENTRANCE Southampton study was that, for the average teleworker, the commuting trip was not fully eliminated, even though the study included only homeworkers. The fact that the average teleworker still commuted an average of eight kilometres per telework day instead of the non-telework 48 kilometres can be explained by the fact that the majority of the sample (70 per cent) occasionally teleworked for only part of the day. On those days, these teleworkers would have still commuted to and from work, just earlier or later in the day than usual. Incidentally, a study on Ericsson had a similar result: a surprisingly high 39 per cent of the teleworkers reported that telework did not change their number of commuting trips. Detailed analysis of the study data suggested the same explanation: this was probably due to a large proportion of half-day teleworkers in the sample (Skåmedal, 2000).

On average, teleworkers have substantially longer commutes than other workers in the same region (Wells et al., 2001; Nilles, 1991; Ritter and Thompson, 1994; Mokhtarian et al., 1995; Lyons et al., 1998).[2] Thus, those employees who choose to telework are more likely to be 'long distance commuters'. This helps explain telework's high impact on commuter travel.

Finally, it is interesting to note that a simple dislike of long commutes is not the only explanation for the correlation between telework and long commutes. The average commuting trip increases with the employee's hierarchical position in an organization. For instance, the commuting trip of an executive is 1.8 times longer than that of a clerical worker (Nilles, 1988). Thus, telework may be more attractive to those in senior hierarchical positions, and employees in these positions tend to live farther away from the workplace.

Work-related Travel other than Commuting

About 10 per cent of intra-city road traffic is associated with business activities other than commuting to work (Nilles et al., 1976; Salomon, 1985). Because this type of travel often occurs for the purpose of FTF social communication, ICT fails to substitute for it as well as it substitutes for commuting travel. Nonetheless, increased use of e-mail, other electronic messaging, and teleconferencing can substitute for some work-related travel. Teleconferencing looks particularly promising in this regard. Instead of travelling to the same location, each teleconferencing participant travels (if necessary) to one of two or more dispersed sites. Often, the dispersed site is the participant's own workplace, so the total travel cost is zero.

One study from the United States suggests that 34 per cent of (non-commuting) business travel could be replaced by telephone conferencing and an additional 10 per cent could be replaced by videoconferencing; the remaining 56 per cent of business travel could not be replaced (Salomon, 1985; La Bella et al., 1990). Kraemer has reached similar conclusions regarding substitution (Kraemer, 1982). Generally speaking, travel is less expensive than telephone conferencing or videoconferencing when the number of participants is low and the duration of the meeting is long (Salomon et al., 1991). Travel is also less expensive when the number of locations involved is large, unless the distance between the locations is also large (Kraemer and King, 1982).

Modal Split

Even if we continue to ignore latent demand, it is clear that not all telework will reduce vehicle-kilometres travelled by car. If telework substitutes for a train or bus ride, or a ride as a passenger, the number of vehicle-kilometres travelled by car will stay the same. In those cases, neither the environment nor traffic flows will be directly affected (Gillespie et al., 1995; Gillespie, 1998; Mokhtarian et al., 1995). A complete assessment of telework's impact therefore requires an examination of the potential teleworkers' modal split (that is, their use of various transport modes – car, train, bus, subway, bicycle, and so on – when commuting) before they started tele-working. Capturing such data is difficult, since teleworkers in informal pro-grams are difficult to locate, and even organizations with formal telework programs rarely keep such records (Nilles, 1988).

The limited data that do exist about potential teleworkers' modal split are less than clear. On the one hand, potential teleworkers are primarily infor-mation workers, with a high proportion of skilled knowledge workers, and research suggests that information workers commute by car more than non-information workers do (Gillespie et al., 1995). Furthermore, in the State of California study, the control group of non-teleworkers used public trans-port more often than the teleworkers (Kitamura et al., 1990). There are also indications that teleworker households tend to be generally more car-dependent (Pendyala et al., 1991). For these reasons, one could conclude that potential teleworkers are more car-dependent than the average worker.

However, a survey of employees working in Brussels found that, of the employees willing to telework, 52 per cent regularly drove to work alone. This number is in line with a national survey conducted by the National Institute of Statistics in Belgium (1991), which reported that 54.7 per cent of the general workforce drive to work alone. This suggests that potential teleworkers use their cars to commute at a rate roughly equal to that of the general workforce.

It has been suggested that partial-day telework can have a negative effect on modal split, because the commuting trip is then made during off-peak hours, when there is less public transport available. In that case, there is a high probability of a modal shift from public transport to car usage (Skåmedal, 2000); this assumption is supported by the empirical results of the Ericsson study in Sweden.

It has also been suggested that telework may lead to the demise of carpool initiatives (Sampath et al., 1991; Garrison and Deakin, 1988). If a potential teleworker previously carpooled to work with another person, the carpool initiative might theoretically end if one of the participants started teleworking. As a result, each employee would drive alone to the conventional office, including the teleworker on non-telework days (Kitamura et al., 1990; Pendyala et al., 1991). However, the empirical results suggest that this does not actually happen. For instance, the San Diego study found that carpool initiatives did not stop when their members started teleworking. Both the Ericsson study (Skåmedal, 2000) and the Minnesota study (Wells et al., 2001) found that telework implementation had no influence on carpool initiatives.

In the absence of high-quality data one way or the other about how telework affects employees' modal split, we assume that potential teleworkers have a modal split approximately the same as that of non-teleworkers, and that teleworking does not significantly affect their modal split.

Non-commuter Trips

Besides influencing commuter trips of teleworkers, telework adoption will also affect two other types of trips: non-commuter trips of teleworkers, and the trips of their household members.

Telework changes the teleworker's trip composition. Between 25 per cent and 50 per cent of all trips are 'linked' or 'chained' (Salomon, 1985). For example, workers often incorporate non-work trips (such as shopping trips, trips to drop off children at school, or personal business trips) into their travel behaviour. When the commuting trip is eliminated or reduced, this reduces trip chaining (Gillespie et al., 1995).

Telework also changes the spatial distribution of the destinations of non-commuting trips in a specific way: the trip destinations become more concentrated around the home location and less around the work location. This redistribution of trips toward the local street network shifts traffic onto the local network, which is usually beneficial from an overall road externality impact perspective (Kitamura et al., 1990; Nilles, 1991; Ritter and Thompson, 1994). The State of California study (USA) showed that telework increased the percentage of non-work trips made to destinations within 20 kilometres of the home from 35 per cent to 42 per cent (Mokhtarian et al., 1995). The Ericsson study also found a reduction in the length of non-work-related trips (Skåmedal, 2000). Owing to this shorter distance, an employee may opt for non-motorized modes or public transport for these trips (Sampath et al., 1991). Even if teleworkers continue to use cars for these trips, to the extent that the teleworkers can now schedule these trips outside peak hours, traffic congestion will be smoothed. Of course, childcare schedules and employers' expectations to maintain conventional work hours can restrict this flexibility (Balepur et al., 1998), in which case these trips may have to continue to take place during peak hours. The Minnesota survey findings further reveal that errand running tends to occur on regular workdays instead of on teleworking days. This phenomenon was especially true for part-time teleworkers that alternated days at home and days in the office. Furthermore, this study confirms the shift of traffic to the local network, because errands tended to be accomplished near the teleworkers' homes rather than their workplace (Wells et al., 2001).

Several empirical studies suggest that teleworkers actually perform fewer non-commuting trips than conventional workers. According to the State of California Pilot study and the Puget Sound study, total travel savings were about 6 per cent higher than the savings in commuting. This implies that telework may have actually decreased non-commuting travel (Mokhtarian et al., 1995). Furthermore, the Netherlands study reported a drop in the number of trips made by teleworkers for purposes other than commuting or business (experiment 1 showed a reduction of 14 per cent, and experiment 2 showed a reduction of 15 per cent) (Hamer et al., 1991, 1992). The Ericsson study also reported indications of a reduction of non-work-related trips (Skåmedal, 2000). The researchers involved in the Ericsson study believed that this could be explained by a streamlining of activities, whereby simple home–activity–home chains were replaced by longer and more complicated ones. However, their own research results tend to undermine this theory, since according to their data teleworkers reduced their average chain length by 12 per cent (Hamer et al., 1992).

Mokhtarian et al. (1995) have noted three methodological reasons why these empirical studies might erroneously report a decline in non-commuting trips. First, participation in a telework program whose main objective is to determine telework's impact on travel may condition the participants to reduce their travel. In psychology this is known as the observation effect. Second, there may be intentional 'cheating', especially if the participants know that the pilot project is trying to determine telework's potential as a trip-reduction measure. Thus, respondents may deliberately under-report their number of trips, especially the ones made during work hours. Finally, the apparent reduction may be the consequence of participant fatigue, leading to an under-reporting of the number of trips made. We conclude that the impact on non-commuting trips appears to be marginal; the main effect of telework seems to be on the commute itself (Mokhtarian et al., 1995).

Beyond non-commuting trips, telework may also influence the commuting behaviour of other members in the household. If there are as many drivers as cars in a household, the ability to telework may eliminate the need for an additional car. Consequently, this could lead to changes in vehicle ownership in the medium term (Sampath et al., 1991). In the short term, when an individual who used to commute by car starts teleworking, the car becomes available to other household members, and this may generate additional trips, particularly in households with fewer cars than drivers (Gillespie et al., 1995; Lyons et al., 1998; Kitamura et al., 1990).

A recent study of employees in Brussels revealed that, in 14.1 per cent of the cases, the commuting trip of a potential regular teleworker could theoretically simply be replaced by a commuting trip of another working member of the household (who previously did not have access to a car) (Illegems and Verbeke, 2004). However, in several other studies, telework did not appear to actually cause additional trips by other household members. The empirical results of the two-year State of California Telecommuting Pilot Project (Sampath et al., 1991; Kitamura et al., 1990) found no evidence that the household members of teleworkers made any additional trips during that time. The same conclusions were also drawn from a project in the Netherlands (Hamer et al., 1991), and from the Ericsson study (Skåmedal, 2000). Some evidence even indicates that the non-work trips of other household members are reduced by telework. This may be due to the observation effect, under-reporting, or participant fatigue – or it may be due to the streamlining of travel patterns by all household members due to the additional flexibility in trip scheduling (Kitamura et al., 1990).

In our view, the evidence suggests that telework does not cause additional trips by other household members. However, predictions are difficult in this area, and new studies should carefully assess car use by other household members.

Latent Demand

Telework may not only substitute for travel; it may also generate travel. As teleworkers leave the roads, other workers will, to some extent, take their place. In the case of mobility demand, the travel time elasticity of demand is often higher than the price elasticity of demand. Since telework reduces the number of commuter trips, the traffic flow during peak hours will temporarily become less congested. However, this initial improvement in traffic flow will then be moderated when a number of new road users perceive the lowered congestion and start using the roads during peak hours (Gillespie et al., 1995; Ritter and Thompson, 1994). Research based on earlier experiences regarding the effect of latent demand when other policies were introduced (but not based on empirical data) indicates that approximately half of the potential reduction in vehicle-kilometres achieved through telework will be replaced by new traffic (Gillespie et al., 1995; Ritter and Thompson, 1994).

Medium-term Impact: Car Ownership

In our effort to establish and then quantify the crucial premise that teleworking reduces total vehicle-trips and vehicle-kilometres, we turn now from telework's short-term impacts to its most significant medium-term impact: does telework lead teleworkers to eliminate a household car? The answer is clearly 'no'. Neither the State of California study, nor the San Diego study, nor the Ericsson study provided any evidence that telework implementation acts as an incentive to eliminate a household car (Skåmedal, 2000).

Long-term Impact: Residential Relocation

As the number of commuter trips decreases owing to part-time or full-time telework, the distance between the conventional workplace and the residence becomes less important. Since a relocation of the workplace is one of the most important reasons to relocate the residence (Brown, 1976), telework could theoretically be a factor leading a teleworker to move to a new residence farther away from the conventional workplace. A decision to move would, in theory, become more likely if the former residence was chosen as the result of weighing convenient commutes against undesirable intrinsic residential characteristics. Such a move would increase the length of the commuting trip on non-telework days, thus generating additional travel on those days (van Reisen, 1997; Lyons et al., 1998).

In the State of California project, 6 per cent of the teleworkers involved did consider moving further away from work after the two-year period. However, of those only 28 per cent reported that the ability to telework played a significant role, and there was no significant difference between the actual moves of the teleworkers and the control group (Mokhtarian, 1991). The Ericsson study reached the same conclusion: although 3 per cent of the sample stated that they had plans to move further away from their conventional workplace, the moves did not actually take place (Skåmedal, 2000). We conclude that the impact of telework on residential relocation is minimal.

Our conclusion is perfectly consistent with the correlation between telework and commute distance. We deny only that telework functions as a cause to increase commute distance. Rather, the causality goes the other way. As we have described, early adopters of telework are often people with long commuting distances. Presumably, telework seemed particularly attractive in part because of the long distance between the residence and the conventional workplace.

TELEWORK'S COMMUTE-RELATED IMPACTS

Let us summarize the above discussion. On the one hand, research clearly suggests that telework directly reduces vehicle commute trips. On the other hand, several indirect factors must also be considered in estimating telework's complete impact on vehicle trips:

1. Not all telework will reduce vehicle-kilometres travelled by car. If telework substitutes for a train or bus journey, or a journey as a passenger, there will be no reduction in vehicle-kilometres travelled by car.
2. Telework also changes trip composition. Between 25 per cent and 50 per cent of all trips are 'linked' or 'chained' (Salomon, 1985). Often, workers incorporate non-work trips (such as shopping trips, trips to drop off children at school, or personal business trips) into their travel behaviour. When the commuting trip is eliminated or reduced, this reduces trip chaining.
3. In the short term, when an individual who used to commute by car starts teleworking, the car becomes available to other household members and this may generate additional trips, particularly in households with fewer cars than drivers (Gillespie et al., 1995; Lyons et al., 1998; Kitamura et al., 1990).
4. Research based on earlier experiences of the effect of latent demand when other transport policies were introduced (but not based on empirical data) indicates that approximately half of the potential reduction in vehicle-kilometres achieved through telework will be replaced by new traffic (Gillespie et al., 1995; Ritter and Thompson, 1994).
5. As the number of commuter trips decreases owing to part-time or full-time telework, the distance between the conventional workplace and the residence becomes less important. Telework could theoretically be a factor causing the teleworker to move to a new residence further away from the conventional workplace. Such a move would increase the length of the commuting trip on non-telework days.

While it is important to incorporate the above factors in assessing telework's total impact on vehicle trip reductions, the overall evidence suggests that the reduction in commuting and work-related travel is dominant and telework does in fact reduce vehicle trips and vehicle-kilometres. The societal impacts from telework's influence on vehicle trips and vehicle-kilometres are outlined in the following paragraphs.

Emissions

According to the US Environmental Protection Agency (EPA) the personal automobile is the single greatest polluter. Annual emissions for an average passenger car include 80 pounds of hydrocarbons (2.9 grams per mile), 606 pounds of carbon monoxide (22 grams per mile), 41 pounds of nitrogen oxides (1.5 grams per mile), and 10 000 pounds of carbon dioxide (0.8 pounds per mile).

Does telework's reduction in vehicle trips and vehicle-kilometres translate into a reduction in vehicle emissions and a corresponding improvement in air quality? The impact of a particular penetration level of telework on air quality depends on a number of parameters such as distance travelled by car, number of cold starts, number of hot starts, speed, type of vehicle, and ambient temperature.

In theory, telework could have a negative effect on air quality. The amount of emissions produced is closely linked to the travel pattern. Since telework implementation reduces trip chaining, this might result in more cold starts and shorter trips, producing higher levels of emissions per vehicle-kilometre (Gillespie et al., 1995).

In reality, however, the small increase in emissions per vehicle-kilometre is overwhelmed by the reduction in vehicle-kilometres. For example, the State of California study found that telework reduced vehicle emissions and improved air quality. This study estimated the total impact of telework on air quality by using air quality models and data from travel diaries regarding number of trips, cold and hot starts, average speed, and vehicle-kilometres travelled before and after telework implementation. To give just one example, the adoption of telework reduced the emission of volatile organic compounds (VOC) by 2.72 grams eliminated per kilometre (in spite of the higher fuel consumption per remaining vehicle-kilometre, as noted above). So far, the State of California study and the Puget Sound study are the only two rigorous studies to estimate telework's impact on emissions (Mokhtarian et al., 1995; Henderson et al., 1996). The Puget Sound air quality models led to the conclusion that, because teleworkers make 30 per cent fewer trips, travel 63 per cent fewer vehicle-kilometres, and perform 44 per cent fewer cold starts on telework days, teleworking substantially reduces the emissions of VOC, CO, NOx, and particulate matter (PM). We note that telework's reduction in emissions will be a positive impact for many employees and organizations as well – another reason we have adopted our 'integrative value proposition' approach.

Road Congestion

Each year, traffic congestion in the United States costs a staggering $63 billion; it causes 3.7 billion hours of travel delay and wastes 2.3 billion gallons of fuel (Schrank and Lomax, 2005). Congestion is measured by the hours of delay drivers face each year. By staying off the roads, teleworkers reduce traffic and decrease commute times for non-teleworkers (Illegems and Verbeke, 2003). As described in the previous section, however, telework's influence on road congestion will be moderated by latent demand, which could counteract telework-induced congestion reduction by approximately 50 per cent.

Road Safety

Road accidents are related to the level of traffic, road and weather conditions, and road user behaviour (Guria, 1999). The relationship between road accidents and traffic flow is nonlinear (Dickerson et al., 2000); that is, the number of road accidents is close to zero for low and moderate traffic flows, but it increases significantly at high traffic flows. By decreasing the level of traffic during peak (that is, high traffic) hours, telework takes cars off the road at the time of day when doing so has the highest beneficial marginal effect on road accidents. Furthermore, telework typically results in fewer employees driving habitual routes during morning and evening rush hours, when they may be fatigued or inattentive (Shafizadeh et al., 2004).

Energy Conservation

By reducing travel, telework could significantly contribute to energy conservation (Kraemer, 1982). It is estimated that each percentage reduction in urban commuting in the United States would save about 8.6 billion kilowatt-hours a year. Therefore, although telework is by no means the most direct or efficient way to save energy, its effect on energy consumption could be significant. For example, it has been estimated that, if 50 per cent of the workforce started teleworking 85 per cent of the work time, the amount of fuel used for commuting in the United States would be reduced by 43 per cent (Salomon, 1984). Of course, penetration levels lower than

50 per cent would bring lower payoffs: it has been estimated that the adoption of telework by 1 per cent of the workforce would reduce the country's total energy consumption by approximately 0.06 per cent, not taking into account the effects of latent demand (Gillespie et al., 1995).

Reduced cooling and heating costs at the (now smaller) conventional office would produce additional energy savings. However, savings in office energy would probably be relatively small, because the use of heating, air conditioning and lights would not decline significantly if only a small number of employees were accessing their work remotely (Mokhtarian et al., 1995). Furthermore, any savings at the conventional office would be partially offset by increased costs of heating and cooling at the teleworkers' homes (where facilities are often less efficient) (Salomon, 1984).

Road Maintenance

Telework-induced commute reductions can also provide significant road maintenance savings. One study concluded that, in 1985, expenditures for road maintenance took up 28.9 per cent of the total road revenue disbursement in the US (Chu and Tsai, 2004). This study used a marginal maintenance cost of 10 US cents per vehicle-kilometre for a standard vehicle.

Road Construction

Telework implementation can also reduce the need for new road construction. As a solution to road congestion, both telework and new road construction face the problem of latent demand: to a large extent, they both simply allow suppressed demand to become actual demand (Romilly, 2004). However, if latent demand counteracts telework-induced congestion reduction by only 50 per cent, telework will still reduce road congestion and thereby reduce the need for new road construction.

Mass Transit Usage

If a geographic area has severe mass transit congestion, telework implementation can relieve this congestion and thereby reduce the need for investment in new mass transit capacity.

On the other side of the ledger, however, telework could have a negative effect on the viability of mass transit because fewer commuters will need it during peak hours, so conceivably services may be reduced. Mass transit supports the quality of life of many older, lower-income, and less healthy residents (Southworth et al., 2004).

Although telework may reduce the viability of mass transit, we believe it is more likely that telework's ability to allow for peak shifting would actually enhance the quality of transit services by smoothing demand for mass transit usage more evenly throughout the day. More study is needed to determine telework's impact on mass transit usage.

TELEWORK'S NON-COMMUTE-RELATED IMPACTS

While the discussion so far has focused on telework's reduction of commuter trips and the societal impacts of those commute trip reductions, telework also has a number of societal-level impacts that extend beyond commute trip reductions. Many of these impacts relate to the ones discussed in the previous chapters on organizational and employee impacts, such as workforce satisfaction and productivity. However, in this section these are discussed from the societal viewpoint. Along with economic impacts, non-commute-related impacts also include new job opportunities, community development, environmental impacts beyond emission reductions, and operational continuity. These societal-level impacts are briefly discussed in the following paragraphs.

Economic Productivity

As reviewed in the previous chapters, telework generally has a positive impact on employee productivity, which is a positive impact at the employee, organizational and societal levels. At the societal level, increases in economic productivity stem from the aggregate influence telework has on work performance, absenteeism, and recruitment and retention. For example, one set of studies analysed 40 case studies and survey data from seven different types of organizations in five countries (Denmark, Germany, Italy, the Netherlands and the UK) (Sustel, 2004). These studies allowed direct comparisons of productivity between teleworkers and non-teleworkers and found teleworkers to be more productive and to have reduced rates of absenteeism and increased job satisfaction.

Further contributing to economic productivity, telework has also been associated with better quality work, higher output and greater creativity. These increases are best exemplified in telework's positive influence on human capital development, the personal competencies and skills needed to create wealth (Sustel, 2004). Telework also has a positive societal impact on increased communication and knowledge sharing, as telework programs require the development and implementation of tools that use ICT.

New Job Opportunities

At the societal level, telework provides new job opportunities for groups formerly excluded from labour markets. For example, workers with disabilities are afforded greater opportunities, as both the communication technology and the reduced need to travel to work open job prospects to them. Telework also affords rural workers the opportunity to join traditionally urban workforces. Assuming the technological infrastructure is in place, rural workers can maintain their rural residence and participate in small rural communities while also sharing in the economic growth often associated with larger urban centres. This impact is particularly salient for countries with dispersed and larger rural populations.

These new job opportunities are a positive impact at the employee, organization and societal levels, and an important reason why we chose to talk about telework in terms of a single integrative value proposition.

Community Development and Quality of Life

In the social dimension, there is a link between telework and a good quality of life (Illegems and Verbeke, 2003). While many teleworkers miss the human interaction at the office, the time saved by not commuting offers the social benefits of reduced stress and a better ability to manage the various demands on one's time. The newly available time also makes it easier for workers to be involved in organized local community activities (Sustel, 2004).

Along similar lines, telework may also produce a safer community. For example, telework reduces the number of latchkey children.[3] This not only increases the safety of the children but may even reduce crime in the larger community (Newman et al., 2000). The National Crime Prevention Council (NCPC) in the US has shown that safe and constructive after-school activities for latchkey children help prevent their involvement in dangerous or delinquent behaviour and support their educational goals (NCPC, 1995). The presence of a teleworking parent may have a similar effect.

An increase in telework and the associated daytime use of residential dwellings may even reduce neighbourhood crime by deterring daytime residential burglaries. The Federal Bureau of Investigation in the US, using 2004 crime statistics, reports that, of the burglaries for which the time could be established, most residential burglaries (62.2 per cent) occurred during the day, between 6 a.m. and 6 p.m. (Federal Bureau of Investigation, 2006).

Environmental Impacts Beyond Emissions

In addition to telework's major environmental impact of emission reduction through commute trip reduction, there are other non-emission-related
environmental impacts. We have previously discussed telework's effect on
energy usage; research suggests that while residential energy usage increases
with telework, this is offset by a reduction in office energy consumption.
Others have also pointed out that telework duplicates office equipment and
computer hardware, clearly a negative environmental impact. On the other
hand, telework and the extensive use of a company intranet (presumably
for electronic document transfer) has been linked to significant reductions
in printing, thus reducing the environmental impact of paper consumption
(Sustel, 2004).

Operational Continuity

Telework has proven to be, and will increasingly be used as, a mechanism
to provide operational continuity at both the organizational and societal
levels. In the final chapter of this book we suggest that as threats to government and business continuity increase, so will the adoption of telework
as a business continuity strategy. Risks to operational functions can come
from internal causes (power grid failures, equipment failures), natural disasters (pandemics, snow and ice storms, floods, earthquakes, hurricanes,
fires) and intentional externally caused disasters (terrorist attacks, acts of
war). Business continuity planning (BCP) and governmental continuity of
operations planning (COOP) develop mechanisms to offer continued operations in the face of disruptive emergencies. Increasingly, we see telework
included in such planning, and at the societal level it offers the potential for
continued service to communities in the face of disruptive emergencies,
which is crucial for the citizens of the affected region. Telework's ability
to offer continuity for both public and private services is illustrated by
its inclusion in many emergency planning policies (for example, Ziegler,
2006).

As flexible replacements for travel behaviour under disruptive emergency
conditions, virtual worksites have already proven themselves, as illustrated
by the great ice storm of 1998 in Eastern Canada, the 1989 California
earthquake, and the New York and Washington terrorist attacks of 11
September 2001 (InnoVisions, 2005).

Finally, it is important to note that while telework increases operational
resilience, by allowing work to be done when office operations are influenced
by disruptive emergencies, it also makes organizations more vulnerable to
disruption of their information systems, such as intranets (ITAC, 2005).

CONCLUSION

In this chapter we have explored the impacts of telework from a societal perspective. First, in order to thoroughly understand the phenomenon of telework, we examined the short-, medium-, and long-term effects of telework adoption. These impacts relate to residential relocation, car ownership, modal splits, non-commute trips and latent demand. Having established that telework reduced both vehicle trips and vehicle-kilometres, we then examined the many societal-level impacts of telework-induced commute trip reductions, including reductions in vehicle emissions, savings on road construction and maintenance costs, and effects on mass transit. Of these, the reduction in vehicle emissions in particular is seen as a positive impact by most employees and organizations as well; this is a major reason for having a single integrative value proposition for telework. Finally, we briefly described additional societal impacts that were not directly related to commute trip reductions, all of which are positive impacts for employees and organizations as well: increased employee productivity, new job opportunities, community development, improved employee quality of life and improved operational continuity. This significant overlap of interests is the reason why we feel it makes more sense to talk about a single integrative value proposition for telework than to try to create three separate value propositions, one for each stakeholder.

This chapter concludes the first part of the book, wherein we have reviewed the impact of telework from all three stakeholder perspectives: employee, organizational and societal. In the next part we turn our attention to the tracking of telework. Such tracking allows us to better quantify, capture, and evaluate the telework impacts reviewed in this first part of the book. This ability is essential in the effort to grow the virtual workplace.

NOTES

1. Penetration level is the percentage of currently employed employees who telework.
2. Against our generalization, the Ericsson study found no significant difference in commuting distance between teleworkers and conventional workers (Skåmedal, 2000). A possible partial explanation may be, again, the high percentage of occasional teleworkers in the sample.
   Furthermore, two time-use studies seem at first glance to go against our generalization; they concluded that the absolute amount of difference in daily travel time between conventional workers and teleworkers is relatively small (Michelson et al., 1999). These studies, however, classified every worker who spent at least one hour per day (excluding overtime) working at home as a teleworker. Thus, a substantial number of nomadic workers (employees who work at various sites in response to changing business needs, at locations generally not chosen by the employee) were included in this sample. This type

of teleworker does more business-related travel than conventional workers. Hence, this may be the reason for the unusual results regarding travel time.

When a teleworker commutes to a telework centre or satellite office, the situation is reversed, and teleworkers have shorter commutes than their colleagues. For example, a 1973 study of Los Angeles found that satellite offices reduced one-way average commuting distance by 65 per cent (Nilles, 1988). The US Residential-Area-Based Offices (RABO) study, conducted in the 1990s, found that satellite offices reduced personal kilometres travelled by 74 per cent and vehicle-kilometres by 65 per cent.

3.   The term 'latchkey children' refers to school-aged children who are at home without adult supervision for part of the day (especially after school until a parent returns home from work).

PART II

TELEWORK TRACKING

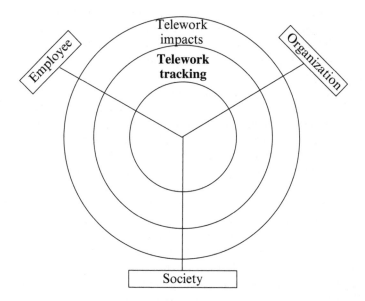

In this part we explore telework tracking from the employee, organizational, and societal perspectives. While often neglected, this tracking is integral to telework adoption and implementation as it provides a mechanism for ongoing feedback to the teleworker, the organization, and government policymakers. Telework tracking also plays a critical role in objectively measuring telework's impacts, many of which were discussed in the previous part of this book. Objective and quantifiable measures of telework penetration and frequency linked to measures of telework's consequences also provides data for analysis of telework behaviour.

As illustrated in the previous part, the impacts of telework are well researched and increasingly popular topics for academics and practitioners alike. As will be described in the last two parts of this book, the implementation and adoption of telework are also areas of increasing interest. In particular, consultants and managers tend to focus on processes for implementing telework programs, while policymakers are particularly focused on telework adoption rates and programs that encourage increased teleworking. Strangely, very little attention is paid to the tracking and measurement of telework. This is unfortunate, as it is our contention that tracking actually forms the linchpin to an integrative view of telework. For example, tracking links the adoption and implementation of telework to the impacts stemming from it. While telework impacts are not caused by its tracking, they are difficult to quantify and identify without the properly constructed tracking of telework behaviour. The importance of tracking also extends in the reverse direction; it provides a feedback mechanism that both will influence further adoption of telework and can be used to adjust telework implementation programs. For these reasons, we feel that the development and use of tracking mechanisms will be critical to growing the virtual workplace.

Not only is there a paucity of attention paid to telework tracking by researchers and practitioners, but the creators of telework tools have produced very few comprehensive telework tracking tools available at each of the three – employee, organizational, and societal – levels. Where tracking does take place, the tracking methods, tools, and benefits vary for each of these levels. In the following three chapters, after reviewing a number of tracking alternatives, we focus on an innovative tracking tool created and administered by Teletrips, Inc. The advantage of focusing on this tool is that it unifies the three perspectives by offering functionality at the employee, organizational, and societal levels. Thus, for illustrative purposes, in Chapter 5 we explore the Teletrips tool from the employee's perspective. This chapter offers a brief overview of telework tracking alternatives and then details the procedures and processes of the tool for the employee.

In Chapter 6 we examine telework tracking from an organizational perspective. We carry forward the Teletrips processes from the employee perspective, and detail how organizations can use the tool to track their employees' telework behaviour. We also discuss how, with proper tracking, organizations can capture and quantify emissions savings from reduced employee commutes. These savings can be credited toward greenhouse gas (GHG) reduction programs and potentially be added to organizational carbon credits.

In Chapter 7 we detail the societal perspective on tracking telework. We first review how the Teletrips tool can provide aggregate data for municipal or regional tracking of telework behaviour. We then use this aggregate data to measure the quantifiable benefits found in savings from transportation externalities. As a continuation from our Chapter 4 discussion of telework impacts at the societal level, we provide several templates that go beyond tracking the frequency and degree of telework to measuring its societal impacts.

5. Telework tracking: the employee perspective

At the employee level, telework tracking lets employees quantify the impacts of their telework. Further, such tracking is integral to both telework adoption and implementation as it provides a mechanism for ongoing feedback to the teleworker. Tracking at the employee level also forms the base from which aggregated data can be used to track telework penetration and frequency at the organizational and societal levels.

In this chapter we first briefly discuss the types of tracking systems available to employees. For illustrative purposes we then focus on an innovative tool developed by Teletrips, Inc. This tool provides many of the features needed in a telework tracking tool and can track from an employee, organizational, or societal level. We introduce Teletrips and then briefly describe the process, backend functioning, and reporting functionality of the Teletrips tool from the employee's perspective. We also discuss a sample of employee-level tracking data from a firm that used the tool. Finally, we end this chapter by reviewing some of the key benefits of this tool for tracking telework from the employee's perspective.

TYPES OF TRACKING SYSTEMS

Telework measurement systems can be placed into four broad categories: none, manual, statistical and technological (Roitz, 2006). Each category has different implications for the teleworker, the organization and society. For example, our research suggests that many teleworkers adopt telework without attempting to quantify the consequences of their telework behaviour – the 'none' tracking system. The key advantages of not using a measurement system are that no additional time, money, or related resources are required to implement such a telework program. Not having a tracking system also avoids the underestimation of telework penetration that can result from teleworkers simply not participating in formal tracking (for example, owing to lack of time or effort). Of course not having a tracking system has the disadvantage of not providing feedback or the ability to quantify telework impacts.

Manual measurement systems are the traditional HR time tracking mechanisms (Roitz, 2006). A good example of this form of tracking is seen in NASA's inclusion of telework tracking on project timesheets (see https://webtads 3.nis.nasa.gov/index.php/Telework). Manual measurement may also take the form of specific databases set up to track only teleworkers. However, manual tracking has several disadvantages (Roitz, 2006). First, any operation (such as manual tracking of telework) that requires teleworkers to do extra work will be a barrier to participation. Second, manual tracking can give both the employee and the manager the impression that a higher degree of supervision is required when an employee works from home. Third, any system that requires manual input from employees will also require a high degree of administrative energy, without which it will not be sustainable. Fourth, such a measure is inherently inaccurate, as manual platforms undercount underground teleworkers who do not see the value in or who do not want to be part of a central registry, and the results do not include occasional teleworkers who forget to enter their data or who are not aware of the formal procedure.

Properly-designed statistical surveys provide the most accurate, useful, cost-effective, and privacy-protecting telework measurement scheme available (Roitz, 2006). This type of tool brings in information from both teleworkers and non-teleworkers, including vital subjective information about the perceived costs and benefits of telework. Of course, these surveys are time and resource-intensive and can be somewhat inaccurate owing to a reliance on employee recall of average teleworking frequency over a given timeframe.

The final category utilizes advanced technology to track telework in real-time. Examples in this category include differentiating locations from which employees sign into LAN networks (local area networks) (home versus office) and using GPS (Global Positioning System) to track real-time locations of workers. The technology behind such tools is available, but is not yet in common use. The advantages of real-time telework tracking are that it is very accurate and not time-intensive for the employee. One potential disadvantage of this type of method is insufficient employee privacy.

INDIVIDUAL TELEWORK TRACKING TOOLS

As an important step towards the fourth system (real-time tracking) described above, several tools can help teleworkers measure and evaluate the impact, or potential impact, of their telework. For example, there are a number of web calculators that provide estimates of emissions relevant to telework. These include http://www.safeclimate.net, which has a tool that calculates carbon footprints using both transport and energy usage inputs.

Using travel records and utility bills, the user supplies the work-related distances travelled by car and plane, and the amount of energy used within the house and at the workplace. Interestingly, and related to our discussion in Chapter 4 on societal impacts of telework, this tool also considers paper usage in its telework impact calculations.

A tool that offers particularly in-depth calculations of telework costs and benefits is the Telework Impact Estimation Tool (TIET). This tool is useful at the employee, organizational and societal levels. The TIET is a web-based tool that utilizes energy consumption data from transportation, electronic equipment, lighting, and heating/cooling and calculates carbon emissions, fuel use, and fuel and energy costs. The TIET also takes into account the amount of space used at home and in the office, the number of hours electric equipment is active, and the sources of heating and cooling. This tool requires users to first answer questions about their daily lives and their work habits before they start teleworking. This is followed by questions about work and daily habits associated with teleworking. If one does not telework, one can still use the tool to quantify the relevant impacts by answering the non-telework portions of the survey. The TIET can be found at http://cgdm.berkeley.edu/telework/.

While both the above tools provide useful calculations of telework impacts, they fail to provide a quick and convenient way to both track ongoing telework behaviour and link this to employee, organizational and societal telework impact calculations. The remainder of this chapter focuses on the patent-pending telework tracking tool by Teletrips, which offers the ability to conveniently track employee-level telework and aggregate these data for organizational and societal reporting.

TELETRIPS BACKGROUND

Calgary-based Teletrips, Inc., founded in 1999, is a group of affiliated businesses providing benefits and services to help reduce commuter traffic, and thereby improve air quality, reduce energy consumption, and improve the quality of life within communities. The core goal of the organization is to promote sustainable urban development through the creation of incentive-based approaches to commuter trip reduction, particularly through implementation of telework programs within both the private and public sectors.

Teletrips provides project management, project consulting, incentives development, telework consulting, and community or program analysis services to develop community-wide and corporate-wide trip reduction programs. The company provides coordination of all aspects of project creation, management and implementation, including planning, policy development, promotion, execution, and post-project analysis. The data collected from the project are used by communities to determine commute patterns and trends for use in transportation infrastructure modelling and subsequent planning.

TELETRIPS TRACKING TOOL

Overview

The Teletrips Tracking Tool is proprietary web-based software that assists with the management and auditing of trip reduction programs. Teletrips software collects data from employees participating in corporate telework/trip reduction programs to track, verify and authenticate kilometres saved from these programs. The information is used to calculate an emissions saving, which can in some cases be used to offset the company's own emissions, or be traded to others. In addition, Teletrips is developing software that will calculate the 'bottom-line' benefits of corporate programs for financial reporting. The reports provided to users of the Teletrips software will demonstrate and quantify the extent of an organization's community responsibility and good governance.

Baseline Emissions is the emissions trading arm of Teletrips, Inc. This division provides emissions trading services to users of the Teletrips software, including the development of a mobile trading incentive, promotion of policies to develop mobile trading, coordination of third-party verification of credits, and representation with buyers of emissions credits.

The Teletrips tool has several features that are particularly useful for both employees and organizations. First, the tool is very streamlined to reduce the time required by employees to track their teleworking. Reducing the tracking burden for the employee encourages tracking participation. Reducing the tracking burden is extended to the organizational level as well by requiring minimal administrative resources to manage organizational tracking programs. Second, the tool allows for tracking by all employees, not just teleworking employees, thus providing baseline measures and increasing the likelihood of capturing underground telework behaviour. Finally, the Teletrips tool has been designed with a focus on potential verification and certification procedures, thus allowing for independent audits of telework programs, tracking and impacts. The ability to audit reported teleworking behaviour will increase in importance as organizations move toward the tracking and trading of GHG emissions.

Tracking Process

At the employee level the first step in using the Teletrips tool is for the employees to complete a profile form. The employees receive an e-mail message indicating that they have been selected for the Teletrips tracking program and that they need to fill out an employee profile to commence tracking. The one-time profile setup takes approximately five minutes. Once employees are set up, they need to spend less than 30 seconds per week filling out a weekly commute log. Figure 5.1 displays the first of three employee profile input screens.

Figure 5.2 displays the second employee profile screen. Fields of particular interest on this screen fall under the 'Telework Info' heading. These fields, which ask for estimates of previous telework frequency, assist in establishing a pre-tracking telework baseline that allows for post-tracking comparisons. This information is largely based on employee estimates, although in some cases the information can be imported from an existing database that might have been used to track telework.

The final screen of the employee profile is shown in Figure 5.3. Under the 'Commute Info' heading, the 'Split-Trips' field allows employees to identify a carpool or transit pickup point, with the next field allowing the employee to identify the distance travelled to that point. As the name

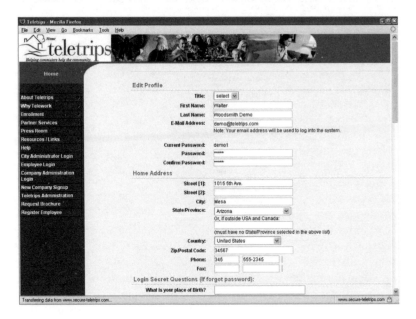

Figure 5.1   Employee profile screen one

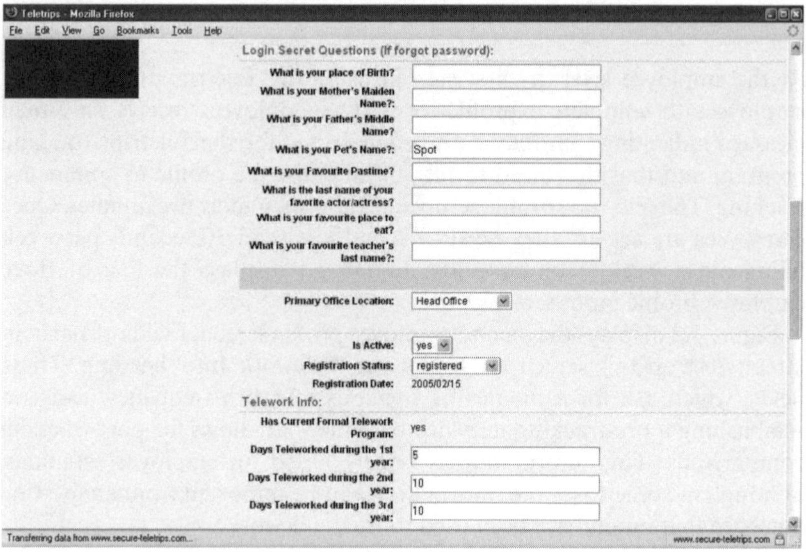

Figure 5.2   Employee profile screen two

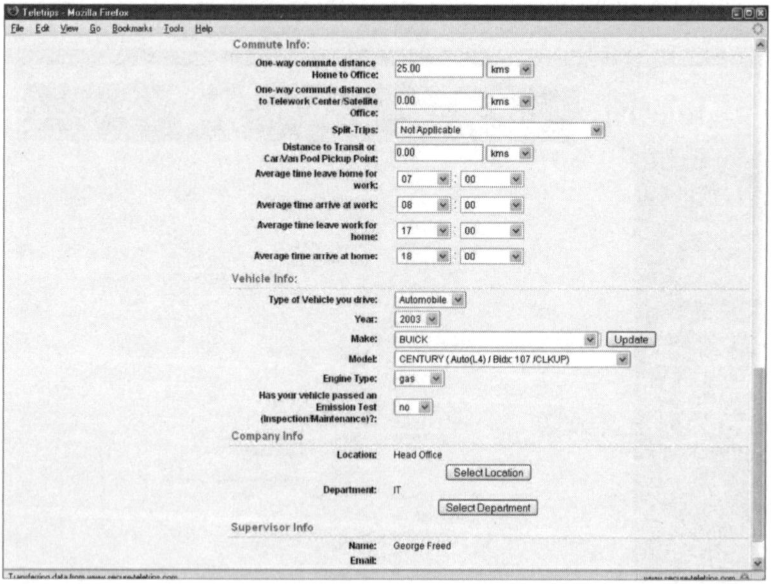

Figure 5.3   Employee profile screen three

suggests, a 'split trip' is commuting behaviour where an employee drives to a bus or train station or alternatively to a carpool pickup point (splitting the commute into driving and another form). Thus, the Teletrips 'Commute Info' fields allow for an accurate estimation of employee commute distances, be it commuting from home or to a split-trip pickup point.

This final profile screen also captures information on the commute times, by requiring employees to estimate the time it takes to go to and from work. These data will allow for calculations of commute time savings. Finally, under the heading 'Vehicle Info,' employees fill in the type of vehicle they drive (that is, year, make, model). This information is linked to a database of vehicles that calculates energy usage and emissions stemming from a given employee vehicle commute trip. The remaining fields of the employee profile can be used by the organization to break down telework tracking by department and supervisor. These fields can assist organizations with tracking compliance by offering an organizational contact to follow up with delinquent tracking behaviour. Supervisor and departmental connections can also be used to track intra-organizational commuter reductions (for example, firms can develop internal commuter challenges pitting departments against each other).

Upon completing the final page of the employee profile, the employee clicks on a submit button which captures the profile in the Teletrips database and sends an e-mail to the organization administrator indicating that the employee has finished the profile form. At this point the organizational administrator can activate the employee's account. Once this is done the employee is completely set up and ready to begin Teletrips tracking.

Once in the system, the employee receives a weekly tracking reminder e-mail from Teletrips (see Figure 5.4). Beyond requesting that the employee complete her weekly commute log, this weekly e-mail also highlights the cumulative distance, dollars, hours and emissions saved. As shown in Figure 5.4, the emission reductions are broken down into pounds or kilograms of VOC, NOx, CO_2 and CO. While these emission reductions are of interest to many teleworkers, the savings in commuting hours and vehicle operating dollars are also frequently of interest. The inclusion of such benefits of commute reductions not only provides weekly feedback to the employee, but also provides ongoing motivation to continue with the Teletrips tracking and presumably the trip reduction behaviour.

The hyperlink from the weekly reminder e-mail takes the employee to the weekly commute log (Figure 5.5). The input fields for the commute logs were designed with speed of use in mind: seven quick clicks of the radio buttons can complete the form in under 30 seconds. Once the weekly commute log is submitted, the data are stored in the Teletrips database and, by linking the commute log data to the employee profile, Teletrips can generate reports for employees, organizations, and municipalities or other regional bodies.

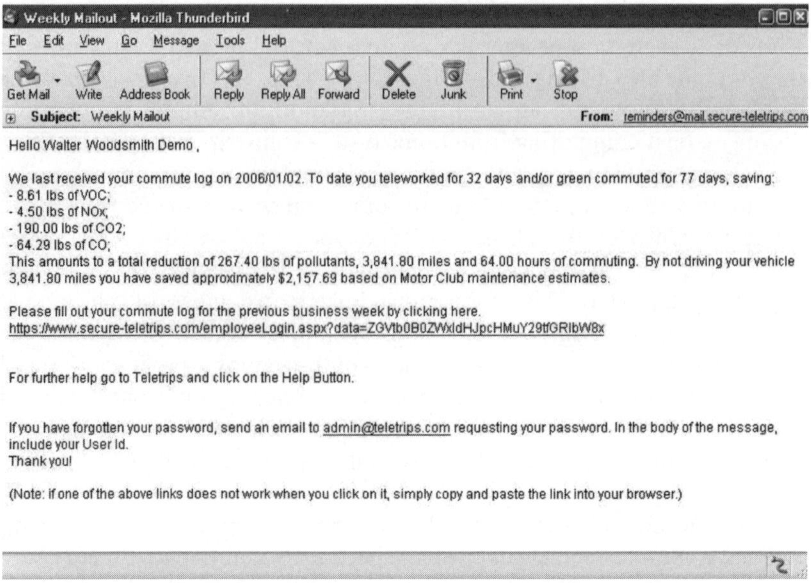

Figure 5.4   Weekly tracking reminder e-mail

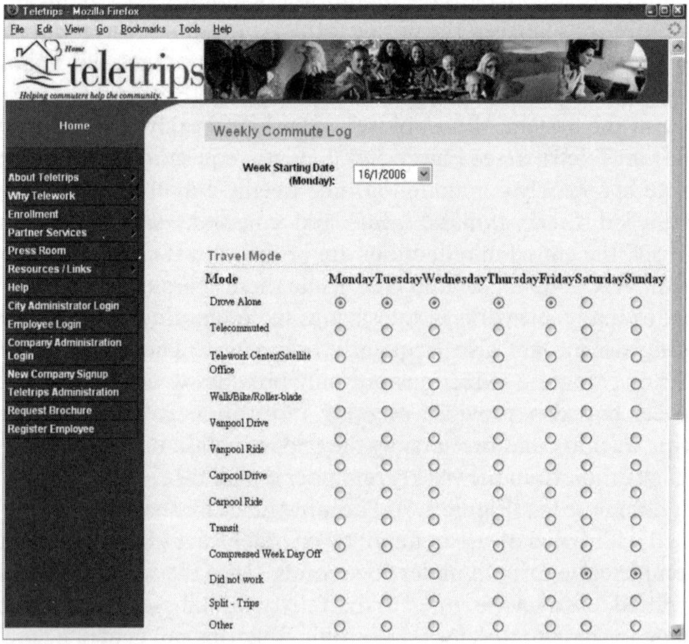

Figure 5.5   Weekly commute log

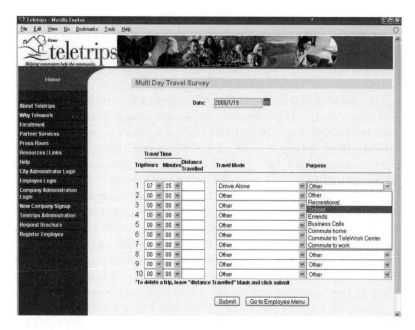

Figure 5.6   Multi-day travel survey

Beyond these basic functions, the Teletrips tracking tool has several advanced tracking options that can provide more detailed information, such as the multi-day travel survey, shown in Figure 5.6. This optional screen, while more time-consuming to fill out, allows employees to capture multi-purpose trips as part of their commute log. Thus, if an employee drops a child off at school on the way to work or stops to buy groceries on the commute home, this screen offers a mechanism for accounting for such dual-use trips. While currently not mandated in the tracking of commute trip reductions, such detailed tracking offers a more precise accounting of the distances and related energy and emissions savings. Of course the trade-off in capturing such detailed data is an increase in the tracking time required for employees, also leading to a likely reduction in employee compliance. Thus, the best use of this form would be on a periodic basis. This would give an indication of the frequency of dual-use trips, from which extrapolations could be made to the weekly commuting behaviour.

Reporting and Backend Calculations for Employee Tracking

The data from the commute logs and the employee profile are stored on the Teletrips servers and can therefore be linked to produce a number of reports.

One report is the weekly tracking reminder e-mail, which summarizes emission, dollar and time savings from commute trip reductions. Beyond this weekly e-mail, employee-level data can also be reported cumulatively in monthly, quarterly, or other specified date ranges. An example of one such report is shown in Table 5.1; the data in this table were produced using the Teletrips tracking tool for a subsidiary of a large multinational enterprise in the energy industry. The collection period was from 1 January 2005 to 30 November 2005. It should be noted that the table is just a sample of employee-level data (from 12 employees) taken from a much larger population of employees who utilized the Teletrips tool. Each row represents one employee.

A number of data sources and calculations are involved in producing reports such as the one shown in Table 5.1. For example, the 'distance reduced' refers to the total kilometres saved by teleworking, using a telework centre or another 'green commute' option. This is calculated for an employee for the period chosen according to the aggregated weekly commute log information and the distance information provided when the employee filled out her initial profile. From these figures the 'employee vehicle savings' columns provide savings calculations based on values for the make/model/year of the employee's vehicle. Further broken down, these savings include gasoline conserved (litres or gallons), which is calculated according to make/model/year data for gasoline consumption and reduced kilometres from teleworking or other green commute options.

It is also important to highlight that the Teletrips tracking tool can capture and break down data into a variety of commute trip reduction, or green commute, forms. While the focus of this book is on telework, employees and organizations are also interested in the savings and benefits accrued from all the possible commute trip reduction options. Table 5.2, drawn from the same sample of Teletrips trackers reported in Table 5.1, illustrates the breakdown of various commute trip reduction options. At the organizational and societal level such detailed data can be used to evaluate the impact of the various commuter reduction options and how the adoption of these options is influenced by a variety of policy initiatives. These implications are further discussed in the following chapters, but once again it is important to note the role that tracking – in this case overall green commute tracking – plays in linking the implementation, adoption and impacts of the commute behaviour.

CONCLUSION

Telework tracking at the employee level is critical to the future growth of the virtual workplace. Employee-level tracking gives feedback and

Table 5.1 Employee-level tracking data

Distance reduced (km)	Telework commute hours saved	Employee vehicle savings				Employee emission savings				
		Gasoline conserved (litres)	Gas ($)	Maintenance ($)	Total ($)	CO_2 (kg)	CO (kg)	VOC (kg)	NOx (kg)	Total (kg)
2 850	196	365	328	416	744	694	19	1	1	716
11 600	138	1485	1336	1694	3030	201	79	6	5	290
2 611	65	334	301	381	682	666	18	1	1	686
1 408	50	180	162	206	368	397	9	1	1	407
3 302	47	423	380	482	862	842	22	2	1	867
5 096	25	652	587	744	1331	1949	42	2	2	1996
1 836	23	235	212	268	480	492	13	1	1	506
672	18	86	77	98	176	105	4	0	0	110
512	16	66	59	75	134	3	4	0	0	7
4 944	13	633	570	722	1291	294	39	3	3	340
412	11	53	47	60	108	3	3	0	0	7
1 613	7	206	186	235	421	11	11	1	1	23

Table 5.2   Green commute tracking

Days teleworked	Compressed workdays	Walk/ bike/ roller	Transit	Vanpool ride	Carpool ride	Total green commute	Total km saved	Total hours saved
18	0	0	99	0	14	113	3 350	235
80	0	0	3	4	46	53	13 300	160
39	0	0	39	1	2	42	1 782	65
63	0	0	0	0	5	5	2 611	65
34	2	0	73	0	1	74	3 744	51
17	0	0	8	0	81	89	5 320	27
9	0	0	0	0	0	0	1 836	23
18	0	103	6	0	0	109	762	20
20	0	0	0	0	0	0	640	20
9	0	85	26	0	0	111	5 355	13

quantifies the personal impacts stemming from telework behaviour. The ability to quantify these impacts and relay this information back to employees will influence the cost–benefit assessment of employees considering telework adoption. Thus, telework tracking at the employee level will ultimately promote the continued and increased adoption of telework.

This chapter has explored telework tracking from an employee's perspective. While there are many forms that such tracking can take, we have focused on the Teletrips tool as a method for tracking employee-level telework. This tool has the advantage of offering speedy and prompted tracking logs that link employee telework behaviour to a set of data obtained from employee profiles. Using a number of assumptions and backend calculations, this tool lets employees track their telework behaviour and quantify its impacts. At the employee level, the key advantages of the Teletrips tool – and criteria that should be applied to other tracking methods – include minimal time requirements, availability of detailed data, telework tracking, and impact measurement and feedback. The Teletrips tool also has the advantage of being able to track and measure telework impacts from multiple perspectives. In the next chapter we move our focus of telework tracking from the employee perspective to that of the organization.

6. Telework tracking: the organizational perspective

In line with the previous chapter on employee-level telework tracking, there are also a number of key advantages to telework tracking at the organizational level. To begin with, telework tracking lets organizations assess the current telework penetration and frequency levels within the organization. Such tracking also offers ongoing feedback that can direct organizational-level telework policies and implementation programs. Finally, an increasingly relevant advantage of organizational-level telework tracking is the ability to capture and calculate the aggregate impacts of employee telework behaviour. For example, with proper tracking, organizations can capture and quantify emission savings from reduced employee commutes. These savings can be credited toward GHG reduction programs and potentially be added to organizational carbon credits.

In this chapter we explore telework tracking from the organization's perspective. We first outline and provide examples of a number of organization-level telework tracking options. Included in this overview are the key data requirements that organizations should consider when evaluating telework tracking options. Next, we highlight the utility and processes involved in using the Teletrips tracking tool at the organizational level. Finally, we end the chapter by analysing a sample of organizational-level data collected with the Teletrips tool.

FACTORS INFLUENCING ORGANIZATION-LEVEL TELEWORK TRACKING

When tracking telework, organizations should consider several key variables. Fortunately, most organizations will already have data on some of these variables, such as energy use in buildings and by equipment, and some organizations may even have information related to employee commute distances (Irwin, 2004). Generally speaking, in order to assess emission savings from teleworking, organizations need some mechanism to track the following key variables: reduction in commute miles, number of days per week or month the person teleworks, mode of travel (including type of vehicle and number of people if by car), and emission factors for mode of travel.

As discussed in the previous chapter, tracking tools fall into a number of categories. The three most common forms available to organizations are manual tracking, statistical (survey) tracking, and technology-focused tracking. Because we have already evaluated these types of tracking categories in the previous chapter, the current discussion will only highlight a few points of consideration for telework tracking at the organizational level. Manual tracking, when combined with the appropriate software, lets organizations aggregate individual-level telework tracking data. Surveys can be conducted periodically (for example, everyone is surveyed quarterly) or cross-sectionally (for example, a sample of employees track all commuting behaviour for a week each year). These results can then be statistically extrapolated to the organization as a whole. Organizations can also obtain data from employee telework agreements, which is less intrusive than other forms of tracking and utilizes pre-existing data. Such tracking, however, has the disadvantages of not capturing informal telework and of relying on *ex ante* estimates of telework behaviour that may be less accurate than *ex post* recollection of actual telework behaviour.

Assuming that the tracking tool accurately captures telework behaviour, two additional factors play a prominent role in evaluating tracking tools at the organizational level. The first factor is cost, to both the individual employee and the organization. From the organizational perspective the costs of tracking include employee and administrative costs that are largely composed of the time required to organize tracking, track, and then analyse and report the results from the tracking. The second factor for organizations to consider is privacy. Invading employee privacy is harmful to intra-organizational trust.

Beyond tracking commute trip reductions, organizational telework tracking can also capture telework impacts on office space and office energy usage and impacts of teleconferencing. It has been noted that not every audio, web, or video conference will replace a trip (Irwin, 2004). Thus, one approach to tracking the impact of virtual meetings is to choose a percentage of remote conferences that will be assumed to replace travel, according to company experience (Irwin, 2004). This percentage could then be used to estimate the reduction of plane or vehicle commuting distances, and these savings could be added to the organization's conventional commute reduction figures.

Regarding office energy use, telework provides the potential for energy savings from the reduction in cooling and heating costs at the (now smaller) conventional office. For small telework programs, however, savings in office energy will probably be minimal, given that the use of heating, air conditioning, and lights will not decline significantly if only a small number of employees telework (Mokhtarian et al., 1995). Telework also impacts the energy needed to run office equipment. For example, organizations may see reductions in energy usage as office equipment is turned off or used less while employees work from home. Of course, the utilization of additional teleconferencing equipment may actually increase equipment-related energy use for the organization. The point to highlight is that organizations should be aware of their potential energy savings from telework programs and factor these estimates into their tracking data and analysis.

One of the more salient organizational-level telework impacts is the potential reduction in office space costs. Flexible office arrangements such as 'hotelling' – where multiple teleworkers share reduced per capita office and desk space – allow organizations to realize substantial real estate savings. It is important that these savings are also captured and included in telework tracking and program evaluations. An innovative example of factoring-in office space savings from teleworking is provided by the Ministry of Public Works and Government Services Canada (PWGSC, 2003). The PWGSC provides a template for calculating a cost–benefit analysis of using temporary telework versus leasing 'swing' space while an organization is moving between locations or waiting for remodelling of existing office space. The use of temporary telework to reduce the need for swing office space is an uncommon but cost-efficient way to telework. The key point is that organizations can and should track the office space savings stemming from telework adoption.

The PWGSC suggests a five-step procedure for calculating the financial benefits of space reduction. The first step requires the user to input the average total space allocation per employee. This figure should include gross-up factors for lunchrooms, conference areas, and meeting facilities. The PWGSC offers the following estimates for different work types: office knowledge worker requirements range between 18 and 28 square metres per employee (or 200–300 square feet), call centre employees take from 14 to 18 square metres (or 150–200 square feet), and government employees average between 12 and 18 square metres (or 125–200 square feet).

The second step of the calculation requires the input data concerning the city where the office is to be located. This, in combination with step three – which requires the market type (for example, urban or suburban) – can be used to calculate the 'all-in rent' costs. These figures, usually supplied on a square foot or square metre basis, can be acquired from such organizations as the Building Owners and Managers Association (BOMA). The fourth step in the calculation is to input the estimated length of time that the swing office space would be needed. Finally, step five takes the all-in rent figure and adds any additional fit-up costs (such as getting the space up to code or organizational specifications). The fit-up costs add an average of $300 per square metre or $30 per square foot to the overall costs (these would be amortized over the life of the lease).

Using the above steps the PWGSC provides the following example to demonstrate the potential savings in swing office space from temporary telework. The calculations are based on an urban location in Ottawa where 10 square metres are needed per employee for a 12-month period with a $25 per square metre fit-up cost. In urban Ottawa, the cost works out to $157.50 per square metre per month, resulting in $18 900 per employee for the one-year duration of the lease. The PWGSC estimates the telework setup costs for each employee to be $2112 for the duration, with a retained investment on the telework equipment averaging $696 per employee. Thus, if telework is used, the savings per employee will be $17 484. Therefore, if the organization had ten employees teleworking instead of using leased swing space, the net savings would be $174 840 over the year.

The above calculations are relevant outside the specific 'swing space versus temporary telework' scenario. The significant cost savings highlight the importance for organizations to factor in potential office space impacts when tracking and assessing any telework program. Naturally, for traditional office space/telework scenarios, the organizational space requirements will rarely be zero, as they were in this scenario. Particularly with part-time telework, the employee will still need office space. Nonetheless, flexible office sharing arrangements can reduce space requirements even for part-time teleworking.

EXAMPLES OF ORGANIZATIONAL TELEWORK TRACKING

Table 6.1 displays some of the key results from an analysis of organizational telework tracking (Irwin, 2004). As the table indicates, three of the 12 companies surveyed do not track the number of teleworkers. Of the firms that do track, it appears that telework is defined either by the number of days a week the employees telework or by whether or not the employee has assigned office space. Ten of the companies had some data on transport and building use related to telecommuting, while none reported collecting data on vehicle-miles avoided by substituting telework for business travel (Irwin, 2004).

Beyond industry, government organizations also provide examples of telework tracking. For example, although there is no requirement for US federal agencies to track teleworking participants, some, such as the

Table 6.1   Approaches to tracking the number of teleworkers

Company	Track telework	Definition of telework	Method of tracking	Number of teleworkers
Apple	Yes	Two or more days a week	Confirming survey twice a year	350
AT&T	Yes	Prefer definition of 1 or more days a week; also track full-time virtual workers	Annual statistical survey	25% once or more a week, 10% full-time; in 2002, 17% full-time virtual and 40% telework some of time
Compaq	Yes	Home-based full-time; office-based part-time	No response	7000 total
HP	No			
Intel	At individual site only		Track number of drivers and miles avoided	No company-wide numbers
IBM	No assigned	Only mobile workers	Office space	58 000 in 1999
Lockheed-Martin	No			
Motorola	Yes	Work from home at least 8 hours a week	No description	No number given
Nortel Networks	Yes	No office space, home office wired	No description	6000
Sun Microsystems	Yes		Annual survey of commuting modes. New data collection system at pilot stage	
Radio Shack	Yes	Staff at call centre		35
Texas Instruments	No			

Source: adapted from Irwin, 2004.

Department of Energy and the Federal Deposit Insurance Corporation, are tracking telework through their time and attendance system. These agencies track employees who are regular and recurrent teleworkers, ad hoc (episodic or situational) teleworkers, and those teleworking for medical reasons.

US federal agencies offer further insight into organizational telework tracking, as these agencies were recently asked to report on the mechanisms used to track the prevalence of telework and the equipment provided to teleworkers. In this survey, 57 agencies reported using the telework agreement as the tracking mechanism, 35 used their current time and attendance system, and 33 had electronic tracking systems in place. Three agencies did not track telework (OPM and GSA, 2006).

To help these governmental and non-governmental organizations track telework, several third-party vendors have created organizational-level telework tracking tools. For example, Teleworking Consulting International (TCI) has developed a tracking tool that is part of the Canadian Standards Association (CSA) Climate Change, GHG Registries. GHG Registries maintains four primary integrated registries that together have been designed to meet the GHG policy registry needs within Canada. The four registries are the Canadian GHG Challenge Registry, the Canadian GHG Reductions Registry, the Canadian GHG Credit Registry and the Canadian Telework Registry. The Telework Registry Administration Console (teleTRAC) is a web-based tool that allows users to create, edit, and manage a telework program within the Canadian Telework Registry. The teleTRAC software provides the tools to measure, report, and manage GHG emissions, reductions, and removals.

Table 6.2 summarizes the data for the projects being tracked by this tool. As the table illustrates, there are only two active projects and 34 total users. That a Canadian national registry would have only 34 total users suggests a lack of telework tracking by both organizations and employees. That said, the tracking tool clearly provides some useful information. For example, it reports commuting distance avoided, commuting costs and commuting time avoided, and emissions avoided. Also of interest from the teleTRAC report is the tracking of costs, time and emissions from continuing commuting. These figures could be used to show the potential for further reduction if the trips in question could be replaced by telework.

Table 6.2   teleTRAC tracking results

Item category	Results
Number of active teleTRAC projects	2
Number of active teleTRAC users	34
Reductions for both active teleTRAC projects:	
Commuting distance (km) avoided	38 074.30
Commuting costs avoided	$559.68
Commuting time avoided	1860 minutes
Emissions avoided	6003.23 kg CO_2
Remaining totals for both active teleTRAC projects:	
Distance (km) commuted	153 931.05
Commuting costs	$10 668.14
Commuting time	32 772 minutes
Emissions generated	46 461.36 kg CO_2

Source: adapted from GHG Registries, 2006.

TELETRIPS TRACKING TOOL AT THE ORGANIZATIONAL LEVEL

In the previous chapter we examined the Teletrips telework tracking tool from the employee's perspective to illustrate the importance and potential of telework tracking tools. For illustrative purposes, we now offer a description of the Teletrips tool from the organization's perspective. The reports generated by Teletrips help a company assess the energy savings of its telework programs, audit their bottom-line impacts, and substantiate actions that reduce business risk through the dispersion of resources. Furthermore, through its proprietary web-based software program, used in conjunction with the US Environmental Protection Agency (EPA)'s Office of Transportation and Air Quality, Teletrips can calculate, validate and aggregate the emission reductions from telework and other trip reduction programs. In tracking NOx, VOC, CO, and CO_2 emission reductions, Teletrips uses established protocols and thereby provides the organization with pollution credits (Mobile Emission Reduction Credits or MERCs). MERCs are a marketable asset because bearers can trade or use them for environmental compliance.

The valuation of these MERCs will vary depending on a number of variables. For example, Teletrips suggests that in the regulated NOx and VOC cap and trade programs, the price variables include:

1. severity of air pollution in the region;
2. local, state, or provincial trading regulations (22 states currently have emissions trading regulations in place, with the Bush administration's Clear Skies Legislation encouraging all states to adopt such flexible approaches);
3. maturity of the air emission trading market in the area.

With GHG open market trading, price variables include:

1. national or international regulatory pressures to limit GHG, such as the Kyoto Protocol;
2. governmental regulatory actions;
3. integrity of protocol used to measure reductions. Emitters who are looking for a hedge against future regulation of GHG (and the resultant expenditures to comply with such regulation) are purchasing GHG options, or futures, now.

Teletrips Process

Organizations participating in a telework or trip reduction program using Teletrips begin by designating an administrator. The administrator enrols the organization with Teletrips and selects the employees to be included in the program. The administrator then receives a security code for gaining access to the data, reviewing and modifying profile information and receiving the summary reports.

The administrator will receive, via e-mail, the necessary information to get the trip reduction program participants registered and track their behaviour. The administrator fills out basic information about the organization and its trip reduction program. Figure 6.1 illustrates the first page of the company profile screen that the administrator completes on behalf of the organization. It is important to note that this process is not resource-intensive, taking approximately five minutes.

Fields of particular interest in Figure 6.1 include the 'Air Attainment Area', 'Mailout Rate' and telework history fields. Air attainment areas are designated by government agencies to help track pollution within a given air region; the designation of these areas is particularly salient in the California system. The ability to track emissions within a given region not only helps regional air planners but in the future may influence the price that organizations receive for their MERCs.

The 'Mailout Rate' field allows the organization to choose the frequency of tracking reminder e-mails that the employees receive. Organizations can, for example, use more frequent reminders early on and then change to

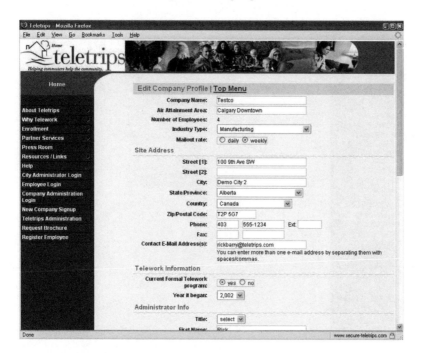

Figure 6.1   Teletrips company profile screen

weekly reminders as tracking becomes habitual. Under the 'Telework Information' fields, organizations can provide background and history of their telework and telework tracking programs. These fields allow for a tracking comparison with a baseline measure. For the organization this is usually the focus of telework tracking, as it is the comparison of period A with period B that reveals additional emission reductions. Finally, it should be noted that much of the remainder of the company profile form allows the administrator to add employees to the tracking database. This can be done manually, but to minimize resource requirements employees can be added by importing their information from a database file.

After completing the enrolment process the administrator receives a security code for gaining access to the data, reviewing and modifying profile information and receiving the summary reports. Figure 6.2 illustrates the administration menu available to the administrator. As displayed in this figure, the administrator can update the company profile, add employees, search for a specific employee and generate a variety of reports.

The reports section contains two key reports: the missing weekly commute report and the emissions report. The missing weekly commute report helps the administrator identify the employees that have not filled

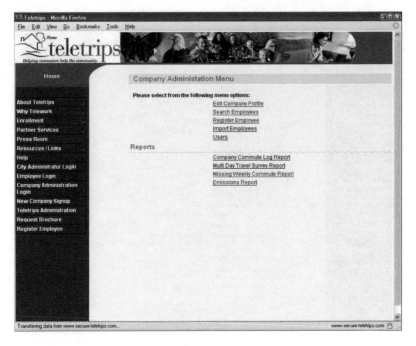

Figure 6.2   Teletrips company administration menu

out their weekly commute log. On the basis of this report the administrator could send a reminder to the non-tracking employees to fill out the weekly commute log. The emissions report provides the aggregate emission savings for the organization. We will review this report in more detail in the following section, which focuses on the Teletrips tool's output.

Teletrips Output

For the organization, one of the most important outputs from the Teletrips tool is the emissions report. This report identifies individual tracking results and aggregates total savings across all employees (savings include miles saved, hours saved, and various emissions saved). A sample emissions report is provided in Figure 6.3. The report gives the timeframe in which the tracking data were gathered and then breaks down each employee's green commutes and associated mileage reductions, and adds these figures in the bottom row to display the values for the telework program as a whole.

It is important to note that in calculating this report only telework and compressed workweeks influence commuter hours and miles saved; the other green commute options do not affect these calculations. The emission reduc-

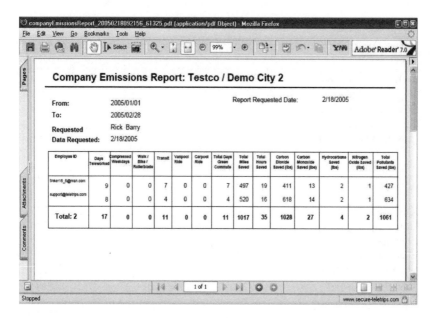

Employee ID	Days Teleworked	Compressed Weekdays	Walk / Bike / Rollerblade	Transit	Vanpool Ride	Carpool Ride	Total Days Green Commute	Total Miles Saved	Total Hours Saved	Carbon Dioxide Saved (lbs)	Carbon Monoxide Saved (lbs)	Hydrocarbons Saved (lbs)	Nitrogen Oxide Saved (lbs)	Total Pollutants Saved (lbs)
tinker16_5@man.com	9	0	0	7	0	0	7	497	19	411	13	2	1	427
support@teletrips.com	8	0	0	4	0	0	4	520	16	618	14	2	1	634
Total: 2	17	0	0	11	0	0	11	1017	35	1028	27	4	2	1061

Figure 6.3   Teletrips company emissions report

tion portion of the report may lead to MERCs. Emission calculations take commute miles saved through green commutes and multiply these figures by emission coefficients taken from the US government and other coefficients specific to the makes and models of the vehicles driven by employees.

The organizational-level functionality of the Teletrips tool is further demonstrated by an analysis of data from a large energy firm whose employees tracked their commuting behaviour over an 11-month period. These data are provided in Table 6.3. As depicted in the table, during the 11-month period 407 telework days were logged (in comparison with 2709 mass transit commutes). The aggregate commute time saved from the 407 telework days was 745 hours. The total value of all green commutes (mass transit, carpool, telework, walking, and so on) was $38 641 and the total amount of pollutants saved was 33 956 kilograms.

Given the potential telework days available (240 days × 84 employees = 20 160), the actual days teleworked (407) represents a low telework level of 2 per cent. This can be compared with the mass transit commute level of approximately 13 per cent. The total green commute level was 25 per cent. These levels offer insight into the potential savings from telework. For example, if this firm could increase its telework to a level equal to that of its mass transit commutes, it could save an additional 4000 hours of commute time. The organization's employees could use those additional

Table 6.3   Aggregated Teletrips data for company emissions report

Item category	Results
Employees tracking	84
Days teleworked	407
Compressed workdays	20
Green commutes:	
Walk/bike/rollerblade	1755
Mass transit	2709
Vanpool ride	79
Carpool ride	559
Total	5102
Km saved	147 937
Hours saved	745
Fuel saved (litres)	18 935.94
Fuel dollars saved	17 042.34
Maintenance dollars saved	21 598.8
Total dollars saved	38 641.14
Pollutants Saved (kg):	
CO_2	32 757
CO	1 060
VOCs	75
NOx	65
Total	33 956

4000 hours either as additional work hours or to enhance their work/life balance.

Benefits of Teletrips

The Teletrips tool provides organizations with an intuitive and low-resource-demand method for tracking telework and other green commute behaviour. Of specific interest to the organization, the Teletrips tool also offers the advantage of capturing GHG savings and through its audit process allows for the savings to potentially count toward an organization's MERCs or carbon credits. Another advantage of the Teletrips tool for organizations is that Teletrips houses and maintains the data on its own server, thus minimizing the IT burden on the organization. The web-based system also allows for tracking from remote locations. Employees do not need to come into the office – or even be connected to it – in order to track their commuting behaviour.

With regard to our earlier discussion of organizational-level telework impacts, the only important feature currently unavailable within the Teletrips tool is the tracking and measurement of potential office space savings. This is understandable, because Teletrips' main focus is now on green commutes in general, which typically do not produce office space savings.

CONCLUSION

Like employee-level tracking, the tracking of telework at the organizational level will influence the growth of the virtual workplace. Organizational telework tracking not only provides performance metrics for telework programs, but also can offer bottom-line benefits in the form of emission credits. The ability of telework tracking to quantify organizational telework benefits, combined with the fact that organizations' telework adoption decisions will be largely based on a cost–benefit calculation, suggests that organizational telework tracking will increase the growth of the virtual workplace.

This chapter has explored the tracking of telework from an organizational perspective. Our analysis suggests that organizations generally fall short in tracking and capturing telework behaviour and benefits. While there are many forms that such tracking can take, for illustrative purposes we focused on the Teletrips tool. This tool offers ongoing, real-time, auditable tracking, yet requires minimal administrative resources. The Teletrips tool provides a good example of the organizational benefits of telework tracking, particularly in calculating aggregated emission reduction figures. As shown in this chapter and the previous one, the Teletrips tool also has the advantage of being able to track and measure telework impacts from multiple perspectives or levels of analysis. In the next chapter we move our focus of telework tracking from the perspective of the organization to that of the society.

7. Telework tracking: the societal perspective

Tracking telework from a societal perspective is important because it allows for the empirical evaluation of telework-focused public policies. Such tracking also allows organizations and employees to see the aggregated effect of their behaviour. The current lack of sufficiently populated employee and organizational-level tracking databases, however, limits the utility of aggregating these databases to produce societal-level tracking. Thus, societal-level quantification of telework penetration and the associated spillover must currently rely on calculations from economic models and standard coefficients. (By standard coefficients we mean values for parameters that have been determined as a result of small-scale telework studies or analyses unrelated to telework. These parameters include items such as productivity increases resulting from telework, and the economic value of pollution reduction per vehicle-kilometre.)

In this chapter we explore telework tracking from a societal perspective. In line with the previous two chapters we first review current attempts to track telework at the societal level. We then describe how the Teletrips tool can assist in tracking telework at the societal level. Acknowledging the lack of societal tracking efforts, we conclude the chapter by offering a number of templates and economic formulas that can be used to calculate telework penetration levels and the associated spillover effects.

TRACKING EFFORTS AT THE SOCIETAL LEVEL

While many levels of government want to track the penetration of telework, the few efforts to develop a unified societal-level tracking system lack widespread use. Without significant participation, these database tools offer little value in measuring societal-level telework impacts or adoption rates. Most societal-level tracking initiatives take a project-by-project form, with little success in advancing a long-term societal-level tracking system.

Examples of societal-level tracking initiatives include the previously discussed teleTRAC tool, the development of which the Canadian government partially supported. Societal-level tracking initiatives also include government agencies' attempts to lead by example. For example, the US government through the Federal Employees Clean Air Incentives Act has an established reporting requirement for telework. Unfortunately, the definition for data to be provided is unclear, as is the type of teleworking that should be reported. Thus, federal agencies report data differently according to their interpretation of the definition of telework. There is also no requirement for federal agencies to establish and maintain records on, or a tracking system of, teleworking participants and relevant variables such as commute miles and commute hours saved by teleworking (OPM and GSA, 2006).

Regional and municipal telework tracking programs have also had limited success. Most of these tracking efforts are on a pilot project basis, with few maintaining a long-term consistent tracking program. Most notably these municipal-level programs revolve around commuter challenges that are designed to run one week to a month. These challenges often track reductions in single occupancy vehicle commute trips, and such programs pit one organization against another to see which one can achieve the greatest reduction in single occupancy commute trips. While such challenges are beneficial in terms of exposing commuters to different commute options, rarely do these challenges continue to track commuter, and specifically telework, behaviour beyond the timeframe of the challenge.

TELETRIPS TOOL AT THE SOCIETAL LEVEL

As in the previous two chapters, the Teletrips tool will serve as a useful illustration of the potential for societal-level telework tracking. The Teletrips tool can aggregate tracking data at the municipal, regional or federal level. As the number of organizations tracking with Teletrips increases, the utility of the regional tracking ability of this tool will become significant. Societal-level tracking is well within Teletrips' mandate, as the firm aims to create, implement, and manage public–private partnership programs to reduce commuter congestion, improve air quality, and reduce energy consumption. Teletrips joins with municipalities, states, provinces, and federal governments to design and implement incentives to encourage a sustainable approach to commuter transportation. These incentives may be achieved through public funding or through pure market-based approaches such as emissions trading. Teletrips recognizes the importance of telework tracking in harnessing the potential of telework programs and helping the community in its planning process. The Teletrips software is designed to complete the public–private goal of assessing community-wide environmental, transportation infrastructure, and health impacts of employees' commuter decisions.

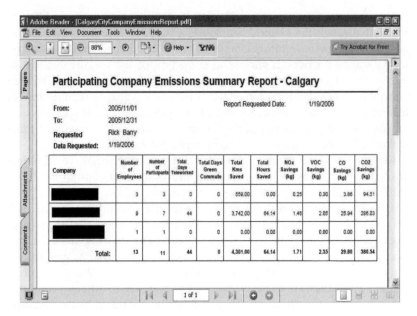

Figure 7.1   Teletrips societal-level reporting

An example of the information that could be gathered at a regional level with the Teletrips tool is provided in Figure 7.1. As this figure shows, the tool allows regional administrators to aggregate company tracking data. Because the tool breaks the data down by company, it can also be used with incentive-based teleworking policies.

Another mechanism that Teletrips offers at the regional level is the ability to track trip reductions by given commuter routes. While this is not an often used feature of the tool, employees can be asked to detail the route that they take to work, thus allowing for analysis of the congestion savings on a given route stemming from green commute behaviour.

MEASURING TELEWORK'S ABILITY TO ALLEVIATE ROAD TRANSPORT EXTERNALITIES

Moving from the Teletrips tool, which can aggregate actual telework behaviour, we now present a model that uses aggregate data to quantitatively estimate telework's potential effectiveness in alleviating road transport externalities. We also provide templates that allow for the calculation of telework's impacts on road maintenance and construction as well as on business continuity and mass transit usage. Readers not interested in quantifying these externalities may wish to skip the rest of this chapter, as it is rather technical.

Assessment of the Reduction in Vehicle Trips

The guideline used for this assessment is a method developed by Mokhtarian (1998). This model takes a fraction of the maximum expected number of teleworkers on a particular workday (M), looking only at those that generate a travel impact T (Formula 1):

$$T = M \times (1 - 0.19) \tag{1}$$

Self-employed individuals are partially subtracted because the majority of these individuals work in or from their homes. According to Pratt (2002) the work-at-home group consists of 68 per cent employees, 19 per cent home-based business owners, and 11 per cent non-home-based self-employed. Thus, for 19 per cent of the telework population there is no reduction in the peak-hour commuter round-trip. Therefore, the maximum expected number of teleworkers on a particular workday (M) is reduced by 19 per cent to obtain the maximum expected number of teleworkers on a particular day that generates a travel impact. M itself is calculated using Formula 2:

$$M = E \times A \times W \times C \times F \tag{2}$$

where
E = the average number of people employed in a certain geographic area and timeframe,
A = the proportion of the workforce that is able to telework,
W = the proportion of the workforce able to telework that is willing to telework,
C = the proportion of the workforce able and willing to telework that actually chooses to telework,
F = the average frequency of telework expressed as a fraction of a five-day workweek.

In order to assess E, the active workforce is multiplied by a coefficient a. This coefficient is lower than 1 because of working days lost on account of illness, leaves and strikes. Normally the necessary statistics can be obtained from the National Statistics Office. Template 1 explains how the value of E can be obtained. If these statistics are not available for a particular geographic region within a country, the national statistics can be used.

Template 1   The average number of people employed in a certain geographic area and timeframe

Item	Coefficient/formulas	Field
The active workforce in the considered geographic region		I
The average number of holidays (including legal holidays)		II
The average number of days that employees are sick		III
The average number of days that employees are on strike		IV
The number of workdays without correction for leave, illness or strikes		V
Correction coefficient = a	$(V-II-III-IV)/V$	VI
E = the average number of people employed in a certain geographic area and timeframe	$VI \times I$	VII

In order to assess A (the proportion of the workforce that is able to telework), Template 2 can be used. Ideally, these numbers should be broken down by sector for the geographic area. However, if these data are not available, the national statistics can be used. These percentages are then used as weights when summing up the percentage of teleworkers usually found in a particular sector.

When estimating W (the proportion of the workforce able to telework that is willing to telework) Mokhtarian suggests that, based on empirical data, this may be as high as 88 per cent (Mokhtarian, 1998). However, Mokhtarian also points out that selection bias in survey-based studies may produce an overestimation of W ($W_1 = 0.8$) (Mokhtarian, 1998). For example, people who do not want to telework are less likely to return a survey related to telework. Hence, Mokhtarian suggests that the proportion of the workforce that is able to telework and is willing to telework is more likely to be close to 50 per cent ($W_2 = 0.5$) (Mokhtarian, 1998).

In some situations, constraints are not powerful enough to eliminate a preference for telework, but they may be sufficient to prevent the person from actually choosing telework (for example, the absence of a separate office space at home may be an insufficient constraint to eliminate the preference for telework but could prevent the person from actually choosing it) (Mokhtarian, 1998). For this reason, C (the proportion of the workforce

Template 2   The proportion of the workforce that is able to telework

NAICS-code	Percentage of employees in that particular sector	Percentage of potential teleworkers in the workforce in that particular sector
11 – Agriculture, Forestry, Fishing and Hunting		
21 – Mining and Oil and Gas Extraction		
22 – Utilities		
23 – Construction		
31–33 – Manufacturing		
41 – Wholesale Trade		
44–45 – Retail Trade		
48–49 – Transportation and Warehousing		
51 – Information and Cultural Industries		
52 – Finance and Insurance		
53 – Real Estate and Rental and Leasing		
54 – Professional, Scientific and Technical Services		
55 – Management of Companies and Enterprises		
56 – Administrative and Support, Waste Management and Remediation Services		
61 – Educational Services		
62 – Health Care and Social Assistance		
71 – Arts, Entertainment and Recreation		
72 – Accommodation and Food Services		
81 – Other Services (except Public Administration)		
91 – Public Administration		
Proportion of the workforce that is able to telework	Sum of the products of the above two columns	

able and willing to telework that actually chooses to telework) comes into play; Mokhtarian's estimate of 76 per cent ($C = 0.76$) can be used (Mokhtarian, 1998).

Studies suggest that employees prefer part-time telework over full-time telework (Yap and Tng, 1990), and the frequency of telework reflects this. A weighted average across various studies worldwide suggests a current average frequency of 1.2 days per workweek. For the United States, Rathbone (1992) reports an average frequency of 1.8 days per workweek, while Handy and Mokhtarian (1996) report a frequency of 1.2 days per workweek. For Singapore, Olszewiski and Lam (1996) estimate the frequency at 2 days per workweek. Lyons et al. (1998) estimate the frequency of telework in the UK at between 1.4 and 1.7 days per workweek. For the Netherlands, the frequency has been estimated at between 1 and 1.5 days per workweek (van Reisen, 1997). Handy and Mokhtarian (1995) surveyed the literature and found that frequency levels range from 0.8 days per workweek up to 3 days per workweek (Handy and Mokhtarian, 1994). For current telework frequency, we use 1.2 days per workweek ($F_1 = 0.24$). In response to suggestions from surveyed HR managers (Illegems and Verbeke, 2003), we also include a plausible frequency of 3 days per workweek ($F_2 = 0.6$).

Template 3 can be used to estimate the maximum number of teleworkers on a particular workday. The lower level of the maximum number of teleworkers on a particular day (M) is given by $E \times A_1 \times W_2 \times C \times F_1$ and the upper level is given by $E \times A_2 \times W_1 \times C \times F_2$. Template 3 also allows for the calculation of the maximum number of teleworkers that generate a travel impact on a particular day (T).

In a second step, the model estimates the impact on transportation by assessing the net reduction in vehicle-kilometres travelled (Z). The model takes into consideration travel-generating effects of telework (Formula 3):

$$Z = V - (N + R + L) \times V \tag{3}$$

where
$V =$ the total expected commuter vehicle-kilometres eliminated on any given weekday (see Formula 4),
$N =$ the expected increase in travel due to non-work trip generation, expressed as a fraction of the reduction in vehicle-kilometres travelled,
$R =$ the expected increase in travel due to longer commute distance as a result of residential relocation, expressed as a fraction of the reduction in vehicle-kilometres travelled,
$L =$ the expected increase in travel due to latent demand, expressed as a fraction of the reduction in vehicle-kilometres travelled.

Template 3 *Estimates of the maximum number of teleworkers on a particular day (*M*) and maximum number of teleworkers that generate a travel impact (*T*), based on previous assumptions*

Item	Coefficient/formulas	Field
The average number of people employed in a certain geographic area (E)		I
The proportion of the workforce that is able to telework (A_1)		II
The proportion of the workforce that is able to telework (A_2)		III
The proportion of the workforce able to telework that is willing to telework (W_1)		IV
The proportion of the workforce able to telework that is willing to telework (W_2)		V
The proportion of the workforce able and willing to telework that actually chooses to telework (C)		VI
The average frequency of telework expressed as a fraction of a five-day workweek (F_1)		VII
The average frequency of telework expressed as a fraction of a five-day workweek (F_2)		VIII
Maximum teleworkers on a particular day (M) $= E \times A_1 \times W_2 \times C \times F_1$	I×II×V×VI×VII	IX
Maximum teleworkers on a particular day (M) $= E \times A_1 \times W_1 \times C \times F_1$	I×II×IV×VI×VII	X
Maximum teleworkers on a particular day (M) $= E \times A_1 \times W_2 \times C \times F_2$	I×II×V×VI×VIII	XI
Maximum teleworkers on a particular day (M) $= E \times A_1 \times W_1 \times C \times F_2$	I×II×IV×VI×VIII	XII
Maximum teleworkers on a particular day (M) $= E \times A_2 \times W_2 \times C \times F_1$	I×III×V×VI×VII	XIII
Maximum teleworkers on a particular day (M) $= E \times A_2 \times W_1 \times C \times F_1$	I×III×IV×VI×VII	XIV
Maximum teleworkers on a particular day (M) $= E \times A_2 \times W_2 \times C \times F_2$	I×III×V×VI×VIII	XV
Maximum teleworkers on a particular day (M) $= E \times A_2 \times W_1 \times C \times F_2$	I×III×IV×VI×VIII	XVI

Template 3   (continued)

Item	Coefficient/formulas	Field
Proportion of self-employed that do not generate travel effects		XVII
Maximum teleworkers on a particular day that generate a travel impact $(T) = M \times (1-0.19)$ and $M = E \times A_1 \times W_2 \times C \times F_1$	IX×XVII	XVIII
Maximum teleworkers on a particular day that generate a travel impact $(T) = M \times (1-0.19)$ and $M = E \times A_1 \times W_1 \times C \times F_1$	X×XVII	XIX
Maximum teleworkers on a particular day that generate a travel impact $(T) = M \times (1-0.19)$ and $M = E \times A_1 \times W_2 \times C \times F_2$	XI×XVII	XX
Maximum teleworkers on a particular day that generate a travel impact $(T) = M \times (1-0.19)$ and $M = E \times A_1 \times W_1 \times C \times F_2$	XII×XVII	XXI
Maximum teleworkers on a particular day that generate a travel impact $(T) = M \times (1-0.19)$ and $M = E \times A_2 \times W_2 \times C \times F_1$	XIII×XVII	XXII
Maximum teleworkers on a particular day that generate a travel impact $(T) = M \times (1-0.19)$ and $M = E \times A_2 \times W_1 \times C \times F_1$	XIV×XVII	XXIII
Maximum teleworkers on a particular day that generate a travel impact $(T) = M \times (1-0.19)$ and $M = E \times A_2 \times W_2 \times C \times F_2$	XV×XVII	XXIV
Maximum teleworkers on a particular day that generate a travel impact $(T) = M \times (1-0.19)$ and $M = E \times A_2 \times W_1 \times C \times F_2$	XVI×XVII	XXV

$$V = T \times f \times D \tag{4}$$

where
f = the proportion of telework occasions that eliminate a vehicle commuter trip,
D = the average round-trip commuter distance.

When estimating V (the total expected commuter vehicle-kilometres eliminated on any given weekday), one has to take into account only the proportion of the vehicle-kilometres travelled. Therefore, f will be less than 1 after eliminating the person-kilometres travelled by soft modes and public transport and correcting for carpooling. Hence f is obtained by dividing the percentage of commuters using a car to travel to work by the average vehicle occupation. When estimating D (the average round-trip commuter distance), one has to take into account that, so far, most empirical studies have concluded that teleworkers face longer than average commuting trips. However, if the teleworkers use telework centres or satellite offices, only some of the commuter vehicle-kilometres are eliminated – roughly 65 per cent (Nilles, 1988; Balepur et al., 1998). In the United States, most current telework is home-based, because this is easy to organize and relatively inexpensive (Mokhtarian and Sato, 1994; Nilles, 1998). Telework is often home-based in the EU as well (European Commission, 1998).

This leads us to Formula 5:

$$V = d_1 \times T \times f \times D + d_2 \times T \times f \times 0.65 \times D \qquad (5)$$

where
d_1 = the percentage of home workers in the total telework population; as an example, the VUB-Brussels employee survey indicates this figure can be estimated at 82.4 per cent (Illegems and Verbeke, 2004);
d_2 = the percentage of centre-based teleworkers in the total telework population; the VUB-Brussels employee survey indicates this figure can be estimated at 17.6 per cent (Illegems and Verbeke, 2004);
D = the average one-way commute distance.

On the basis of an aggregate time series analysis and of the limited empirical evidence available, Choo et al. (2005) concluded that it can be assumed that the travel-generating effects of telework implementation are small relative to the savings. They concluded that the reduction in vehicle-kilometres due to a reduction in commuting can be seen as a reasonable upper bound of the effect of teleworking implementation on vehicle-kilometres travelled.

When estimating the increase in non-commuter travel (N), one must note that no empirical evidence confirms this hypothetical increase. On the contrary, evidence seems to point in the opposite direction. Hence we assume that N equals zero. Similarly, no evidence supports an increase in travel due to residential relocation. Hence we assume that R is also zero.

At this point, no empirical evidence exists regarding the impact of latent demand (L) on travel savings due to telework. However, a number of researchers have suggested that approximately half of the potential reduction in vehicle-kilometres will be replaced by new traffic (Gillespie et al., 1995; Ritter and Thompson, 1994). Hence L is estimated at 0.5. Template 4 allows for calculating the reduction in vehicle-kilometres per day.

Template 4   Reduction in vehicle-kilometres

Item	Coefficient/formulas	Field
Maximum teleworkers on a particular day that generate a travel impact (T) (see Template 3)		I
Percentage of commuters using a car to travel to work		II
The average vehicle occupation		III
The proportion of telework occasions that eliminate a vehicle commuter trip (f)	II/III	IV
The average round-trip commuter distance (in kilometres) (D)		V
The percentage of home workers in the total telework population (d_1)		VI
The percentage of centre-based teleworkers in the total telework population (d_2)		VII
Correction factor for commuting to a centre		VIII
The total expected commuter vehicle-kilometres eliminated on any given weekday (V)	$(VI \times I \times IV \times V)+$ $(VII \times I \times IV \times VIII \times V)$	IX
The expected increase in travel due to non-work trip generation (N)		X
The expected increase in travel due to residential relocation (R)		XI
The expected increase in travel due to latent demand (L)		XII
The net reduction in vehicle-kilometres travelled per workday (Z)	$IX-(X+XI+XII) \times IX$	XIII

SOCIETAL IMPACT

Once we have figured out these telework-induced reductions in vehicle-kilometres travelled, what is the monetary impact of consequent reductions in road congestion, air pollution, noise pollution, and road accidents, as well as the monetary impacts related to energy savings, road maintenance, new road construction, business continuity, and usage of mass transit?

Note that our analysis does not include telework's positive impact in other macro-level areas, such as workforce satisfaction, workforce productivity, and aggregate new job opportunities for groups formerly excluded from the labour markets (for example, disabled people, parents with young children, and people in rural areas).

Road Congestion

To estimate the monetary savings in external costs related to road congestion due to a particular level and frequency of telework, we use Formula 6:

$$MC = Z \times C \qquad (6)$$

where
MC = monetary savings in external costs related to road congestion due to a particular level and frequency of telework,
Z = savings in vehicle-kilometres due to a particular penetration level and frequency of telework,
C = marginal external cost of road congestion per vehicle-kilometre.

Template 5 allows for calculating the monetary savings in external road congestion costs for different penetration levels and frequencies of telework.

Template 5 Monetary savings in external costs related to road congestion due to a particular penetration level and frequency of telework

Item	Coefficient/ formulas	Field
The net reduction in vehicle-kilometres travelled per workday (Z) (see Template 4)		I
Marginal external cost of road congestion per vehicle-kilometre (C)		II
Monetary savings in external costs related to road congestion due to a particular level and frequency of telework per workday	I×II	III
The number of workdays in a year		IV
Monetary savings in external costs related to road congestion due to a particular level and frequency of telework per year (MC)	III×IV	V

Emissions

Telework reduces the number of daily commuter trips, thereby reducing the total emissions caused by vehicle activity (Henderson et al., 1996). As noted earlier, the impact of a particular level of telework on air quality depends on a number of parameters, such as:

- *Distance travelled by car or vehicle-kilometres*: the greater the distance travelled by car, the greater the total emission volumes will be.
- *Number of cold starts[1] and number of hot starts*: when a vehicle with a warmed-up engine is started, it produces a lower emission of pollutants than a vehicle with a cold engine. Therefore, if teleworking causes people to make more unlinked trips, this might actually increase pollution (Henderson et al., 1996).
- *Speed*: a U-shaped relationship exists between speed and emission levels. Up to around 80–96 kilometres per hour, the emission of pollutants decreases as the speed increases. Above 80–96 kilometres per hour, the emission of pollutants increases as speed increases. In addition, multiple accelerations and decelerations during a trip increase the emission of pollutants. Stop-and-go travel (in traffic jams, for example) is particularly bad with respect to certain pollutants; for example, it is the worst for emitting carbon monoxide (CO) and hydrocarbons (Salomon, 1984).
- *Type of vehicle*: the emission of pollutants caused by vehicle activity varies with the type of vehicle. For example, a catalytic converter lowers the emission of pollutants.
- *Ambient temperature*: the emissions generated by a cold start are highly correlated with the temperature of the surrounding air at that time. Therefore, cold starts caused by a trip to work early in the morning or late at night produce higher emissions than cold starts during regular daytime hours. Telework reduces such early and late night commuter trips (Sampath et al., 1991; Henderson et al., 1996).

Road transport is the primary cause of the emission of nitrogen oxides (NOx), volatile organic compounds (VOC), carbon monoxide (CO), and particulate matter with a diameter of less than 10 micrometres (PM10). Road transport also contributes to the emission of sulphur dioxide (SO_2), tropospheric O_3 (ozone), and carbon dioxide (CO_2). Tropospheric O_3 is a secondary pollutant caused by the emission of VOC and NOx. VOC and PM10 can cause cancer. NOx, O_3, SO_2, and CO_2 may cause respiratory infections, chronic obstructive pulmonary diseases, and asthma. O_3 also has a negative effect on the growth of vegetation. SO_2 is a soured component

*Table 7.1   Monetary valuation of specific emission factors for an urban
            area*

	NOx	VOC	CO	PM10
Euros (1990) per kg	13.8	2.96	0.01	83.20

Source: Mayeres et al., 1996.

that affects buildings as well as soil and water (B.I.M., 1996). Mayeres et al. (1996) have estimated the monetary value of the emission factor per kilogram of NOx, CO_2, VOC, CO, PM10, and SOx in a peak period in an urban area (Table 7.1).

It is important to note one reason why telework may increase the emissions per vehicle-kilometre. As discussed in Chapter 4, the amount of emissions produced is closely linked to the travel pattern. Since telework implementation reduces trip chaining, this might result in more cold starts and shorter trips, producing higher levels of emissions per vehicle-kilometre (Gillespie et al., 1995). In reality, however, the small increase in emissions per vehicle-kilometre is overwhelmed by the reduction in vehicle-kilometres.

To date the State of California study and the Puget Sound study are the only two rigorous studies to estimate telework's impact on emissions (Mokhtarian et al., 1995; Henderson et al., 1996). In the Puget Sound study, the analysis of air quality impact is based on 72 telecommuters (these persons did not necessarily participate in all survey waves) of whom eight teleworked from a centre and ten teleworked only partial days (Henderson et al., 1996). The air quality models used in the State of California study (EMFAC 7E and BURDEN 7E) have estimated a reduction in VOC of 1.1 grams eliminated per kilometre, a reduction in NOx of 0.9 gram eliminated per kilometre and a reduction in CO of 9 grams eliminated per kilometre (Mokhtarian et al., 1995).

The Puget Sound air quality models led to the conclusion that, because teleworkers make 30 per cent fewer trips, travel 63 per cent fewer vehicle-kilometres and perform 44 per cent fewer cold starts on telework days, teleworking substantially reduces the emissions of VOC, CO, NOx, and PM (Table 7.2).

The estimates obtained in the Puget Sound study were based on the same type of air quality model as the State of California Study, namely EMFAC and BURDEN, but using a later version (7F). Although these models are among the most advanced mobile source emission models available and probably provide the best estimates of the impact of telework implementation on vehicle emissions for air basins in California today, they tend to

Table 7.2   Reductions in the emission of several pollutants*

Pollutant	State of California study	Puget Sound study
VOC	70.2	25.96
NOx	62.0	27.32
CO	581.2	204.15
PM	–	6.92

Note: * Measured in grams per telework occasion on a particular day.

Sources: State of California study: Mokhtarian et al., 1995; Puget Sound study: Henderson et al., 1996.

underestimate the amount of emissions caused by vehicle activity (Henderson et al., 1994, 1996).

The models take into consideration the season as well as the fleet age mix. Summer and winter are the two seasons for which vehicle activity patterns and atmospheric conditions result in the worst air quality. In the summer the greatest concern is ozone precursors (VOC and NOx), while in the winter the CO level is of greatest concern. No conclusions were drawn about the emission of sulphur oxides (SOx) or lead, because the small population involved in this study did not generate measurable amounts of these pollutants. The emission of PM and NOx, which is primarily related to running-exhaust, decreased owing to the reduction in vehicle-kilometres travelled. The reduction in cold starts, of which the largest reductions were in the morning, contributed mainly to the reductions in the emissions of VOC and CO.

The values reported in these studies may be too high owing to the fact that the emissions of these pollutants per vehicle-kilometre have dropped since this assessment, because modern vehicles pollute much less. However, these figures still allow us to estimate the magnitude of the reduction in emissions. These figures are also substantiated by recent evaluations of VOC and NOx emission reductions per telework occasion in five US e-commute pilot cities. These cities issued emission credits for telecommuting and the data revealed that the reductions in these five cities are below the impact estimated in the State of California Study but above that of the Puget Sound Study. Table 7.3 gives an overview of the reduction in the different cities assuming that the employees would have driven alone to work on conventional workdays. Hence the Puget Sound study values can be used as conservative defaults.

In order to assess telework's effect on the emission of certain pollutants, we use the data from the Puget Sound study. In this case, estimates are available only for PM, NOx, VOC and CO. An estimation of the monetary

Table 7.3   Reductions in the emission of VOC and NOx*

City	VOC	NOx
Washington, DC	63.05	57.15
Denver	71.21	55.34
Houston	48.53	44.0
Los Angeles	55.79	28.12
Philadelphia	54.43	63.50
Average	64.4	56.25

Note: * Measured in grams per telework occasion on a particular day.

Source: Nelson, 2004.

savings in the external costs related to emissions due to a particular level and frequency of telework can be made using Formula 7:

$$TE_i = T \times PS_i \times 1/1000 \tag{7}$$

where
TE_i = the total reduction in emission for a pollutant i on a peak period on a particular day in kilograms,
T = the maximum number of teleworkers on a particular day that generate a travel impact,
PS_i = the reduction in emission of a pollutant i per telework occasion according to the Puget Sound study (in grams).

To assess the monetary impact of a specific penetration level of telework on emissions in kilograms for a certain geographic area, we use Formula 8:

$$MVE_i = MVE/g_i \times TE_i \tag{8}$$

where
MVE_i = the total monetary impact of a particular penetration level of telework on the particular emissions of NOx, VOC, CO, or PM10,
i = a particular pollutant,
MVE/g_i = the monetary value of the marginal external cost for a specific pollutant in dollars per kilogram.

Template 6 can be used to calculate the monetary savings due to a reduction in emissions caused by a particular penetration level and frequency of telework.

*Template 6   Reduction in emissions resulting from a specific level of
            telework*

Item	Coefficient/formulas	Field
The reduction in emission of VOC per telework occasion (in grams)		I
The reduction in emission of NOx per telework occasion (in grams)		II
The reduction in emission of CO per telework occasion (in grams)		III
The reduction in emission of PM per telework occasion (in grams)		IV
Maximum teleworkers on a particular day that generate a travel impact (T) (see Template 3)		V
The reduction in emission of VOC on a particular day (in kg)	$(I \times V)/1000$	VI
The reduction in emission of NOx on a particular day (in kg)	$(II \times V)/1000$	VII
The reduction in emission of CO on a particular day (in kg)	$(III \times V)/1000$	VIII
The reduction in emission of PM on a particular day (in kg)	$(IV \times V)/1000$	IX
The number of workdays in a year		X
The reduction in emission of VOC for a year (in kg)	$VI \times X$	XI
The reduction in emission of NOx for a year (in kg)	$VII \times X$	XII
The reduction in emission of CO for a year (in kg)	$VIII \times X$	XIII
The reduction in emission of PM for a year (in kg)	$IX \times X$	XIV
The monetary value of the marginal external cost of VOC in $/kg		XV
The monetary value of the marginal external cost of NOx in $/kg		XVI
The monetary value of the marginal external cost of CO in $/kg		XVII
The monetary value of the marginal external cost of PM in $/kg		XVIII

Template 6   (continued)

Item	Coefficient/formulas	Field
The monetary value of the reduction in emission of VOC for a year	XI×XV	XIX
The monetary value of the reduction in emission of NOx for a year	XII×XVI	XX
The monetary value of the reduction in emission of CO for a year	XIII×XVII	XXI
The monetary value of the reduction in emission of PM for a year	XIV×XVIII	XXII
The monetary value of the reduction in emission of VOC, NOx, CO and PM for a year	XIX+XX+XXI+XXII	XXIV

Road Safety

Road accidents are related to the level of traffic, road and weather conditions, and road user behaviour (Guria, 1999). The relationship between road accidents and traffic flow is nonlinear (Dickerson et al., 2000); that is, the number of road accidents is close to zero for low and moderate traffic flows, but it increases significantly at high traffic flows. By decreasing the level of traffic during peak (that is, high traffic) hours, telework takes cars off the road at the time of day when doing so has the highest beneficial marginal effect on road accidents. In order to estimate the monetary savings related to road accidents we use Formula 9:

$$MA = Z \times A \tag{9}$$

where
MA = monetary savings in external costs related to road accidents due to a particular level and frequency of telework,
Z = savings in vehicle-kilometres due to a particular penetration level and frequency of telework,
A = marginal external cost of road accidents per vehicle-kilometre. We note that Mayeres et al. (1997) estimated these costs at 0.1036 euros per km.

Template 7 can be used to assess the monetary savings in external costs related to road accidents.

Template 7   Monetary savings in external costs related to road accidents
due to a particular level and frequency of telework

Item	Coefficient/formulas	Field
The net reduction in vehicle-kilometres travelled per workday (Z) (see Template 4)		I
Marginal external cost of road accidents per vehicle-kilometre (A)		II
Monetary savings in external costs related to road accidents due to a particular level and frequency of telework per workday	I×II	III
The number of workdays in a year		IV
Monetary savings in external costs related to road accidents due to a particular level and frequency of telework per year (MA)	III×IV	V

Noise Levels

In order to estimate monetary savings due to a reduction in noise pollution, we use Formula 10:

$$MS = Z \times S \tag{10}$$

where
MS = monetary savings in external costs related to noise due to a particular level and frequency of telework per workday,
Z = savings in vehicle-kilometres (per workday) due to a particular penetration level and frequency of telework,
S = marginal external cost of noise per vehicle-kilometre; we note Mayeres et al. (1997) provided an estimate of approximately 0.0015 euros per km.

Template 8 allows for calculating the monetary savings in external costs related to noise.

Energy Usage

Transport accounts for a substantial part of total energy end use. Despite fuel efficiency improvements, Salomon forecasts only small further improvements (Salomon, 1984). Hence, if telework is an effective substitute for travel, it could significantly contribute to energy conservation (Kraemer,

*Template 8   Monetary savings in external costs related to noise due to a
particular level and frequency of telework*

Item	Coefficient/formulas	Field
The net reduction in vehicle-kilometres travelled per workday (Z) (see Template 4)		I
Marginal external cost of noise per vehicle-kilometre (S)		II
Monetary savings in external costs related to noise due to a particular level and frequency of telework per workday	I×II	III
The number of workdays in a year		IV
Monetary savings in external costs related to noise due to a particular level and frequency of telework per year (MS)	III×IV	V

1982). In the United States, the transportation sector comprises 28 per cent
of the total energy consumption (Energy Information Administration,
2006). At high telework penetration levels, the energy effects would be very
substantial. As suggested in Chapter 4, if 50 per cent of the workforce
started teleworking 85 per cent of the time at home or in a telework centre,
the amount of fuel used for commuting in the United States would be
reduced by 43 per cent (Salomon, 1984). Further, it has been estimated that
the adoption of telework by 1 per cent of the workforce would reduce the
country's total energy consumption by approximately 0.06 per cent, not
taking into account the effects of latent demand (Gillespie et al., 1995). It
has also been estimated that each percentage reduction in urban commuting in the United States would save about 8.6 billion kilowatt-hours per year
(Energy Information Administration, 2006).

Various methods have been used to assess the savings in energy consumption per telework occasion due to the elimination of the commuting trip.
These methods are illustrated in Table 7.4. Because early adopters tend to
have a longer commuting trip, this table's 'average reduction in energy use' is
likely to be an overestimation with respect to all potential teleworkers. In
order to avoid this problem, an estimation of average fuel saving per kilometre due to telework would be more appropriate (Mokhtarian et al., 1995). It
should also be noted that only the third method takes into account lower fuel
efficiency for the remaining distances covered by car after the introduction of
telework (this would be due to a higher number of short, non-linked trips).

As previously stated in Part I, reduced cooling and heating costs at
the (now smaller) conventional office would produce additional energy

Table 7.4   Impact of telework implementation on energy use for travel

	Average fuel efficiency (km/litre)	Average reduction in energy use (in litres) per telework occasion (with correction for vehicle-kilometres)
Method 1: average fuel efficiency multiplied by the average number of kilometres saved by not performing a commuting trip		
Arizona AT&T study	11 (researchers did not elaborate on how this figure was determined)	3.4 l
Puget Sound study	10.6 (researchers did not elaborate on how this figure was determined)	3.4 l
Method 2: average of the self-reported fuel efficiency multiplied by the self-reported savings in commuting		
SCAG study	10.1	5.3 l
Method 3: fuel savings estimated according to the results of air quality models		
State of California study EMFAC 7E air quality model	7.6 (after introduction of telework)	8.3 l
	7.9 (before introduction of telework)	

Source: adapted from Mokhtarian et al., 1995.

savings. However, savings in office energy would probably be relatively small, given that the use of heating, air conditioning, and lights would not decline significantly if only a small number of employees were teleworking (Mokhtarian et al., 1995). Furthermore, any savings at the conventional office would be partially offset by increased costs of heating and cooling at

Table 7.5   Impact of telework implementation on home energy use

Research study	Home energy increase in kilowatt-hours (kWh/ telework occasion)
Puget Sound study method: the researchers did not elaborate on the method used	+ 5.5 kWh
SCAG study method: energy use is estimated based on hours of use of different appliances (e.g., heating, air conditioning, computers)	+ 7.9 kWh
State of California study method: comparison of monthly energy bill of teleworkers and non-teleworkers (in order to translate this cost into kilowatt-hours, the average cost for one kilowatt-hour in the investigated area was used)	+ 20.5 kWh

Source: adapted from Mokhtarian et al., 1995.

the teleworkers' homes (where facilities are often less efficient) (Salomon, 1984). Three studies have estimated the increased use of energy in the home due to telework, as shown in Table 7.5. According to these findings, the extra energy used at home will offset between 11 per cent and 25 per cent of the travel energy savings (Gillespie et al., 1995; Mokhtarian et al., 1995).

We conclude that, even taking into consideration increased energy use in the home, telework still reduces overall energy use. We view the State of California study as the most scientifically rigourous, because it uses the most scientifically-grounded methods to estimate both the reduction in gas consumption and the offsetting increase in energy use at the teleworker's home. The California study results in the highest net energy savings (Table 7.6), largely because the teleworkers in that study had the highest average commuting distance. Consequently, average net energy savings for teleworkers in general may be much lower. Thus, we suggest a reasonable average value for net reduction in energy usage of 43.7 kWh per telework occasion.

To estimate the reduction in energy usage per day and per year, we look at the savings in energy usage (as reported by several studies) as well as the cost of a kilowatt-hour. Thus, we use the following formula:

$$TEU = EU \times T \tag{11}$$

where
TEU = total reduction in energy usage on any particular day due to a particular level and frequency of telework (in kWh),

Table 7.6   Impact of telework implementation on energy use

Research study	Travel energy reduction (in kWh/telework occasion)	Home energy increase (in kWh/telework occasion)	Net energy savings (in kWh/telework occasion)
Puget Sound study	33	5.5	27.5
SCAG study	51.4	7.9	43.5
State of California study	80.6	20.5	60.1

Note: The energy savings in kilowatt-hours (kWh) due to reduced vehicle-kilometres were obtained by assuming 9.7 kWh per litre.

Source: adapted from Mokhtarian et al., 1995.

EU = reduction in energy usage per telework occasion (in kWh),
T = total number of telework occasions on a particular day that generate a travel impact.

In order to assess the monetary savings in energy usage due to a particular level and frequency of telework, the total reduction in energy usage expressed in kWh should be multiplied by the electricity tariff applicable in the geographic region, using formula 12:

$$MTEU = TEU \times M \qquad (12)$$

where
$MTEU$ = monetary savings in energy use due to a particular level and frequency of telework,
TEU = total reduction in energy use on any particular day due to a particular level and frequency of telework (in kWh),
M = the cost of a kilowatt-hour.

Template 9 allows for the calculation of the monetary savings related to a reduction in energy use for different penetration levels and frequencies of telework.

Road Construction

Road construction costs can be unbundled into investment costs on the one hand and maintenance costs on the other. The maintenance costs have both a fixed and a variable component. The fixed component is incurred

Template 9   Monetary savings in energy use due to a particular level and frequency of telework

Item	Coefficient/formulas	Field
Reduction in energy use per telework occasion on a particular workday (EU) (in kWh)		I
Maximum teleworkers on a particular day that generate a travel impact (T) (see Template 3)		II
Total reduction in energy use on a particular workday (TEU) (in kWh)	I×II	III
The number of workdays in a year		IV
Total reduction in energy use per year (in kWh)	III×IV	V
The cost of a kilowatt-hour		VI
Monetary savingsper year for a particular level and frequency of telework ($MTEU$)	V×VI	VII

each year, and is independent of the number of vehicles using the road. This cost component results from the impact of weather conditions, corrosion, and so on. The variable part of the maintenance costs, on the other hand, depends upon the usage of the road network. More traffic leads to more wear and tear and therefore higher variable maintenance costs. By reducing the number of vehicle-kilometres, telework reduces variable maintenance costs. If we assume, for simplicity, a linear relationship between the percentage reduction in traffic volume due to telework and the level of the variable maintenance costs, then the total savings on road construction costs can be calculated as follows. Obviously, if a fraction of the investment costs can be postponed because of a slower increase in traffic growth, this will lead to additional savings, not included in the formulas below.

$$TC_{RC} = C_I + (C_{MV} + C_{MF}) \qquad (13)$$

where
TC_{RC} = total cost of road construction ($ per year)
C_I = investment cost of road construction ($ per year)
C_{MV} = maintenance cost (variable) ($ per year)
C_{MF} = maintenance cost (fixed) ($ per year).

$$m = Z_Y / K \qquad (14)$$

where
m = percentage of the total vehicle-kilometres that will be reduced in one year due to telework
Z_Y = net reduction of total vehicle-kilometres due to telework
K = total vehicle-kilometres in one year.

$$TC_{RCT} = C_I + ((1-m) \times C_{MV} + C_{MF}) \tag{15}$$

$$MG_{RCT} = TC_{RC} - TC_{RCT} \tag{16}$$

TC_{RCT} = total cost of road construction if implementing telework (\$ per year)
TC_{RC} = total cost of road construction without implementing telework (\$ per year)
m = percentage of the total vehicle-kilometres that will be saved in one year due to telework
C_I = investment cost of road construction (\$ per year)
C_{MV} = maintenance cost (variable) (\$ per year)
C_{MF} = maintenance cost (fixed) (\$ per year)
MG_{RCT} = monetary gains regarding road construction maintenance due to telework (\$ per year).

Template 10 can be used to calculate monetary gains regarding road construction and maintenance due to telework.

Business Continuity

At the moment no clear methodology exists for assessing the impact of telework on a business's continuity after an emergency. Thus, we propose a methodology that allows for rough estimates of the positive effect of telework on employees' productivity in the face of an emergency or disruption to the traditional workplace (Formula 17). It should be noted that we do not include telework's positive effect on potentially reducing emergency-related casualties.

$$MBC = P_E \times t_e \times T \times W_T \times q \tag{17}$$

where
MBC = monetary savings per year due to enhancement of business continuity due to a particular level and frequency of telework,
P_E = probability that an emergency takes place in a particular geographic area, expressed per year; the value needs to be divided by 365 to obtain a daily probability,

*Template 10   Monetary gains regarding road construction due to a
                particular level and frequency of telework*

Item	Coefficient/formulas	Field
Investment cost of road construction (C_I)		I
Maintenance cost (variable) (C_{MV})		II
Maintenance cost (fixed) (C_{MF})		III
Total cost of road construction (TC_{RC})	I+II+III	IV
Net reduction of total vehicle-kilometres due to telework (Z_Y)		V
Total vehicle-kilometres in one year (K)		VI
Percentage of the total vehicle-kilometres that will be saved in one year due to telework (m)	V/VI	VII
Total cost of road construction if implementing telework (TC_{RCT})	I+(1−VII) ×II+III	VIII
Monetary gains regarding road construction and maintenance due to telework (MG_{RCT})	VIII−IV	IX

t_e = average duration of an emergency in a particular geographic area (in days),

T = the maximum expected number of teleworkers on a particular workday,

W_T = average daily wage of an information worker,

q = correction factor that takes into account that the average productivity of employees in case of a catastrophe is not reduced to zero, even without a telework program; according to the information of ITAC (2005) this value can be reasonably set at 0.62.

Template 11 allows for calculating the monetary impact due to enhancement of business continuity given a particular level and frequency of telework.

Mass Transit Usage

If a certain geographic area has severe mass transit congestion, telework implementation can relieve this congestion and/or avoid investment in new mass transit capacity. The following calculation assesses the positive monetary impact of telework on mass transit congestion. This assessment should only take place if the congestion level of mass transit is higher than 100 per cent (see Formula 18).

Template 11   Monetary savings due to enhancement of business continuity given a particular level and frequency of telework

Item	Coefficient/formulas	Field
Probability that an emergency takes place in a particular geographic area $(P_E/365)$ (per day)		I
Average duration of an emergency in a particular geographic area (t_e) (in days)		II
Maximum expected number of teleworkers on a particular day (T) (see Template 3)		III
The average daily wage of an information worker (W_T)		IV
Correction factor for partial reduction in productivity (q)		V
Monetary savings due to enhancement of business continuity due to a particular level and frequency of telework per day	I×II×III×IV×V	VI
The number of workdays in a year		VII
Monetary savings due to enhancement of business continuity due to a particular level and frequency of telework per year (MBC)	VI×VII	VIII

$$\text{congestion level of mass transit} = \text{number of commuters} \\ \text{in peak hours}/(\text{transportation capacity per hour} \times \\ \text{number of peak hours}) \qquad (18)$$

In order to assess the monetary impact of relief of mass transit congestion, we use the methodology developed by Mitomo and Jitsuzumi (1999). This methodology assesses the commuter disutility of time spent on congested trains (expressed in minutes). We describe a simplified version of this approach below. Thus, the difference in commuter disutility is calculated for non-teleworkers as well as for teleworkers before and after telework implementation. For the teleworkers it is assumed that after telework implementation their commuter disutility becomes 0 minutes. Formula 19 calculates the commuter disutility per commuter before telework implementation as a function f of the time spent on a commuter trip and the congestion level before telework implementation:

$$U_{CBT} = f\, t\, (C_{BT}/100) \qquad (19)$$

where
U_{CBT} = the commuter disutility per commuter (expressed in minutes),
C_{BT} = congestion level before telework implementation (as a percentage),
t = the average time spent on a commuter trip by mass transit; if this figure is not available, the average commuting time could be used as a proxy.

In order to estimate the commuter disutility per commuter before telework implementation, the congestion level before telework implementation needs to be assessed (Formula 20). The number of commuters in peak hours is multiplied by a factor of 2 to take into account a commuter round-trip.

$$C_{BT} = ((p \times E \times 2)/(CAP_{MT} \times h_p)) \times 100 \tag{20}$$

where
C_{BT} = congestion level before telework implementation (as a percentage),
p = the proportion of the active workforce that uses mass transit for their commuter trip,
E = the average number of people employed in a certain geographic area,
CAP_{MT} = the mass transit transport capacity per hour (number of rides per hour),
h_p = the number of peak hours; this is set at six hours as a default value, assuming that the morning peak is between 6 and 9 a.m. and the evening peak between 3 and 6 p.m.

Formula 21 assesses the commuter disutility per commuter after telework implementation for non-teleworkers as a function f of the time spent on a commuter trip and the congestion level after telework implementation.

$$U_{CAT} = f\, t\, (C_{AT}/100) \tag{21}$$

where
U_{CAT} = the commuter disutility per commuter (expressed in minutes),
C_{AT} = congestion level after telework implementation (as a percentage),
t = the average time spent on a commuter trip by mass transit; if this figure is not available, the average commuting time could be used as a proxy.

In order to estimate the commuter disutility per commuter after telework implementation for non-teleworkers, the congestion level after telework implementation needs to be assessed (Formula 22). Hence, the number of teleworkers who used mass transit before teleworking reduces the total who will be using it afterwards.

$$C_{AT} = (((p \times E \times 2) - (p \times T \times 2))/(CAP_{MT} \times h_p)) \times 100 \tag{22}$$

where
C_{AT} = congestion level after telework implementation (as a percentage),
p = the proportion of the active workforce that uses mass transit for their commuter trip,
E = the average number of people employed in a certain geographic area,
T = maximum number of teleworkers on a particular day that generate a travel impact,
CAP_{MT} = the mass transit transport capacity per hour (number of rides per hour),
h_p = the number of peak hours; this is set at six hours as a default value, assuming that the morning peak is between 6 and 9 a.m. and the evening peak between 3 and 6 p.m.

Finally, the monetary value of the change in commuter disutility for teleworkers and non-teleworkers who use mass transit can be calculated (MMT_1) (see Formula 23):

$$MMT_1 = [(U_{CBT} - U_{CAT}) \times number\ of\ remaining\ commuters + (U_{CBT} - 0) \times number\ of\ teleworkers)] \times (S_h/60) \qquad (23)$$

where
MMT_1 = the monetary value of the change in commuter disutility for teleworkers and non-teleworkers,
S_h = average salary per hour. If available the salary for information workers should be used. Since the commuter disutility is given in minutes this value is divided by 60.

Template 12 allows for the calculation of the monetary savings in commuter disutility for teleworkers and non-teleworkers using mass transit for their commuter trip.

On the other side of the ledger, however, telework could have a negative effect on the viability of mass transit because fewer commuters will use it during peak hours, so conceivably services may be reduced. Any such reduction in mass transit would have a societal impact, as mass transit supports the quality of life of many older, lower-income, and less healthy residents (Southworth et al., 2004). Southworth et al. (2004) have estimated the urban public transit benefits per trip at US$6.70. Their estimates take into account user mobility benefits, congestion mitigation, safety benefits, air quality benefits, transportation efficiency benefits, and expenditure multiplier benefits. Hence the negative impact of telework implementation on mass transit could be assessed using Formula 24:

Template 12   Monetary savings in commuter disutility for teleworkers and non-teleworkers using mass transit for their commuter trip

Item	Coefficient/formulas	Field
The proportion of the active workforce that uses mass transit for their commuter trip (p)		I
The average number of people employed in a certain geographic area (E) (see Template 1)		II
The mass transit transport capacity per hour (number of rides per hour) (CAP_{MT})		III
The number of peak hours (h_p)		IV
Maximum number of teleworkers on a particular day that generate a travel impact (T) (see Template 3)		V
The average time spent on a commuter trip by mass transit (t)		VI
Congestion level before telework implementation for non-teleworkers and teleworkers (expressed as a percentage) (C_{BT})	$[(I \times II \times 2)/(III \times IV)] \times 100$	VII
Congestion level after telework implementation for non-teleworkers (expressed as a percentage) (C_{AT})	$\{[(I \times II \times 2)-(I \times V \times 2)]/ (III \times IV)\} \times 100$	VIII
The commuter disutility per Commuter before telework implementation (expressed in minutes) (U_{CBT})	$f\, VI \times (VII/100)$	IX
The commuter disutility per commuter after telework implementation for non-teleworkers (expressed in minutes) (UC_{AT})	$f\, VI \times (VIII/100)$	X
Average salary per hour (S_h)		XI
The monetary value of the change in commuter disutility for teleworkers and non-teleworkers (MMT_1)	$\{(IX-X) \times [(I \times II)-(I \times V)]+ [IX \times (I \times V)]\} \times (XI/60)$	XII

$$MMT_2 = p \times T \times 2 \times c \qquad (24)$$

where
MMT_2 = monetary valuation of the loss of the benefits of mass transit per workday,

p = the proportion of the active workforce that uses mass transit for their commuter trip,
c = estimated benefits of mass transit per trip,
T = maximum number of teleworkers on a particular day that generate a travel impact. The amount is multiplied by 2 because it is assumed that commuters make two commuter trips per day.

Template 13 estimates the monetary value of the loss of the benefits of mass transit for a particular level and frequency of telework per year.

Template 13   Monetary value of the loss of the benefits of mass transit due to a particular level and frequency of telework

Item	Coefficient/formulas	Field
The proportion of the active workforce that uses mass transit for their commuter trip (p)		I
Maximum number of teleworkers on a particular day that generate a travel impact (T) (see Template 3)		II
Estimated benefits of mass transit per trip (c)		III
The monetary value of the loss of benefits of mass transit due to a particular level and frequency of telework per day	I×II×III×2	IV
The number of workdays in a year		V
The monetary value of the loss of benefits of mass transit due to a particular level and frequency of telework per year (MMT_2)	IV×V	VI

CONCLUSION

This chapter has explored the tracking of telework from a societal perspective. We noted that the lack of tracking efforts at the employee and organizational levels negatively influences societal-level tracking. This largely stems from a reduced ability to aggregate individual tracking to a regional level. This is unfortunate as the tracking of telework provides the link between telework impacts and telework adoption, which owing to environmental impacts is particularly salient at the societal level.

In place of real-time tracking data, we offered a number of economic formulas and templates that rely on standard coefficients to estimate telework frequency and societal impacts. First we offered formulas and templates that allow for an estimation of the level of commute reductions for a given level of telework. These estimates then allow for calculations of the yearly monetary savings resulting from the reduction in external costs related to road congestion, air pollution, noise pollution, and road accidents. We also outlined methods for calculating the monetary savings from telework's influence on energy consumption, road maintenance, business continuity and mass transit, and the one-time benefits of telework implementation on road construction.

This chapter concludes the telework tracking part of this book. It is our contention that the employee, organizational, and societal tracking of telework is critical to the growth of the virtual workplace. Telework tracking is the linchpin in our EOS telework integrative framework as it connects telework adoption to telework impacts, thus further reinforcing continued telework adoption. Telework tracking also provides a mechanism to evaluate and adjust telework implementation. Thus, in the next part we explore the telework implementation construct from the three perspectives of the EOS integrative telework framework.

NOTE

1. By 'cold start' we mean a start when the vehicle's engine is cold. An engine is considered cold if it has been turned off for more than one hour for vehicles with a catalytic converter and four hours for vehicles without a catalytic converter.

PART III

TELEWORK IMPLEMENTATION

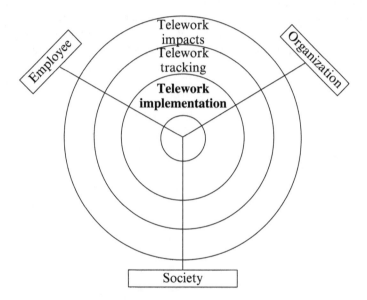

This part explores the factors enabling telework implementation from each of the three EOS perspectives. While in the previous part we stressed the importance of telework tracking in growing the virtual workplace, telework implementation plays a critical role in translating the telework adoption decision into a viable and successful form of work. Telework implementation's effect on the success of telework will, through the desire to reinforce successful strategies, further influence subsequent telework adoption. Thus, proper telework implementation will assist in growing the virtual workplace.

Factors determining the optimal implementation of telework become progressively more complex as one moves from the employee level to the organizational level and finally to the societal level. At the employee level, there are key factors to pay attention to when implementing telework. While important, these recommendations are fairly straightforward and produce consistent, predictable results. As one shifts to the organizational perspective, suggestions for telework implementation become more complex, as the number of stakeholders and intervening variables are greater than with a single employee. This is evident in the decisions organizations make regarding the selection of teleworkers, telework policies, and the management of virtual teams. At the societal level, telework implementation, manifested through public policies, laws, and incentives, is immensely complex; the results of varying policies often remain ambiguous. It is important to note that – particularly at the societal and organizational levels – the implementation of telework policies must be continually monitored to measure their impact. Based on such measurements, continuous feedback can be used to adjust the current and future implementation policies.

8. Telework implementation: the employee perspective

Employees' perceptions of telework implementation play a critical role in the demand for and adoption of telework. If employees decide to adopt telework but fail to properly implement it, future adoption and its resulting impacts will be short-lived. While there is no definitive guide for implementing telework at the employee level, a number of procedures and assessments are available that the literature consistently suggests will lead to success.

In this chapter we summarize a number of key considerations for helping employees implement this work option. We first review the important process of self-assessment for telework suitability. This self-assessment should be the first step for employees considering virtual work. We then offer some practical advice on setting up an appropriate home office. Finally, we cover a few of the daily working processes and policies that employees should consider in carrying out effective telework. In what follows, we will not repeat our earlier discussion of telework tracking. Naturally the incorporation of some form of tracking mechanism is important in implementing telework, and we refer the reader back to the previous part of this book for an in-depth review of telework tracking alternatives.

SUITABILITY SELF-ASSESSMENT

The Realities of Telework

The first step to implementing telework at the employee level is for employees to evaluate their own characteristics, job situation, and work style to see whether these fit with some of the unique demands that telework presents. Part of this assessment is for employees to educate themselves about the realities of a virtual office. For example, La Gioia (2004) highlights that during telework no one is around to offer constructive feedback to the employee. Another reality of telework that La Gioia emphasizes is that at the home office family and friends are often oblivious of the fact that they are disturbing work time when they call or barge into the office to ask a question.

Employees can further educate themselves about the realities of telework by considering a few general questions, such as:

- Are you happy working by yourself?
- Would you miss regular contact with other people at work?
- Are you self-motivated?
- Are you good at time management?
- How does your family feel about you working from home?
- Are you technically competent (for example, in the use of a PC)?
- Are you happy communicating by telephone instead of FTF?

(adapted from MIRTI, 1998)

Another method for employee self-assessment is for employees to create a list of 'pros and cons'. In Chapter 2 we gave an in-depth review of potential telework impacts from the employee perspective and in Chapter 11 we offer an analysis of telework impact perceptions for teleworker adopters and non-adopters. With regard to self-assessment, it is important for individual employees to assess whether telework will have a positive or negative impact on their life. Some very practical factors to consider in self-assessment are suggested by Public Works and Government Services Canada (PWGSC). These factors include the cost of transportation between home and workplace; availability of transportation; savings on food and clothing; proximity of stores, banking, and other services; increase in heat and water costs; costs to ensure a practical, pleasant work area; possible increase in insurance; additional tax-deductible expenses; and savings gained through flexible working hours (for example, reduced need for after-school childcare) (PWGSC, 2006). PWGSC also suggests that employees consider work environment factors in assessing their situational fit with telework. These factors include family obligations such as child care, children's lunches and return from school, as well as care of elderly relatives; social aspects such as the cooperation and presence of colleagues; and access to work tools, such as a library, reference books, photocopiers, computers, and expert colleagues (PWGSC, 2006).

Characteristics of a Successful Teleworker

Specific employee traits lend themselves to successful telework. Many researchers have emphasized the need to select 'appropriate' teleworkers (for example, Harpaz, 2002; Manoochehri and Pinkerton, 2003). In the following paragraphs we offer five key differentiators of teleworker success that have been discussed in the literature. These five differentiators are the ability to separate work from home life, working without close supervision/self-discipline/finding work intrinsically rewarding, overcoming isolation, organizational abilities, and need for autonomy.

1. Separating work from home

According to Raghuram and Wiesenfeld (2004), telework can potentially increase or decrease job stress, depending on the person's ability to set boundaries that separate work from non-work life. They use the terms 'segmentation' or 'structuring behaviours' to describe the ability to separate work from non-work domains so that they do not affect each other. These proactive strategies aimed at planning and organizing the workday include having a daily task schedule, setting daily performance goals, and establishing a work area free from distractions (Raghuram and Wiesenfeld, 2004). The office provides temporal and spatial cues to facilitate this separation or segmentation (that is, work is physically separate from home), but in a telework situation the employees must create their own segmentation. Employees whose personal attributes allow them to segment work and non-work domains experience less conflict between work and non-work (Raghuram and Wiesenfeld, 2004).

2. Need for achievement/self-discipline/finding work intrinsically rewarding

Another differentiator between successful and unsuccessful teleworkers is their ability to function when they are not under close supervision or direction (Manoochehri and Pinkerton, 2003). Working independently increases an employee's autonomy, control, and responsibility (Harpaz, 2002). This requires self-discipline and the ability to work according to a self-imposed schedule. Teleworkers should ideally be able to work independently and have no history of performance problems (Harpaz, 2002).

In general, self-disciplined employees find work intrinsically rewarding. Thus, these workers might be expected to score higher on need for achievement (NAch) scales. Individuals high in need for achievement are typically characterized as goal seekers who react positively to competition and consistently aspire to accomplish difficult tasks (Steers and Braunstein, 1976). Of course, the question arises whether employees actually expect they can fulfil such high needs for achievement outside the main office; if this were not the case, and the office context were actually important to satisfy needs for achievement, one might find a negative linkage between NAch and telework adoption. In connection with this point, La Gioia (2004) suggests that each employee assess whether his ego gets deflated when a colleague or supervisor fails to mention his major contribution to the success of a project, or whether she is sufficiently satisfied just by knowing that she did a great job. If the employee is unable to stay motivated by simply knowing she did a great job, she might have a difficult time maintaining a high level of performance when she is teleworking alone, possibly without as much acknowledgment of her accomplishments.

The self-discipline characteristic is also related to the diligence trait. Individuals that score high on diligence scales are probably better able to separate work from non-work life. They will work harder and be disciplined enough not to be easily distracted by non-work issues or temptations (such as television). Diligent employees are more likely to want to work hard regardless of whether they are in the office or teleworking, and will structure their telework days to maximize productivity.

3. Overcoming isolation

A third differentiator between successful and unsuccessful teleworkers is the ability to overcome social isolation. The isolation resulting from separating the teleworker from her social network in the traditional office is one of the most commonly expressed challenges of telework (Kurland and Bailey, 1999). This isolation can lead to social as well as professional isolation. Teleworkers who feel isolated may become frustrated and dissatisfied with their telework arrangement. These negative effects can potentially overshadow the benefits of telework (Apgar, 1999, as cited in Manoochehri and Pinkerton, 2003), particularly for people who have a strong need for social interaction. For many people, the workplace is an important source of social interaction and friendship, which may be difficult to replace in a telework arrangement (Potter, 2003).

4. Organizational abilities

Being organized is a key trait of successful teleworkers. Few things consume precious time more than hunting down a document or telephone number that should have been filed neatly away in the first place. And hardly anything is worse than beginning a day unsure of what you will be doing first, second, third, and so on (La Gioia, 2004). Individuals who are organized are likely to be better at separating their work and non-work life because they are able to plan and structure their day when teleworking. They would probably be better at setting daily performance goals and establishing a work area free from distractions than would those who are less organized. Further, organized teleworkers would probably function better than less-organized teleworkers when not under close supervision or direction. The increased autonomy, control, and responsibility that come with telework require greater organization in order to get things done.

5. Need for autonomy/independence

Individuals high in need for autonomy generally value independence of thought; they prefer self-directed work, care less about others' opinions and rules, and prefer to make decisions alone (Steers and Braunstein, 1976). In a telework situation an individual is expected to work without direct supervision, and to set her own schedule and method for getting things done. Teleworkers higher in need for autonomy are more likely to perform effectively and be satisfied with telework than those with a lower need for autonomy. Employees should assess how many opinions they weigh before they get moving on something or make a decision. If an employee feels she is not confident enough to think through a problem and make a decision about it on her own, she might be too dependent to work alone from home (La Gioia, 2004).

Assessment Mechanisms

The above personality characteristics and associated questions offer an informal method for employees to gain insight into their own fit with telework. More formal mechanisms for employee telework self-assessment include a number of web-based and downloadable assessment questionnaires. For example, a brief interview self-assessment tool can be found at the Portuguese Telecentro website. This site is maintained by InterWork, a network of highly-recognized consultants and specialists who provide services concerning teleworking. The assessment tool asks a series of questions relating to a person's fit with telework, after which a score is automatically calculated. The tool can be found at http://www. telecentro.pt/ingles/products/teste_perfil_ing.asp.

Another example of a telework self-assessment questionnaire comes in a paper-and-pencil form and was devised by Telework Consultants International (TCI, 2003). The questionnaire is designed to rate an employee's suitability for telework, and offers a suitability rating. Questions from this instrument generally fit into one of three categories: the employee's circumstances or environment, the employee's traits or characteristics, and the demands or characteristics of the job. A sample of the content of these three broad categories covered by the self-assessment questionnaire is provided below:

1. *Employee's environment or personal circumstances*

- Childcare arrangements and home care of special-needs individuals.
- Spouse or partner's current work arrangements.
- Availability of separated and dedicated quiet space for a home office.
- The time it currently takes to commute to and from work.

2.   *Employee's traits or characteristics*

- Current degree of socializing at work.
- Comfort level with working alone.
- Comfort level with sharing office space.
- Computer and technical literacy of the employee.
- Employee's organizational skills.
- Employee's propensity to become a workaholic.

3.   *Demands or characteristics of the job*

- Does the job demand short-notice meetings and frequent FTF interactions?
- Does the job require the expertise of and interaction with managers and peers?
- What is the level of trust between manager and employee?
- Is the completion of job tasks easily measured?
- How flexible is the scheduling of job tasks?

For each of the three broad categories listed above there are several points to consider that affect an employee's suitability for telework. For example, employees assessing their suitability for telework must also take into account the characteristics of the job itself (category 3 in the above assessment questionnaire). In general, jobs that require less FTF contact and that have more flexibility in scheduling tasks are more appropriate for telework. The employee's level of expertise also impacts suitability for telework, as employees who are new to a job and need further training are not as suitable for telework as those who already possess the required knowledge. Jobs that have definable and easily-measured task outcomes might also lead to more successful teleworking, as performance of the work is easy to evaluate. Finally, the levels of shared values and trust between management and employees influence the suitability of telework.

With regard to the employee's current circumstances, it is generally agreed that the motivation to telework increases the likelihood of telework success. As La Gioia (2004) suggests, desire is a key attribute of successful teleworkers, as it motivates them to plan for the drawbacks that come with working from home. Circumstances that increase the motivation to telework include the need for flexibility to care for children or other special-needs individuals. Of course, this motivation must be tempered with proper preparation for reducing interruptions during the work hours. In other words, telework should not be used as a substitution for child, elder, or special-needs care. Additional sources of care would be needed, as the teleworker would be unavailable during the workday, except for breaks and lunch.

Commute distance also influences motivation – the longer the distance, the greater the motivation. Beyond employee circumstances that motivate teleworkers, a work environment conducive to telework will also increase the chances of telework implementation success. Thus, in the following section we discuss the requirements of a home office.

HOME OFFICE DESIGN

As mentioned previously, one factor in employee self-assessment of tele-work suitability is the availability of a separate and quiet workspace. In the following paragraphs we will expand on this suggestion, to further outline prescribed requirements in setting up a home office for telework.

As with the self-assessment, there are a number of important questions to consider when setting up a home office for telework. These questions fall broadly into workspace and work equipment requirements. Workspace questions include:

- Do you have a separate room available in your home?
- Is there enough working space and storage space available?
- Is the space a pleasant place to be working in? (Lighting, room temperature, and so on.)
- Can you keep work information confidential?
- Can you shut the door of your office at the end of the workday?

(adapted from MIRTI, 1998)

Beyond the space requirements for a home office, consideration of equipment and furniture is important in implementing telework for the employee. General questions around the type of equipment that will be needed include:

- What type of computer will you use?
- What sort of telecommunications will you need? (Separate telephone line? ISDN (integrated services digital network)? Fax? Answering machine?)
- Is the furniture suitable?
- What type of stationery do you require?

(adapted from MIRTI, 1998)

Expanding on the above questions on telework home office equipment, it is generally agreed that the equipment needed for the home office will

Table 8.1   Equipment usage for teleworkers

Equipment	% used
Telephone	94
Pager/cell phone	71
Fax	66
Internet access	64
Teleconferencing	26
Videoconferencing	7

Source: adapted from ITAC, 2000.

vary by the job. Basic office furniture, such as an ergonomically correct chair and sturdy desk, will be needed by most teleworkers. For some of the more technologically advanced jobs, the particular nature of the equipment needed and the cost/benefit for each piece will influence the decision. For example, a software developer would have greater computer requirements, and a sales executive would require greater voice functionality. Further, the needs of a part-time teleworker may be fewer than or different from those of a full-time teleworker. Beyond computer equipment, Table 8.1 details findings of the most-used equipment for teleworkers.

However, equipping teleworkers involves much more than just physical equipment (Allenby and Roitz, 2006). Beyond the physical equipment, computer applications and databases must be accessible from the Web through intranets, and communication tools must be available to replace FTF discussion. Allenby and Roitz further suggest that the foundation for both access and communication is bandwidth in the home, and that the lack of high-speed Internet access has historically been the main barrier to telework. In line with this argument, Gartner (2000) reports that high-speed access by teleworkers and home office customers is more than double the traditional residential level. Among teleworkers and home office customers, the penetration level was 18 per cent in Gartner's study and has increased dramatically since.

Even if the space and equipment are adequate, the home office still needs to be designed properly. Public Works and Government Services Canada (PWGSC, 2006) recommends that home offices be set up where there is plenty of natural sunlight, as this will make for more pleasant work, especially during the long and dull winter months. It is also suggested that a good supply of fresh air should be available for the workstation, which is preferably near a window that can be opened. PWGSC further recommends that teleworkers acquire good ergonomic furniture (desk and chair) and use a proper wrist support to prevent fatigue and possible nerve damage. Thus, it is strongly advised not to work at the kitchen table or card table, as keyboarding when your hands are not in a neutral position puts stress on the nerves in the arms and could lead to carpal tunnel syndrome.

To further assist teleworkers in the setup of their home office, several resources are available. For example, ITAC offers a brochure on setting up a home office; this brochure includes not only suggestions for equipment but also diagrams of proper ergonomic office furniture setup: http://www.workingfromanywhere.org/resources/homeoffice.htm.International Telework Consulting (ITC) also offers a number of home office planning tools, one of which provides for planning the layout of the room. Another valuable resource for employees setting up a home telework office is published by MIRTI and can be found at http://www.telework-mirti.org/handbook/inglese/ergo.htm. This site offers detailed information on the ergonomics, both physical and cognitive, of setting up an office. For example, it is suggested that the distance from seat surface to desktop should be between 270 and 300 mm and that the seat surface should measure 400–450 mm across and 380–420 mm from back to front. Regarding the ergonomics of computer usage, MIRTI suggests the monitor should be at an 88°–105° inclination to horizontal, while the screen distance to table edge should be 500–750 mm and the keyboard (home row) to table edge should be 100–260 mm.

PREDEFINING TELEWORK PROCEDURES AND POLICIES

Having considered employee telework suitability, self-assessment, and the proper layout and equipping of the home office, we now focus on the importance of developing proper teleworking procedures and policies. In undertaking telework, the employee should ensure that many of the work expectations and telework procedures are defined before the work arrangement begins. There are a number of questions regarding telework procedures that the employee should ask herself prior to commencing telework. These questions can be organized into ones surrounding communication with the office, work expectations, and contingencies. The following are adapted from PWGSC (2006):

1. *Communication with the office*

   - Can telephone calls to your office number be switched to your home easily?
   - How will you be informed if there are developments or problems in your company?
   - Can you ask for team meetings during your office visits?

- Will you be regularly in contact with colleagues, and through what communication technologies?
- Are there certain periods of the day when you are expected to be accessible?

2. *Work expectations*

- Is there any type (not necessarily formalized) of work record?
- Do you feel that the work tasks you have set are feasible within the available working time?
- Is the agreement transparent about the work to be undertaken?
- What arrangements regulate hours worked at home?
- What arrangements are there for holidays, illness, and so on?
- How are performance tasks set?
- How is work performance monitored? What performance indicators are used?

3. *Contingencies*

- What arrangements have been made in case of illness?
- Who is available to help you with hardware or software problems at home?
- Is the employer legally liable for any work-related injuries or illness?
- What insurance measures have been taken?
- Will there be additional household insurance required? Who pays the premium?
- Does the employer hold family members or visitors liable for damages (for example, to equipment)?
- Is it possible to return to the original office workplace? (This is known as the 'voluntary principle'.)
- Is there a time limit on the right to return to working in the office?
- Will a space in the office be maintained for part-time teleworkers?

Consideration of the above questions will lay the groundwork for commencing a satisfying telework program. It is generally agreed that answers to many of these questions should be captured formally, and that a telework agreement should be signed to make sure that both employee and organization understand the work arrangement. Telework agreements offer a mechanism for predefining telework procedures and expectations, thus resolving potential ambiguities and reducing potential conflicts between the employee and organization.

Simple telework agreements are widely available on the Internet; for example, the Office of Personnel Management (US Government Services)

Table 8.2   Pre-telework checklist

Item	Needs attention	Completed
Work area is set up, including table/desk, comfortable chair, good lighting, bookshelves and storage space		
Telephone is installed, and as needed, electrical outlets near workstation		
Implications of telework with your insurance company: do you have liability insurance?		
Tax implications: can you deduct certain expenses?		
Discussions completed for possible arrangements regarding daycare, children, elderly relatives, and so on for telework days (in addition to days in the office)		
Schedule known by supervisor and colleagues (accessibility to schedule and work areas)		
Arrangements made with other occupants of the telework place		
Ways of communicating, sharing documents and work tools with colleagues are clarified and agreed to		
Information on by-laws obtained and these are properly observed (for example, installation of smoke detectors)		
Necessary office supplies and tools are available		
Telework arrangement document is completed		
Telework training has taken place or has been scheduled		

Source: adapted from PWGSC, 2006.

offers a concise telework agreement at http://www.telework.gov/ documents/ tw_man03/appd_h.asp; and the National Institutes of Health in the US provides a comprehensive agreement at http://wlc.od.nih.gov/work-life/ sample_telework.doc. This latter agreement includes exhibits that detail the work schedule, provide a telework office evaluation (focusing on office setup, safety, and security), and supply an equipment inventory.

With the completion of a suitability self-assessment, the design of a proper home office, and predefined work procedures and policies, the employee is ready to commence a telework arrangement. As final verification, employees can review the checklist shown in Table 8.2 to ensure they are well prepared to implement their telework program.

ONGOING TELEWORK PROCEDURES

Moving from preparing for and defining telework procedures in advance of implementation, in this section we now offer a number of prescriptions surrounding ongoing telework policies and arrangements. In line with the previous sections in this chapter, there is a series of questions that employees should ask themselves while they are actively involved in teleworking. These include:

- Do I feel a part of the firm, even though I am are not physically present in the office?
- Do I feel my colleagues accept the telework arrangement?
- Do my family and friends accept the telework arrangement?
- Is my work properly valued by my manager and colleagues? Are arrangements for setting and monitoring my performance tasks working adequately?
- Are there enough opportunities to meet informally with my colleagues?
- Do I manage to separate my professional and private life?
- How productive is my work?
- Am I able to participate in my company's new initiatives?

(adapted from MIRTI, 1998)

Telework Tips

While the above questions serve as a useful guide during teleworking, there are also a number of agreed upon 'telework tips' (adapted from Dinnocenzo, 1999) that may guide the employee through the telework process. These tips can be categorized into time management, work/life balance, communication and socialization.

Time management

It is important that the teleworker develop a time-management system to manage her daily priorities and achieve her goals. This system should help the employee organize her work into manageable pieces and set deadlines for accomplishing tasks. Employees should avoid time wasters such as answering the door or home telephone, watching television and running 'quick' errands.

To further avoid interruptions at work, teleworkers should establish set times to check e-mail (that is, they should not allow e-mail to constantly interrupt their work). Frequently checking e-mail can substantially slow down productivity. It is also recommended that employees establish clear 'interruption rules'. Interruptions are a major complaint of teleworkers, and can be managed by agreeing with their families about when, how, and for what types of issues interruptions are justified. A related point to family interruptions is the importance of not using telework as a substitute for childcare. Although telework will allow more time with family (for example, lunches together, time saved because of no commuting), employees still need to make childcare arrangements. Childcare is a full-time job, and no one should expect to telework and take care of children at the same time.

Work/life balance
Employees must also be cognizant of the risk of working too much while teleworking. It is suggested that employees maintain a healthy work/life balance by setting reasonable limits on their work hours. When teleworking, it is easy to work into the evening and skip breaks. Establishing work hours and reasonable breaks is important, as breaks are necessary to relax, re-energize, and recover. Another way to avoid overworking and to maintain a work/life balance is for the virtual worker to establish a ritual to end her telework day, such as turning off the computer, turning off her business line, and closing her home office door. It is important to avoid the temptation of checking e-mail throughout the evening.

Communication
While teleworking, it is vital that the employee maintain open and frequent contact with her colleagues and managers. To facilitate this communication, it is suggested that employees post their telework schedule in the office and provide co-workers with their telework location phone number. It is also important to encourage office workers to continue to interact regularly with teleworking employees. The teleworking employee should also be diligent in checking, confirming and responding to voice messages left at her office or home work numbers (PWGSC, 2006).

Socialization
While working from home, employees must be proactive in maintaining a social network and FTF contact with colleagues. Experts suggest teleworkers avoid isolation by keeping in touch through phone and e-mail and scheduling FTF meetings (breakfast or lunch, exercise, coffee, and so on) with co-workers, colleagues, associates, and friends on a regular basis. Teleworkers should inform their supervisor if they find they are feeling isolated and losing sufficient interaction with co-workers. The supervisor can then help them find methods to ensure active and frequent communication and involvement with their co-workers (PWGSC, 2006).

CONCLUSION

In this chapter we have explored telework implementation from the employee's perspective. The prescriptions for successful implementation at this level are straightforward, particularly when compared with the complexities surrounding implementing telework at the organizational and societal levels. That said, the importance of successful employee-level telework implementation cannot be overstated. Implementing telework in a fashion amenable to the worker herself is a critical step in the overall telework framework. If employees are not satisfied with their experience, adoption rates of this work behaviour are likely to decline and efforts to grow the virtual workplace will falter.

To facilitate the successful implementation of telework it is important for teleworkers to self-assess their personality and situational telework suitability. Prior to implementing telework it is also important for employees to set up proper home offices and predefine much of their telework arrangements. Finally, during the actual process of teleworking, several factors should be continuously evaluated to increase the likelihood of telework success.

As with all the constructs and perspectives in the EOS integrative telework framework, employee implementation cannot be considered in isolation. As seen in this chapter, the details of the employee's implementation affect employee impacts and adoption, as well as the organization's impacts, implementation and adoption. In the next chapter, we provide more explicitly the complement to the employee's perspective by examining telework implementation from the organizational perspective.

9. Telework implementation: the organizational perspective

The successful implementation of telework at the organizational level is important because such programs can influence employee morale, retention, productivity, and ultimately firm-level performance. Effective telework implementation at the organizational level will also influence the success of employee-level telework implementation by creating the appropriate environment for teleworking, thus increasing the growth of the virtual workplace. As discussed in Chapter 6 on tracking telework from the organizational perspective, the success of organizational telework programs will influence the extent to which organizations can capture emission credits from employee commute reductions. These credits may also have a direct impact on the bottom line.

Implementing telework from the organizational perspective can involve both induced and autonomous programs. A business undertaking an autonomous telework program encourages its employees to express their interest in participating in telework. Induced telework programs are much more top-down, in that they start at the strategic HR level and filter down through the organization.

In either case several factors will influence successful implementation. We place the factors involved in a company's implementation into five broad categories: job selection, employee selection, the design of the program, evaluation concerns, and the management of virtual teams. In this chapter we explore these five categories and offer suggestions for improving organizational telework implementation within each category.

TELEWORK JOB SELECTION

In implementing a telework program, an organization is usually aware that some jobs are better suited to this work arrangement than others. Just as employees should undergo telework suitability self-assessment exercises, so too should managers determine and assess the various positions within the organization for their telework suitability. While it may seem difficult to assess the viability of various positions for potential teleworking, several guidelines can help managers through the process.

In general, telework is feasible for work that requires thinking and writing, such as data analysis, reviewing grant applications or cases, and writing regulations or reports. Essentially, almost any computer-oriented task or telephone-intensive task is compatible with telework. Examples of such tasks include setting up a conference, obtaining information, contacting customers, and entering information into a database (VIACK, 2006). PWGSC (2006) offers the following checklist to assess a position's telework compatibility:

- The tasks are quantifiable.
- There is minimal requirement for FTF contact with other employees or the public.
- There are minimal requirements for the employee to be located in the central workplace.
- Trips can begin or end at the remote workplace rather than at the central workplace.
- Tasks can be completed at the remote workplace without violating security requirements.

Managers should not only assess which jobs are most compatible with telework but also unbundle jobs to identify individual tasks that are amenable to telework. Even if the overall job is not compatible with telework, specific tasks within the job may still be handled through a part-time telework arrangement. For example, a multi-country survey across Europe asked employees whether they spent at least six hours per week on office work that could be done at an office desk or on an office computer. The suggestion was that these tasks allow for telework, and the survey found that two-thirds of all jobs are technically compatible with telework, at least part-time (ECaTT, 2000).

Although most jobs are compatible with some form of telework arrangement, certain job characteristics are generally incompatible with telework. For example, jobs requiring a great deal of FTF interaction are not good candidates. Jobs where security is of high importance and jobs that use materials that cannot be moved from the office are also less appropriate. (Both of these characteristics are becoming more amenable to telework with the increased sophistication of ICT. Improvements in the technology and affordability of videoconferencing and data encryption are making FTF-reliant or highly secure jobs more compatible with telework.)

Finally, we note that while *a priori* job selection is important to successful telework implementation, organizations can always implement telework on a trial basis for any given position. Temporary implementation of telework, if matched with sufficient tracking and evaluation mechanisms, allows for more accurate assessments of a job's telework suitability. Beyond assessing suitability, such trials also allow for learning and adaptation to implement more effective telework arrangements.

TELEWORK EMPLOYEE SELECTION

There are a number of characteristics that make some employees more suited for telework than others. That is why, in addition to assessing a job's suitability, successfully implementing telework involves evaluating each candidate. Organizations can screen potential teleworkers according to the same criteria that the employees use for self-assessment. (We refer the reader to the self-assessment portion of the previous chapter for many of these details.)

An appropriate method for determining employees that are best suited for a telework arrangement is to determine criteria to be eligible for telework and to evaluate each employee's working style and personality against these criteria. Those employees who are highly focused, self-sufficient and flexible, have great organization skills and enjoy the solitude of working at home may be the most adaptable to telework (VIACK, 2006). It is also suggested that workers who are likely to succeed while telecommuting are typically proven performers with strong past job reviews and high levels of shared values and trust between worker and supervisor. Other important characteristics include being strong in terms of oral and written communications, decision-making, and problem-solving skills (Davis, 2006; PWGSC, 2006). Chapter 11 provides a further description of characteristics found in telework adopters. That description is based on our primary research which analysed data from 284 employee-level surveys.

To assist managers in assessing employee telework viability, T Manage Inc. evaluates potential teleworkers with survey-based software called TeleProfiler. This instrument measures the employee's ability to work independently according to certain characteristics, skills and relationships. T Manage Inc. suggests that successful teleworkers are typically self-disciplined and able to work independently with a limited need for feedback, but able to ask for it if necessary. The TeleProfiler software also suggests that the most successful teleworkers are proven performers who are experiencing success in their current positions (Davis, 2006).

Beyond selecting the appropriate employee for telework, organizations should also assess the suitability of the telework supervisor in implementing a telework arrangement. Telework supervisors, much like teleworkers, must possess above-average planning and organizational skills (Davis, 2006) and they require above-average coaching and communication skills owing to the lack of consistent and FTF contact with the employee. These supervisors should also possess the ability to establish and evaluate well-defined measurable objectives and goals (Davis, 2006).

DESIGN OF THE TELEWORK PROGRAM

Predefining the Program

After selecting the jobs and employees most suited for telework, organizations still have a number of choices to make in three key areas: the type of telework program, equipment issues and security issues.

Type of telework program

There are many options available to organizations in designing a telework program. Employers can choose from a combination of full-time and part-time telework arrangements that can base the employee at home, at a telework centre, or in a satellite office. Regional infrastructure may dictate the telework program options available to the organization. For example, most urban centres in Canada do not have a telework centre in place, so that option may not be feasible; the prevalence of telecentres and telecottages in Europe makes this a more viable option for organizations there. (A telecottage is usually a community-based and community-supported facility that assists learning, access to technology, and access to work for its local community, whereas a telecentre is more commercially focused – that is, organizations pay per teleworker for use of the telecentre. The telecottage movement started in Sweden and has been taken up most notably in the UK, where there are over 200 telecottages (Simmins, 1997).)

As with telecentres, an organization's ability to choose a satellite office arrangement may be limited by the size of the organization. In general, only large organizations in very large metropolitan areas are likely to have satellite offices or wish to create them for teleworking purposes. For these reasons, most Canadian teleworkers are likely to be home-based (Transport Canada, 2006).

While preconceptions of telework usually focus on the home office teleworker, satellite office programs can also have significant benefits for an organization. In an analysis of a recent satellite office program within the Industry Canada ministry, PWGSC (2003) found that satellite office telework contributes to staff retention, maintains client service levels, and dramatically reduces commute times.

For illustrative purposes we offer the following brief description of the Industry Canada satellite office case. Industry Canada has two large offices in Toronto (a city with high levels of road congestion) and three small shared satellite offices in the outlying municipalities of Burlington, Aurora, and Pickering. Almost 30 members of the Industry Canada staff use these satellite offices as their primary or alternate work location, attending the Toronto offices only as required. The intent of this alternative work strategy was to retain qualified staff, to better serve clients in these respective areas, and to help staff avoid long daily commutes into the main offices (PWGSC, 2003). PWGSC assessed the value of these satellite office sites through a survey designed to capture the experiences of the participating staff. Key findings from the survey were:

- Satellite offices significantly reduced traffic commute times. Approximate commute time savings ranged between 45 and 67 hours per month, per staff member.
- Satellite office staff tended to use mass transit to get to the main (Toronto) office. While staff used their own vehicles to cover the distance between home and the satellite site, the majority reverted to mass transit when heading for Toronto.
- Staff who worked at satellite offices did not have duplicate space at a Toronto office. If staff had workspace at one location, they had to use shared space when attending another.
- Satellite staff seemed to have maintained levels of client service. There was no indication that the use of satellite offices produced negative impacts on individual or team output to clients.
- The use of satellite offices did not disrupt team cohesion. Both staff and managers consistently reported that the satellite location had a positive effect on team cohesion and the team's ability to meet.
- The use of satellite offices contributed to staff retention. Almost 75 per cent of respondents indicated they would consider changing jobs if they were unable to continue to work from a satellite site.
- The use of satellite offices contributed to work/life balance. Staff indicated they elected the satellite office arrangement because they wanted to reduce commute times, thereby obtaining a better work/life balance.

(PWGSC, 2003)

Equipment

As another part of predefining the type of telework arrangement, organizations should consider and accommodate telework equipment requirements before implementing the telework program. The first decision the organization must make is whether the organization or the employee is purchasing the equipment. In assessing the provision of telework equipment the organization should consider issues around taxes, procurement, maintenance and support, insurance, and arrangements for the eventual return of the equipment (PWGSC, 2006). If the organization is purchasing the equipment for the home office, it should provide mobile solutions that can be networked anywhere, thus reducing redundancies between office and home equipment (Goodman 2004). Furthermore, to minimize the environmental impact of the equipment purchase, the organization should ensure that the equipment is energy efficient and will suffice to do the job over the medium term.

In assessing equipment requirements, an organization should give the teleworker the technology she needs to be just as efficient working remotely as in the main office. The inherent technology needs of a teleworker include a computer, Internet connectivity (high-speed broadband is best), e-mail software, telephone, fax machine, and collaboration software (VIACK, 2006). The importance of collaboration-enhancing equipment and software cannot be overstated, as it will assist in reducing common weaknesses associated with telework, such as employee isolation, managerial concerns of lost control, and diminished innovation and knowledge sharing. We suggest that to ensure collaboration each teleworker and non-teleworker be equipped with high-speed Internet, a Web camera, a headset/microphone, and collaboration software.

Effective collaborative software includes features such as real-time video, telephone-quality audio, and presence detection systems to allow better interaction between the main office and the teleworker (VIACK, 2006). Other features of effective collaborative software include instant messaging, joint editing, whiteboarding, live view, chat, and secure file sharing/storing. VIACK further suggests that such software should allow teleworkers to replicate an in-person meeting and easily contribute to the discussion when joining meetings at the office via the Internet. Managers should be able to both see and hear teleworkers during online meetings, and both teleworkers and managers should be able to check each other's availability for meetings or quick discussions (for example, through instant messaging). From the manager's perspective, presence detection software will further alleviate the 'out of sight, out of mind' concern with managing a remote workforce, as the manager will quickly be able to determine which of her workers are online, offline, in meetings, away from the computer, or wishing not to be disturbed (VIACK, 2006).

Security

A primary concern for organizations implementing a telework program centres on security issues. Security issues such as secure document disposal, locking or encryption of data, antivirus protection, data backups, and confidentiality or non-disclosure agreements should be addressed by the organization before starting a telework program (Transport Canada, 2006). To protect the security of organizational data and networks, organizations should include in the telework setup provisions for lock-tight password protection, comprehensive encryption systems using Advanced Encryption Standard (AES), public key encryption, and encrypted file storage (VIACK, 2006). A common threat to organizational security stems from the e-mail systems used by home-based teleworkers. Highly confidential information, such as financials, salary data, strategic plans, or budgets, should not be transmitted via unprotected e-mail; instead, encrypted methods of sharing and storing information should be used (VIACK, 2006). Organizations should also ensure the security of online meetings, either through AES or public encryption keys.

In addition to purchasing security technology, organizations should keep firm control over who has access to what information and collaborative tools. VIACK (2006) suggests that effective collaboration software should allow the manager to designate which employees have access to what files. Finally, it should be noted that the increasing use of wireless networks at remote locations, while convenient, introduces specific security issues.

Setting up the Program

The first step most organizations should take when setting up a telework program is to create a telework policy. A good telework policy should provide employees with the guidelines and expectations for the program and its participants – and guarantee teleworkers the same rights, opportunities, and benefits afforded to employees on-site (Transport Canada, 2006). Telework policies should define the program parameters, including which positions are best suited for telework, and include the necessary forms or documentation required to participate in the program (VIACK, 2006). The following is an outline of some of the most important sections in a telework plan:

- General telework policy statement with program definitions.
- Program goals and objectives.
- Explanation of the process for program participation.
- Review of program benefits.
- Identification of positions or aspects of positions appropriate or inappropriate for a telework arrangement.
- Review of time, pay, and attendance issues.
- Sample agreement to be completed by the employee and supervisor.
- Checklist of technology and equipment needs.

(VIACK, 2006)

Beyond telework policies, organizations can also form telework commit-tees and select telework coordinators as an initial step to setting up their telework program. If organizations are implementing telework programs with ten or more employees, one of the employees should be identified as the telework coordinator. Typically an employee from HR is responsible for organizing telework schedules, arranging equipment and tracking program progress (VIACK, 2006). The telework coordinator can also establish a planning committee, including legal, IT, management and HR personnel. This committee can establish the telework program goals, policies, training and evaluation (VIACK, 2006). We will discuss these issues, particularly training and evaluation, in the next section.

ADMINISTERING AND EVALUATING A TELEWORK PROGRAM

The ongoing administration of a telework program includes training employees and managers on the telework policies, procedures, and tech-niques for managing remote workers. Since telework typically involves a cultural change within the organization, each employee and manager should receive consistent training on the telework policy, procedures, and techniques for managing remote workers (VIACK, 2006). Such training may also help reduce managers' feelings of being overwhelmed by the implementation of new work arrangements.

Administration of the telework program should also include the setting of expectations, measurement, and evaluation of the program, with a particu-lar focus on the communication effectiveness of the program. Especially in the early stages of implementing a telework program, it is important to keep the communication channels open for both teleworkers and non-teleworkers. Organizations can take advantage of collaborative software to post notices and updates on telework procedures and evaluation of the program.

In monitoring the performance of employees participating in a telework program, it is important for organizations to recognize that teleworkers' absence from the office prevents them from receiving quick, informal feed-back. Therefore, a conscious effort should be made to provide teleworkers with ongoing feedback so that they know where their performance stands. Also, managers should focus on results (such as accomplishments, products or services provided) to measure employee performance, since it will be more difficult to observe activities, behaviours, or demonstrated competen-cies (VIACK, 2006).

Beyond evaluating the employees in the telework program, the organiza-tion should also evaluate the telework program itself. Program evaluation, perhaps developed by the telework committee, should be based on quantifiable program goals and objectives (VIACK, 2006). Key areas of program evaluation from the organization's perspective include effects on productivity, operating costs, employee morale, recruitment and retention (VIACK, 2006). For example, operating costs can be measured by pre- and post-program measures of sick leave, workers' compensation costs, and office space needs. VIACK (2006) also suggests that morale, recruitment and retention dimensions of performance can be measured through questionnaires, surveys, focus groups, and analysis of turnover rates. As outlined in Part II of this book, the presence of an effective telework tracking mechanism will be critical to the program evaluation process. Tracking mechanisms will also allow the telework program to be evaluated on societal level impacts such as reductions in air pollution and traffic congestion.

To conclude this section on implementing telework from the organization's perspective we provide a telework program implementation checklist in Table 9.1.

VIRTUAL TEAMWORK

Managing Virtual Teams

Organizations implementing telework programs need to pay particular attention to the management of virtual teams and the effectiveness of virtual leadership. A virtual team is a team with one or more members in a different location. Not all virtual teams include teleworkers (for example, a virtual team could have members in offices in different cities, none of whom are teleworking). However, by virtue of working out of the office, almost all teleworkers are members of virtual teams. This section gives an overview of virtual teams, along with their benefits and challenges.

Overview of virtual teams

With advances in communication technology, teams are now able to work beyond the limitations of geographical locations, time zones and organizational boundaries. Such teams have been termed 'virtual teams', and are becoming a more common type of work unit, predicted to play a key role in organizations (Bell and Kozlowski, 2002). To be considered a *team*, a group of individuals must have specific tasks to perform, be interdependent, and have shared outcomes (Gibson and Cohen, 2003).

What often leads a team to be considered 'virtual' is if some or all members work from dispersed locations, which may be from their homes, in different buildings or cities, and in many cases different organizations,

Table 9.1   Telework program implementation checklist

Item	Item description and associated tasks
Form a strategic planning group	Bring together all of the key groups of your organization. HR, facilities management, information technology, and legal and business units all have a critical stake in the success of teleworking.
Evaluate your organization	Which jobs are most suited to teleworking? A quick initial assessment will determine the potential scale of a teleworking program. A company with 20 employees is not going to require the same infrastructure as one with 20 000 employees.
Define program goals and objectives	Because clear statements of program rationale enable future monitoring and evaluation, it is important to identify the key reasons your organization is interested in teleworking. Where objectives exist, quantify them and ensure their achievement can be measured.
Define program scope	Initiating a telework pilot project with a limited number of individuals allows the measurement of costs and benefits on a small scale before larger-scale implementation is considered.
Estimate program costs	Once the goals, nature, and scope of the program are established, the costs can be estimated on the basis of a detailed review of technology, legal, HR and facility issues.
Monitor and evaluate the program	Monitoring and evaluation help the telework program to evolve according to actual experience and the organization's evolving needs.
Evaluate the employee's situation	The onus will be on the employee to ensure that her personal and home circumstances permit effective teleworking. Inspections by the employer can verify the adequacy of facilities in the home.
Establish a communication policy	Telecommunication is integral to teleworking, although the specific equipment and applications required are highly variable. A communication policy outlining which type of tool to use for which purposes would be useful.
Review liability	Review the employer's liability insurance with regard to worker's compensation, equipment coverage, and any responsibilities that teleworkers may have to update their home insurance policy.

Table 9.1 (continued)

Item	Item description and associated tasks
Review safety	The teleworker's safety, and the ergonomics of her workplace, should conform with organizational guidelines.
Review taxes	There may or may not be tax advantages to teleworkers, so teleworkers should obtain professional tax advice.
Undertake training	An internal training program will create better teleworkers and enhance managers' ability to remotely manage employees. Training can address issues such as computer and time management skills, overcoming feelings of isolation, management by results, and health and safety.

Source: adapted from Transport Canada, 2006.

states/provinces, countries, or continents (Avolio et al., 2001; Gibson and Cohen, 2003).

Virtual teams communicate mainly through ICT. As noted previously, these technologies may include multiple communication channels and involve text, graphics, audio and video communication (Avolio et al., 2001). Specific examples include e-mail, videoconferencing, teleconferencing, discussion groups, chat rooms, project management software, collaborative design tools, knowledge management systems and message boards. Along with these more advanced technologies are less sophisticated but widely-used communication technologies such as the telephone and fax machine (Bell and Kozlowski, 2002). Although virtual teams may occasionally meet FTF, their interactions take place primarily through communication technologies.

Benefits of virtual teams
Virtual teams offer many potential benefits to organizations. A recent field study of virtual teams in a large, global organization found that virtual team members were more satisfied with their projects than members of co-located teams (Webster and Wong, 2003). This finding may be due to a number of factors, or benefits, which have been brought forth in the literature. One benefit of virtual teams is the increased flexibility and responsiveness that geographically dispersed individuals with complementary competencies tend to achieve. In other words, talent can be rapidly drawn together from different functions, locations, and organizations, thereby

leveraging intellectual capital to efficiently solve business problems, create products, and deliver services (Duarte and Snyder, 1999; Gibson and Cohen, 2003). Organizations can access the most qualified people for a particular job or project regardless of their location (Bell and Kozlowski, 2002; Zaccaro and Klimoski, 2002).

Another potential benefit of virtual teams is the cost savings from fewer plane fares, hotels, rental cars and other business travel expenses (Baltes et al., 2002). Meeting virtually when airlines supply the only other reasonable option is often more cost-effective and potentially safer. It also avoids many coordination and logistical challenges, and minimizes time away from the job. Organizations can therefore utilize virtual teams to gain a competitive advantage by producing innovative solutions at a lower cost (Gibson and Cohen, 2003).

Challenges of virtual teams

Virtual teams encounter many of the same challenges as teams that interact primarily FTF. Common challenges include building norms of conduct, establishing team cohesion, appreciating each team member's ideas and talents, and developing trust (Avolio et al., 2001b). For a manager, further challenges include determining performance standards and metrics, and accountability issues (Potter et al., 2000). Having fewer FTF interactions may make these tasks more difficult.

Other challenges are more specific to and prevalent in the virtual context, such as problems with technology. Although various technologies offer many benefits, difficulties with technology can result in delayed communication, frustration and decreased productivity. Members who are not competent at using certain technologies can present a significant barrier to productivity and team satisfaction (Arnison and Miller, 2002).

Another challenge of virtual teamwork involves relationship development. The lack of social and nonverbal cues inherent in working virtually can slow down the formation of interpersonal relationships among team members (Weisband and Atwater, 1999). Virtual teams tend to deal more with logistics and task requirements, with much less focus on relationship building than in FTF teams (Kimball and Eunice, 1999). An insufficient focus on interpersonal processes may lead to less effective team development over time (Wakertin et al., 1997).

An underlying challenge of working virtually is developing appropriate levels of shared values and trust, which arguably can be more difficult than in an FTF context, and which may ultimately affect team performance (Avolio et al., 2001). Related to that and commonly cited in the telework literature is the issue of team members feeling isolated from one another owing to a lack of FTF social interaction (Arnison and Miller, 2002).

One final challenge cited in the literature is that of teamwork role ambiguity (Potter et al., 2000). Role clarity may be more difficult to establish virtually, especially if individuals have not identified socially with each other in an FTF context (Arnison and Miller, 2002). In a virtual team, therefore, role expectations may need to be even more explicit.

Virtual Leadership

Given the increase in virtual teamwork, more leadership is taking place through the use of communication technologies. Virtual leadership is particularly relevant to telework implementation at the organizational level. Avolio and colleagues define virtual leadership as 'a social influence process mediated by advanced information technologies to produce changes in attitudes, feelings, thinking, behaviour, and/or performance of individuals, groups, and/or organizations' (Avolio et al., 2000, p. 617). According to these authors, virtual leadership (a) can occur at any level in an organization, (b) can involve one-to-one or one-to-many interactions within and across large units and organizations, and (c) may be associated with one individual or shared across several individuals.

A recent study sought to improve our understanding of virtual leadership as it occurs within existing virtual teams in a range of organizations (Hambley et al., 2007). This study will be discussed here, as the findings can be directly applied to leading or managing teleworkers. The authors collected qualitative data through comprehensive interviews with nine virtual team members from six different organizations. The researchers used a semi-structured interview format to elicit extensive information about effective and ineffective virtual leadership behaviours and leading teams through different communication media. Using content analysis to code the interview transcripts, the authors obtained detailed notes from these interviews. Two independent raters categorized results into themes and subthemes. The most important findings can be placed under the following four overarching headings: (1) leadership in virtual teams, (2) virtual team meeting effectiveness, (3) personalizing virtual teamwork and (4) learning to effectively use different media.

1. Leadership in virtual teams
The necessity for strong leadership of virtual teams was highlighted throughout the interview data. This corroborates a field study in which employees rated leadership as critical to the success of their virtual teams (Webster and Wong, 2003). Participants provided numerous examples of effective and ineffective virtual leadership and were able to describe the behaviours that they believed exemplify strong leadership in virtual

contexts. They emphasized the necessity of a leader building the virtual team and the fact that she needs a certain set of virtual leadership skills, some of which are qualitatively different from those used in FTF settings. Interviewees mentioned the leader's role in providing vision and direction as very important to virtual team success, supporting the findings of a recent field study by Staples et al. (2004). Interestingly, participants noted that ineffective leadership is amplified or compounded in virtual settings. Virtual leaders must understand the challenges associated with different communication media and learn the behaviours and skills necessary to lead virtual teams effectively. Leaders cannot simply lead virtual workers exactly as if they were FTF.

2. Virtual team meeting effectiveness

Another theme recurring throughout the interviews was the importance of running effective virtual team meetings. Given the frequent lack of FTF contact in virtual teams, meetings take on increased importance as a chance to collaborate, build relationships, and make sure everyone is on the 'same page'. Participants emphasized the importance of the leader in establishing regular virtual team meetings and ensuring that these meetings are well organized. Many specific recommendations were provided on exactly how virtual team meetings can be successfully conducted, many of which require skills above and beyond those needed to facilitate FTF meetings. For example, the leader needs to use virtual-specific techniques to deal with aggressive and passive (for example, introverted) team members in virtual meetings.

These data indicate that one should not simply apply FTF meeting facilitation skills when conducting a virtual meeting. Indeed, the importance of carefully orchestrating conference calls was found to be important for virtual team success in a recent case study by Majchrzak et al. (2004). Researchers have recommended various aspects of facilitation that improve effectiveness of virtual team meetings (Rangarajan and Rohrbaugh, 2003). The leader would be wise to receive coaching or training on the techniques of facilitating virtual team meetings to maximize productivity.

3. Personalizing virtual teamwork

Another recurring theme was that the virtual leader needs to ensure the team goes beyond solely focusing on the work itself to personalizing virtual work relationships. Participants noted that it is easy to become too task-focused, in which case virtual work becomes depersonalized and lacks a 'human element'. Personalizing the relationships between the leader and her virtual team members, as well as between the team members, was deemed important. This finding corroborates past research by Kimball and

Eunice (1999), who found that virtual teams are more prone to lose focus on relationship building. Moreover, Jarvenpaa and Tarniverdi (2002) noted that electronic communication methods coupled with compressed project deadlines may impair team member relationships. Leaders who personalize relationships, however, can increase virtual team trust. That trust can then feed back and personalize relationships: teams with higher levels of trust tend to engage in more personalized, social communications (Jarvenpaa and Leidner, 1999).

Recommendations to enable the leader to build strong relationships with team members included conducting regular one-on-one meetings with them, investing time getting to know them, and periodically visiting them in their own environments if possible. These suggestions can help alleviate the challenge other researchers have noted: that the spatial distance between team members and using non-FTF communication can impede the ability of the virtual leader to mentor and develop team members (for example, Bell and Kozlowski, 2002). Building relationships with team members reflects individualized consideration, a factor of transformational leadership, and enables the leader to better understand and accommodate individuals' needs, abilities, and goals (Bass and Avolio, 1993).

Participants recommended that the leader should also facilitate the building of social connections between virtual team members so that their relationships become personalized as well. Effective relationships between team members was mentioned by participants as a component of successful virtual teamwork that leads to team satisfaction and the desire to continue working together (that is, team cohesion). These observations are in agreement with previous findings that leaders need to allocate more time for communication and be proactive in pursuing relationships (Hart and McLeod, 2003). Taken together, these findings affirm that virtual team leaders who explicitly cultivate team member relationships will foster team member satisfaction and development, and the building of shared values and trust.

4. Learning to effectively use different media
The final recurring theme and major item of learning from the study was that virtual leaders and team members need to examine how to use different media effectively. Different communication media and technologies require particular rules and norms for use, and cues and behaviours occur differently through these media. Virtual leaders and workers must learn how to 'read' and 'hear' body language through non-FTF media. Interview data indicated that different skills were required to effectively work FTF compared with interacting via telephone, teleconferencing, e-mail, videoconferencing, chat, instant messaging and other non-FTF media.

Participants suggested that virtual leaders and team members should be trained on how to use these communication media effectively. In their field study of six virtual teams, Staples et al. (2004) also found that virtual team members need to find the best communication and IT tools for their needs, and receive the training necessary to effectively use these systems. Additionally, Hart and McLeod's (2003) findings from a study of 126 virtual team member relationships suggested that the use of appropriate communication methods was key to developing effective work interactions. As described by Wakertin et al. (1997), it is important for virtual teams to foster familiarity and proficiency with these new tools and techniques of social interaction.

In addition to learning to effectively use various media, the leader needs to establish norms and ground rules for their use. Virtual leaders and team members need to learn that computer-mediated communication may be more appropriate for some tasks than for others (Wiggins and Horn, 2005). Disagreements, for instance, should be discussed over the telephone or in a conference call rather than handled through text-based media (Majchrzak et al., 2004).

Overall, these recommendations for virtual team leaders can be directly applied to leading and managing teleworkers. Organizations implementing telework should ensure that the leaders/managers of teleworkers abide by these and other recommendations from current research on virtual work, and receive appropriate training/coaching in how to lead from a distance.

CONCLUSION

In this chapter we have explored telework implementation from the organization's perspective. The prescriptions for successful implementation at this level are more complex than those found at the employee level. Nonetheless, we identified several steps that organizations can take to increase the success of implementing telework programs. As with the employee perspective, the first steps for the organization are to assess the jobs and employees best suited for telework.

Organizations can also carry out a number of procedures prior to and during the implementation of a telework program that will potentially increase the success of the program. These procedures include developing telework policies, addressing equipment issues, and assessing security issues prior to the launch of a telework program. Organizations should also focus on managerial and teleworker training, at the minimum making both groups aware of the program's expectations and procedures. Once the program has been launched, the organization should monitor and evaluate both the teleworker's and the overall telework program's effectiveness.

We ended this chapter with a focused discussion on virtual teams and virtual leadership. Both these phenomena are relevant to telework implementation at the organizational level, as whenever telework is in place virtual teamwork usually occurs. Findings suggest that virtual teams benefit from strong leadership, effective meeting techniques, personalized virtual meetings, and the effective use of different media.

As with all the constructs and perspectives in the EOS integrative telework framework, organization implementation cannot be considered in isolation. As seen in this chapter, the details of the organization's implementation affect employee impacts, implementation and adoption, as well as the organization's impacts and – importantly – subsequent telework adoption. The greater the adoption of telework at the organization level, the greater the impact on growing the virtual workplace. In the next chapter, we continue to look at telework implementation's role in growing the virtual workplace, but in this case from the societal perspective.

10. Telework implementation: the societal perspective

Societal-level telework implementation, which largely manifests as various forms of government policy, is highly complex owing to the numerous stakeholders, objectives, and intervening variables. Telework policies are further complicated by their interaction with larger environmental objectives as well as more specific policies such as labour regulations and tax codes. While an analysis of macro policies such as the Kyoto Protocol is beyond the scope of this book, it is important to recognize that telework implementation at the societal level is often nested within these broader policies, and thus significantly influenced by their direction and effectiveness. The most salient example of this would be GHG emission reduction policies, such as carbon taxes, credits, and trading regimes. If such policies were inclusive of telework, the GHG savings could significantly influence telework adoption, assuming costs are internalized by organizations.

Societal implementation and the associated public policies regarding telework set a framework that influences telework adoption. In this context, the main challenge for society in growing the virtual workplace is to induce demand for the practice by employees and organizations through appropriate public policies.

Accordingly, this chapter outlines options for societal-level telework implementation that will facilitate and possibly increase telework demand. We first outline the relationship between societal-level telework implementation and public policy and further describe elements of basic policy analysis. With a basic policy analysis framework at hand, we then turn our attention to telework-specific policy options for governments. We broadly classify these options in six categories: government moral support for telework, disseminating information on telework, leading by example, supporting enabling infrastructure, creating regulations and tax codes, and providing incentives and disincentives.

SOCIETAL TELEWORK IMPLEMENTATION AND PUBLIC POLICY

Six-step Policy Analysis Tool

Telework implementation, particularly induced implementation, is largely influenced by government policies. Thus, assessment of societal-level telework implementation focuses on policy analysis. Policy analysis refers to both the process of assessing policies or programs, and the product of that process. There are a variety of policy assessment and implementation models, but most conventional models involve the following six steps:

1. Verify, define and detail the problem.
2. Establish evaluation criteria.
3. Identify alternative policies.
4. Assess alternative policies.
5. Display and distinguish among alternatives.
6. Implement, monitor, and evaluate the chosen policy.

(Susskind et al., 2001)

To assess policy options for growing the virtual workplace we offer the following brief descriptions and potential telework policy applications for the six steps in policy analysis.

1. Verify, define, and detail the problem

This first step in policy analysis is also conceptualized as goal definition – defining the problem, or problem analysis. This step is one of the most important because successful policy analysis requires a clear identification of the problem to be resolved. In terms of policy analysis for growing the virtual workplace, we could define the problem as insufficient telework adoption. Detailing this problem we would contend that, among other things, there is a lack of awareness, infrastructure, and telework-friendly regulations and incentives to produce growth in the virtual workplace.

2. Establish evaluation criteria

In order to compare, measure, and select among alternatives, relevant evaluation criteria must be established (Susskind et al., 2001). Evaluation criteria can include net benefit, effectiveness, equity, political acceptability, and economic benefits. The evaluation criteria can also vary from short- to long-term. In the case of growing the virtual workplace, appropriate evaluation criteria would include telework adoption and frequency rates. Further criteria would be the many impacts discussed in the first part of this book. For example, policies can be evaluated on their ability to reduce emissions, create work/life balance, and increase employee productivity. As these examples illustrate, the selection of evaluation criteria is entwined with telework tracking. Without effective telework tracking it is almost impossible to evaluate telework policies.

3. Identify alternative policies

In order to generate alternatives in this third step, it is necessary to have a clear definition of the problem. In this step policymakers should consider a wide range of options, including the status quo or no-action alternative. In an effort to grow the virtual workplace, we offer the six previously-listed policy options for consideration: providing moral support for telework, supplying information on telework, leading by example, supporting telework enabling infrastructure, creating regulations and tax codes, and providing incentives and disincentives. Of course, maintaining the status quo is always an alternative, wherein governments do nothing to try to increase or facilitate telework growth. It is possible that the virtual workplace would still grow even in the face of a no-action policy by governments. This is particularly possible given our contention that telework growth will mostly come from the 'ground up' (employee level). Of course, it is equally imaginable that a no-action policy would at the very least slow the growth of the virtual workplace (for example, by having no infrastructure available to allow for telework).

4. Evaluate alternative policies

In this step of policy analysis each possible alternative is assessed on its ability to fulfil the evaluation criteria previously established in step 2. Policy options can be analysed through quantitative and qualitative analyses that identify the costs and benefits of each alternative (Susskind et al., 2001). In evaluating alternatives, one should first calculate the cost of each alternative and attempt to predict the consequences of each. With regard to the six telework policy options previously identified, we note that policies such as moral support and providing telework information have the lowest implementation costs; of course, in isolation these two policies also possess small virtual workplace growth benefits. When we review the six policy options later in this chapter, we will briefly evaluate each one.

5. Display and distinguish among alternative policies

Comparison schemes used to summarize benefits of each policy alternative are of great help in distinguishing among several options. These comparison schemes can include the results from quantitative methods, qualitative analysis, and complex political considerations, and ideally will meld these results into a general policy analysis framework (Susskind et al., 2001). To assist in distinguishing among policy alternatives, matrices, lists and charts can be used to show the strengths and weaknesses of each alternative or to describe the best- and worst-case scenario for each one. For our purposes, we briefly outline the six policy categories in this chapter and offer considerations of their utility in growing the virtual workplace. Later in this chapter, we display these options graphically in a policy pyramid.

6. Monitor the implemented policy

The final step in policy analysis is to actually monitor or measure the impacts from the implemented policy. This step assesses whether the policy is having the intended impact and assists in deciding whether a policy should be modified, continued, or terminated. This final step once again highlights the importance of establishing telework tracking mechanisms. Without tracking telework, we would be unable to monitor and would have only a limited ability to assess related policy impacts.

Potential and Procedural Effectiveness

We believe that, in concert with the above six-step policy analysis tool, policymakers should use both potential and procedural effectiveness as evaluation criteria in policy option assessment. Potential effectiveness is determined by a purely technical evaluation: the policy tool with the lowest relative costs for a particular expected level of goal achievement has the highest potential effectiveness. Procedural effectiveness, on the other hand, looks at the realities of both the choice and implementation of policy tools. Specifically, procedural effectiveness takes into account the psychological, sociological, and institutional impediments facing effective policy implementation, including such behavioural constraints as bounded rationality (incorrect beliefs or beliefs based on incorrect information) and opportunism (Illegems and Verbeke, 2003). With these constraints in mind, policymakers can evaluate telework policy options according to their 'real effectiveness', or goal achievement in practice, which is a function of both potential effectiveness and procedural effectiveness.

In developing their conception of procedural effectiveness, Illegems and Verbeke (2003) highlight the behavioural constraints facing the decision-makers and the actors involved in the administrative implementation system. Specifically, the authors highlight that decisions are made and implemented in a context of bounded rationality and, often, opportunism. Ideally, procedural effectiveness would take into account all effects associated with the implementation of a policy tool. However, because gathering information can be costly, decision-makers must implement policies on the basis of an incomplete understanding of these sorts of details. Opportunism can also significantly undermine a policy tool's procedural effectiveness in that policymakers might select and support tools that fulfil their own goals rather than societal ones. For example, a policy tool with high public visibility may be the preferred choice of politicians, because it enables them to gain votes.

Illegems and Verbeke also note that legitimacy is an important consideration in policy implementation. Individuals who think that a policy tool has been chosen using a fair procedure are more likely to consider the tool legitimate, even in the face of negative personal impacts from the policy.

Using the concepts of procedural and potential effectiveness, together with the six steps of policy analysis, we now turn our attention to exploring six potential telework policy options.

POLICY OPTIONS

There are many policy options (both theoretical and already in practice) that aim to increase the growth of the virtual workplace. As previously mentioned, we have broadly classified these in six categories, displayed graphically in Figure 10.1. As illustrated in this figure, we envision the six policy options progressively building from moral support up to incentives and disincentives. It is our contention that policies at the base of the pyramid must be put in place first before the next level of policy alternatives can be implemented. Thus, no policy options can be implemented without the foundation of government moral support, the very first and foundational policy alternative. Moral support signals that the government has at the least made the decision to support growing the practice of telework.

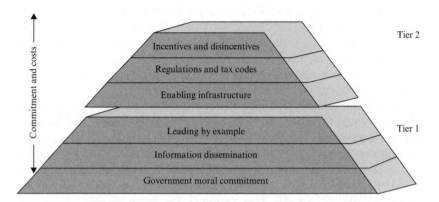

Figure 10.1   The policy option pyramid

From there the government can provide information on *how* to grow the virtual workplace. Disseminating information is the first actionable policy alternative, and it requires the smallest commitment on the government's part (next to moral commitment), thus serving as the second foundation of policy options. All future alternatives will rely on the dissemination of information to inform policy stakeholders of the procedures and benefits involved in subsequent policy decisions.

The next policy option level, leading by example, requires even more commitment on the part of the government. Such leadership grows the virtual workplace directly by moving the large government workforce into telework arrangements, and indirectly by providing a telework implementation model for other organizations to follow.

As illustrated in Figure 10.1, the next three policy options are in a second tier of government commitment to growing the virtual workplace. While the previous three policies form an adequate foundation for increasing telework adoption, they are more passive in nature if enacted without the upper tier. Implementing the second-tier policy options would indicate a shift in policy stance from a passive intention to grow the virtual workplace to an aggressive stance, involving expenditures and logistical commitments.

The first level within these second-tier policies is about infrastructure. Creating enabling infrastructure can require large monetary commitments (for example, developing regional broadband access). This policy level also highlights the sequential development of the policy pyramid, as the base level policy of information dissemination is needed to generate interest in telework prior to the development of an enabling environment; if the enabling environment is pushed forward before information dissemination, governments will spend capital on infrastructure that remains underutilized until information on the availability and utility of such infrastructure is conveyed to potential telework adopters. Infrastructure is in turn a precondition for other policies: for example, governments would be ill-advised to implement tax and regulatory policies to encourage telework if the infrastructure needed for such an arrangement were not in place.

The final two policy options require the most commitment from governments. Regulatory and tax code instruments can create a telework-enabling regulatory environment. These types of policies use monetary incentives to shape potential telework adoption, but they are still less directed than the top-level (incentives and disincentives) policies.

It should be noted that individual policy analysis could be conducted on the many specific policies that fit within each of the six broad policy option categories. For example, within the regulations and tax code category a policy analysis could compare the effect of employee home office tax incentives with that of worker's compensation extending beyond the office workplace.

Because each individual-level policy alternative is highly influenced by the context in which it is developed, we will instead maintain a higher level of analysis that looks only at the six broad policy option categories.

Table 10.1 summarizes the six policy options' effectiveness in growing the virtual workplace, highlighting the use of potential effectiveness (input costs and goal achievement), procedural effectiveness (bounded rationality and opportunism constraints) and overall real effectiveness for evaluating policy alternatives. The table also displays our assessment of whether a policy alternative is necessary and/or sufficient to grow the virtual workplace; we conclude that, while some of the policies are necessary to grow the virtual workplace, none is sufficient. This finding indicates that the six policy options should not be treated in isolation from one another, but rather should be viewed as a potential mix of options that can work synergistically to grow the virtual workplace.

Option 1: Moral Commitment

The base level policy option of moral commitment to growing the virtual workplace usually takes the form of expressions of support without associated actions. While an important first step, and one of the least costly implementation tools, simple moral commitment without follow-up policies has low potential effectiveness. Moral commitment to growing the virtual workplace is often manifested in policymakers' use of press releases, speeches, and interviews with the media. For example, quotes from Canadian policymakers supporting telework include:[1]

> The economic and social advantages of teleworking are core to our ability to transform our society into a knowledge-based economy, from the convenience of home . . . By teleworking . . . Canadians can demonstrate they are using information technology to compete and innovate in their daily lives. (former Canadian Minister of Industry John Manley)

> Telework is one of the many activities communities are encouraging to help improve the health of our environment. While the application of the policy is subject to employee and management approval, I believe this innovative way of working can have a significant impact on our communities. (former Canadian Environment Minister David Anderson)

> Telework Day offers the opportunity to review past successes and to identify current trends that will make you more competitive in the global marketplace . . . [it] offers a wonderful opportunity to recognize the important work carried out every day by those Canadians who function outside the traditional office setting as teleworkers. (former Canadian Prime Minister Jean Chrétien)

Table 10.1 Assessment of policy options to grow the virtual workplace

Policy option	Input costs (potential effectiveness)	Goal achievement (potential effectiveness)	Bounded rationality constraints (procedural effectiveness)	Opportunism constraints (procedural effectiveness)	Real effectiveness	Necessary condition	Sufficient condition
Moral commitment	Low	Low	Low	High	Low	Yes	No
Disseminating information	Low	High	High	Low	High	Yes	No
Leading by example	Moderate	Moderate	High	High	Moderate	No	No
Creating enabling infrastructure	High	High	Low	Low	Moderate	Yes	No
Tax and regulatory codes	Moderate	High	High	High	Moderate	No	No
Incentives and disincentives	High	High	High	High	Moderate	No	No

Another example of moral commitment to telework can be seen in Member of Congress Frank Wolf's petition to president Bush:

> Mr. President, your voice of support for a strong telework system can transform the federal government to be able to respond quickly and to continue to operate in the event of an emergency. The additional benefits which come with telecommuting are also worthy of promotion. (Wolf, 2005)

Examples from the EU of moral commitment to telework also abound. For illustrative purposes we provide the following excerpt from a letter written by Prime Minister Tony Blair announcing the Telework 2000 assembly in the UK:

> I have a simple vision for teleworking. I want everybody to be able to communicate with anybody, wherever they might be. I also want information, arguably the world's most important resource, to be easily accessible for as many people as possible. Knowledge gives us the ability to make informed decisions and fosters democratic debate.[2]

We could provide hundreds, if not thousands, of further examples of moral commitment to growing the virtual workplace. For policymakers, moral commitment is a low-cost way to support telework. Thus, in assessing the potential effectiveness of moral commitment as a policy tool we recognize the key advantage of low-cost inputs. Unfortunately, the lack of action stemming from such policies does not produce a significant level of goal achievement, thus lowering the overall potential effectiveness of this policy tool. From a procedural effectiveness point of view, moral commitment policies are generally effective (as there are minimal procedural implementation factors involved in this type of policy).

Overall, though, the low potential effectiveness of moral commitment policies reduces the real effectiveness of such policies. We argue that moral commitment is a necessary but insufficient policy option for growing the virtual workplace. Moral commitment indicates awareness and potential desire to grow the virtual workplace on the part of policymakers, but this policy alternative must be used in combination with a more actionable policy tool to produce any substantive movement.

Option 2: Information Dissemination

A relatively cost-effective policy tool is the dissemination of information on telework. Such information can include best practices, guidelines for implementation, and results of telework programs. (In some cases, information dissemination programs will first require collection programs to gather the information, such as the development of central registries to track and report telework penetration and frequency rates. Because such information collection programs are preconditions to information dissemination, they will be considered part of this policy alternative.) The effectiveness of disseminating information can be seen in survey results of HR managers, which indicate that the distribution of information about best practices in telework would lead to increased adoption rates (Illegems and Verbeke, 2003).

Examples of information dissemination abound at the national, regional and municipal levels in Canada, the United States and the EU. For illustrative purposes we will focus on a few of the Canadian government's initiatives to disseminate telework information. The Canadian government provides telework resources through such agencies as Transport Canada, which offers publications, web-based information, and commuter options courses. For example, Transport Canada offers assistance in setting up workshops that provide essential guidance for employers who aspire to improve commuter options for their employees. The person from the organization who will lead the workshops ideally requires two to three days of preparation to become familiar with the lecture content and exercises. Transport Canada also offers a commuter options guide that provides the business case for commuter options and includes telework as an alternative work arrangement and commute reduction option. In a similar vein, the Government of Canada's Public Works and Government Services (PWGSC) Human Resources Bureau (HRB) provides a Telework Guide that contains the following key information headings (http://www.hrma-agrh.gc.ca/survey-sondage/1999/tew-pmte-050101_e.asp):

1. about telework
2. weighing the advantages and disadvantages of telework
3. steps to follow for employees
4. checklists
5. tips for successful teleworking.

The Canadian government has also supported the development of the federal GHG registry (Chapter 7). This project developed out of an eight-year $6.4 million investment in a partnership between industry, the Canadian government and the provinces and territories across Canada. This registry is a good source of – and vehicle for collecting – telework information. At the same time, the registry paves the way for more active policy alternatives such as the trading of emission credits.

In assessing the real effectiveness of information dissemination as a policy option for growing the virtual workplace, we note that this policy tool, much like moral commitment, has relatively low-cost inputs. Compared with moral commitment, however, information dissemination offers greater potential effectiveness, as increased awareness and knowledge about teleworking will drive demand for this work arrangement. From a procedural effectiveness viewpoint, information dissemination does encounter problems related to bounded rationality, as telework stakeholders have a limited capacity to capture and integrate the vast amounts of information on telework.

Taking into consideration procedural and potential effectiveness, our overall assessment of the real effectiveness of information dissemination as a policy tool is positive. This policy option, like moral commitment, is a necessary condition to grow the virtual workplace.

Option 3: Leading by Example

Progressing from moral commitment and information dissemination is the more active policy tool of leading by example. This takes the form of governments inducing telework programs within their own agencies. This policy is more challenging in procedural effectiveness, but offers a dual punch in potential effectiveness. First, leading by example increases telework adoption directly, because governments are large organizations and often some of the biggest employers in a given region – thus, by adopting telework, governments directly increase the growth of the virtual workplace. Second, by implementing telework programs, governments provide an implementation model for other organizations. Government experiences in telework provide information on telework impacts and potential implementation hurdles, thus reducing uncertainties and risks for private organizations that are considering telework adoption.

The United States federal government provides a powerful example of such a government-leading-by-example policy. The US Department of Transportation and Related Agencies Appropriations Act (Section 359 of Public Law 106-346) states, 'Each executive agency shall establish a policy under which eligible employees of the agency may participate in telecommuting to the maximum extent possible without diminishing employee performance.' While the government did not reach its goal of applying the law to 100 per cent of the workforce by 2005, 84 per cent of US government agencies have telework policies in place, and 40 per cent of US government agencies provide telework equipment or cost sharing (OPM and GSA, 2005). More than 140 000 of 1.7 million workers across 86 US government agencies have already adopted telework. The US government's efforts provide valuable insight into tracking the growth and organizational buy-in stemming from induced, or top-down, telework poli-

Table 10.2   US government employees teleworking per year

Year	Number of government employees teleworking
2001	73 000
2002	90 010
2003	102 921
2004	140 694

cies. Table 10.2 highlights the growth of telework in the US government, as reported by the US Office of Personnel Management (OPM and GSA, 2005).

The US provides examples of policies at the state level as well. The first formal state telework implementation plan, in California, not only demonstrated that telework was a practical work arrangement, but also revealed to other organizations the significant benefits that telework has for the employer, workers, the environment and the community. The State of Arizona provides another illustration of leading by example: every agency in the state government is required to implement a telework program. The ultimate goal of the program is to have 20 per cent of state employees teleworking. Current assessments of this initiative have not been reported, but the last assessment (updated in 1996) indicated state teleworkers annually drove 3.2 million fewer miles, generated 86 133 fewer pounds of air pollution and saved 106 336 hours of commute time.

These reports from the US government and Arizona illustrate how policy options can be used in tandem for greater effectiveness. In this case, the policy to lead by example is enhanced by also utilizing information dissemination as a policy tool. This 'spreading the word' of the benefits and impacts from government-led telework initiatives increases organizational and employee-level motivation to implement similar telework programs.

Assessing the leading-by-example policy alternative in isolation from other policy options, we conclude that it is moderately effective at growing the virtual workplace. The input costs for implementing this policy are moderate, although the procedural effectiveness of the policy may be reduced or constrained by government employee resistance to change.

Leading-by-example policies' real effectiveness for growing the virtual workplace is closely tied to the adoption of the dissemination of information policy alternative. Without the dissemination of information on government initiatives these initiatives are not able to serve as models to other organizations. Thus, leading by example is not a sufficient condition for growing the workplace. Although it is an effective policy tool, we also do not see it is a necessary condition to grow the virtual workplace.[3]

Option 4: Creating Enabling Infrastructure

Moving into the second tier of policy options – those associated with significant monetary outlays – governments can create an enabling infrastructure to grow the virtual workplace. Enabling infrastructure includes the widespread availability of ICT networks (both voice and Internet). Often governments are best positioned to develop such infrastructure, given the interregional nature and the public benefits derived from these resources.

The important role of telework-enabling infrastructure is supported by Illegems and Verbeke's (2003) survey of 83 organizations, which found that future telework adoption will be influenced by the availability of electronic communication. These findings are supported by the results of another survey assessing the role of broadband access in telework. This survey found a direct correlation between success in working from home and broadband productivity, with 88 per cent of respondents citing broadband as essential to teleworking success.[4]

There are many examples of government initiatives that create a telework-enabling infrastructure. In many cases the development of such infrastructure is a spillover advantage from a policy focused on something beyond telework. For example, the US Federal Communications Commission (FCC) and US Department of Agriculture (USDA) launched a rural wireless community VISION Program. The program aims to help US rural communities set up their own broadband wireless networks. While this program definitely provides the infrastructure needed to support telework, telework infrastructure was not the sole purpose behind the initiative. Another interesting example comes from the United Kingdom, where a policy to encourage more mass transit usage resulted in the development of mobile networks along transit routes. The rationale for these networks was to allow employees to work while commuting, hopefully moving commuters from their car to the mass transit system. Of course, the creation of such network infrastructure also encourages telework as it reduces the need for the traditional office (IPTS, 2004).

In assessing the creation of enabling infrastructure as a policy option for growing the virtual workplace, we note that this policy tool has moderate potential effectiveness, with high potential for achieving telework growth but at significant input costs. Procedural effectiveness for this policy tool is not particularly limited by bounded rationality or opportunism constraints. Thus, creating an enabling infrastructure is overall moderately effective in growing the virtual workplace. Again this policy tool is most effective when used in combination with other policy tools. Creating an enabling environment will enhance most other initiatives by providing a fertile environment for achieving virtual workplace growth. This suggests that creating an enabling infrastructure is a necessary but, by itself, insufficient condition to grow the virtual workplace.

Option 5: Regulations and Tax Codes

Policymakers can influence telework adoption by removing both regulatory and tax barriers and by developing new telework-friendly tax and regulatory codes. These policy tools have high potential effectiveness, but are mired by bounded rationality and opportunism when it comes to procedural effectiveness. With respect to regulatory codes, in particular labour laws, it is becoming increasingly apparent that many of the laws, having their origins in neutralizing abuses of the industrial revolution, have become outdated by the work practices made possible by the digital revolution. These antiquated labour laws are now becoming a barrier to future telework adoption (TelCoa, 2006). Thus, amending labour laws that require stringent tracking of overtime or workplace safety to accommodate the home office worker would have a positive effect on telework adoption.

Illegems and Verbeke (2003) suggest that creating an adequate legal framework for teleworking is an important policy tool. They contend that, as labour markets are deregulated, many forms of work protection traditionally embodied in national statutory provisions are being challenged. Thus, governments must now adapt the regulatory framework to ensure that teleworkers are adequately protected without creating rigidities. Unfortunately, current laws often create substantial institutional barriers to telework; for example, Sweden has a law that entitles union representatives to visit teleworkers in their telework environment at the employer's expense. Of course, laws can also be designed to encourage telework; telework adoption increased in Denmark when home computers supplied by employers to employees were exempted from taxation if the computers were used for work-related tasks. Illegems and Verbeke (2003) suggest that, in general, efforts in Denmark and the Netherlands to eliminate institutional barriers to telework have resulted in the highest telework penetration levels in the EU.

In the US, telework proponents are encouraging the adjustment of tax allowances to include pre-tax deductions for employee-paid telework expenses, such as high-speed connectivity, computers, ergonomic office furniture, lighting and related training. The Telework Coalition (TelCoa, 2006), in concert with a number of US senators, also strongly supported the Telecommuter Tax Fairness Act. This Act would essentially prohibit a state from applying its tax rules and taxing nonresident employees for work performed when they were not physically present in that state. This would prevent telecommuters being taxed twice (without a tax credit): first, by the state where they reside (for example, Connecticut), and second, by the state to which they may commute once or twice a week (for example, New York).

As the Telework Coalition notes, many of the laws and institutions surrounding the concept of work break down when applied to home office models. The following list illustrates some of the areas that require reconsideration in a telework environment:

- *State tax issues* What constitutes interstate business? Does telework establish a physical business presence?
- *Home office safety* What liability should employers have for the safety of an employee's home office?
- *Federal taxes* Home office equipment given to teleworkers is a taxable fringe benefit. Employees face complicated home office deduction rules.
- *Labour* Overtime and record-keeping requirements make it difficult for non-exempt employees to telework.
- *Americans with Disabilities Act* What is a reasonable accommodation? Should a firm pay for the cost of building wheelchair ramps in an employee's home?

(adapted from TelCoa, 2006)

There are yet more ways to adjust regulations and tax codes to produce a more telework-friendly environment. For example, in the US a common barrier to telework is the threat of double taxation. This issue arises when the telecommuter's home state differs from the employer's state; the income the telecommuter earns while working at home is subject to income tax in both states without corresponding credits in either. Thus, the interstate telecommuter may be subject to double taxation solely because she telecommutes across state lines some of the time.

In Canada double taxation is not as much a concern; instead, the problems centre on the teleworker's ability to receive work-related tax credits. For such credits to be claimed, the teleworker's home workspace must be her 'principal' place of employment; she must use it exclusively for earning business income; and the teleworker must obtain, complete, and have her employer sign a Canada Customs and Revenue Agency form certifying that the employee is required to keep a workspace at home. Obtaining this form from the employer may create problems, as telework is often a voluntary arrangement.[5]

The key consideration illustrated in the above two examples is that existing policies and tax regulations often create barriers to telework adoption. Governments can utilize regulations and tax codes as a policy tool to grow the virtual workplace by streamlining, clarifying and amending existing tax codes to support increased telework adoption.

Further examples of the potential for utilizing regulatory and tax policies to grow the virtual workplace are revealed in US regulations surrounding the security of information. The US Treasury Board produced an implementation notice (No. 1993-04) on Security and Telework, which states that, given the high risks involved, telework should not involve access to information that is designated as extremely sensitive or classified as top secret. The Government Security Policy, Ch 2.1, subsection 5, states that information classified in the national interest should never be removed from the workplace. In the light of new technologies not envisaged by earlier lawmakers, such regulatory barriers could be amended.

Regulatory and tax policies have a high potential effectiveness, due to their high potential for goal achievement with only a moderate level of input cost. Unfortunately, this policy option can have a low procedural effectiveness: high bounded rationality and opportunism constraints reduce the ability of policymakers to amend current regulations and tax codes to encourage further telework adoption. Opportunism constraints can be seen in the multitude of lobby and interest groups petitioning for favourable tax and regulatory codes to suit their interests, and the influence these efforts have on policymakers. Bounded rationality constraints are manifested in the suboptimal development of tax and regulatory codes to encourage the growth of the virtual workplace (due to environmental complexity and limited cognitive processing abilities).

Option 6: Incentives and Disincentives

Related to tax codes and regulations, the most proactive and complex policy tool at the government's disposal is financial incentives and disincentives. We distinguish this level of policy options from the previous discussion on tax codes and regulations by its degree of explicit intention to effect change in the virtual workplace. Thus, our conception of the tax code and regulatory policy option is one of relatively passive intent, wherein barriers are removed and a telework-friendly regulatory framework is developed. The incentives and disincentives policy option, by contrast, is much more active and direct, with penalties and incentives explicitly intended to drive increased telework adoption.

Given this definition, we note that very few disincentive policies specifically target increased telework adoption. Most disincentive policies focus on reducing GHG emissions or possibly road congestion; as a consequence, they may have the indirect effect of encouraging telework. One disincentive policy that directly encourages telework is the 2006 US State-Justice-Commerce appropriation bill, which requires five federal agencies to prove that the number of employees working away from the office has risen from fiscal year 2005. If the agencies fail to prove this increase in telework, they forfeit $5 million in funding.

Congressman Wolf commented on the above appropriation bill:

> I do not like having to be so heavy-handed and threaten to withhold funding, but if that is what it is going to take to get more people teleworking, then that is what I will continue to do . . . There simply is just no magic in strapping ourselves in a metal box every day and driving ourselves to the office only to sit behind a computer or talk on the phone for eight hours. (quoted in Pulliam, 2005)

Interestingly, Illegems and Verbeke's (2003) survey of HR managers assessed the effectiveness of a number of policy tools, including road pricing, a disincentive policy. Road pricing, which would increase the cost of using private road transport, was not generally perceived as a measure that would enhance telework adoption. It is noteworthy, however, that managers of organizations that suffer the most from road congestion stated that telework implementation would be enhanced by the introduction of road pricing (61 per cent versus 29 per cent, a statistically significant difference).

Incentive-based policies, on the other hand, offer payment for adopting telework. While such policies can increase telework adoption, they also come with the greatest input costs, thus negating much of their potential effectiveness. Nonetheless, a recent Gartner Dataquest report (2005) suggests that countries that achieve the greatest levels of telework have governments that offer incentives to businesses that set up flexible work programs. The report recommends that governments provide financial incentives for companies that promote telework as part of corporate environmental policies. Incentive programs could also include allowing companies to claim credits for emissions saved from teleworking employees and offering employers subsidies for having employees telework.

In assessing the incentive and disincentive policy option, we rate it high in its ability to achieve the goal of growing the virtual workplace but with an associated high input cost. These high input costs include not only the payee's costs (the payee being the organization in the case of disincentive policies and the government/taxpayer in the case of incentive policies) but also the costs of the oversight and implementation of such policies. This policy alternative has low procedural effectiveness because it is highly constrained by bounded rationality and threats from opportunism. For example, threats from opportunism often arise with incentive-based policies, as self-interest can influence the magnitude and direction (that is, potential recipient) of subsidy programs.

Once again, we stress that our evaluation of the incentive and disincentive policy option, as with the other five policy options, considers the policy only in isolation. As our analysis suggests, the majority of policy alternatives considered in isolation are poor tools for growing the virtual workplace. Utilizing a combination of these policy options, however, is likely to produce the greatest real effectiveness for growing the virtual workplace. The optimal mix and combination of these option will vary for each government's unique situation and environment, so policymakers must be aware of and consider each policy alternative in their attempts to grow the virtual workplace.

CONSIDERING THE EXTERNALITIES

It should be noted that even policies that effectively target telework adoption may have unintended and possibly negative consequences. For example, a potentially negative externality to increased telework adoption is that teleworkers generally use more computer hardware than non-teleworkers (presumably because of duplication of equipment at home and at the traditional office) (Arnfalk, 1999). Producing this extra hardware requires more resources and energy, and creates more electronic waste.[6] A recent study found that manufacturing a 24 kg computer and monitor uses more than 240 kg of fossil fuels, 22 kg of chemicals and a tonne and a half of water. In total the materials used to make a computer weigh 640 times as much as the computer itself (the equivalent ratio for a car is between one and two times its weight; for a refrigerator two times its weight) (Williams et al., 2002). On the disposal side, waste electrical and electronic equipment (WEEE) now constitutes one of the fastest growing waste streams in the EU, with current estimates indicating a rate of growth three times that of municipal waste. In 1998, WEEE accounted for 4 per cent of the municipal waste stream (6 million tonnes), and this is projected to double by 2010 (Churchman-Davies, 2002).

Our analysis of the six policy options was based on the policies' effectiveness in growing the virtual workplace. Policymakers must be prepared to amend effective policies to ameliorate externalities that may arise from achieving the policy objective of growing the virtual workplace. A simple example, from the computer hardware externality presented above, would be to shift the focus from increasing telework adoption to increasing telework adoption that utilizes portable devices such as laptops (which are less energy and material intensive, and also reduce the need for equipment duplication).

Finally, the potential externalities created by telework policy initiatives illustrate the complexities involved in societal-level telework implementation and the constraints of bounded rationality on policymakers' abilities to develop effective policy options.

CONCLUSION

In this chapter we have explored telework implementation from a societal perspective. At the societal level, telework implementation largely manifests as various forms of government policy. This level of implementation is the most complex of the three discussed in this part of the book, as there are numerous stakeholders, objectives, and intervening variables involved. This complexity is highlighted by the potential externalities that arise from effective policies, from the interaction between policy options, and from the multiple criteria that can be used to evaluate policy effectiveness.

This chapter has outlined and briefly evaluated six policy option categories: government moral support for telework, disseminating information on telework, leading by example, supporting enabling infrastructure, creating regulations and tax codes, and providing incentives and disincentives. We assessed the policies' potential effectiveness, including their ability to meet the goal of growing the virtual workplace and the input costs associated with implementing them. We also assessed their procedural effectiveness, taking into account constraints resulting from bounded rationality and opportunism.

Overall, our analysis suggests that none of the policy alternatives is sufficient as a standalone policy to effectively grow the virtual workplace. Disseminating information and creating an enabling infrastructure, however, are necessary conditions for growing the virtual workplace. Thus, our analysis indicates that it will be a combination of policy alternatives, one that specifically matches the unique circumstances faced by each government (local, regional, national and global), that will provide the most effective mechanism for growing the virtual workplace.

This chapter concludes the third part of this book. The objective of this part was to explore telework implementation and its relationship to growing the virtual workplace. Much of the part focused on prescriptions and evaluations of telework implementation options, particularly options that would lead to successful telework implementation and the subsequent continued and further adoption of telework. In the following, and final, part of this book we continue our exploration of growing the virtual workplace by analysing what differentiates telework adopters from non-adopters.

NOTES

1. As reported by InnoVisions Canada, 2006 (http://www.ivc.ca/governments/canada/federal/index.htm).
2. As reported by InnoVisions Canada, 1999 (http://www.ivc.ca/teleworkday/td1999/Blair.htm).
3. One could imagine a scenario whereby a telework conducive environment existed and virtual workplace growth was driven by the demand from employees regardless of government employee telework programs.
4. Survey results reported at http://www.businesswire.com/cgi-bin/f_headline.cgi?bw.062502/221762368.
5. It should be noted that the Canada Customs and Revenue Agency generally interprets 'required to keep workspace at home' to be inclusive of voluntary telework arrangements.
6. Electronic waste, or e-waste, is loosely defined as business and consumer electronic equipment that is near or at the end of its useful life.

PART IV

TELEWORK ADOPTION

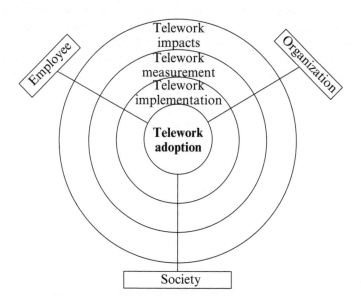

The final part of this book focuses on telework adoption from all three perspectives of the EOS integrative framework. As noted in the Introduction, the traditional telework model starts with the telework adoption decision. In an effort to grow the virtual workplace, however, we developed the EOS integrative telework framework, which inverts the traditional model and starts by exploring telework impacts, tracking and implementation. It is the increase in telework adoption, however, that we ultimately equate with the growth of the virtual workplace.

The first chapter in this part, Chapter 11, explores the telework adoption decision from the employee perspective, presenting an in-depth analysis of our primary research comparing telework adopters and non-adopters. This analysis provides guidance for employees, organizations and government policymakers about the factors that are most likely to increase the adoption of telework by employees. Because telework impacts have a critical impact on the adoption decision, we analyse which impacts are perceived as positive and which as negative by employees.

Recognizing that employee telework adoption decisions are also influenced by organizational adoption decisions, in Chapter 12 of this part we explore the role that organizations play in telework adoption decisions. This analysis, also based on our primary research, assesses perceived negative and positive telework impacts from the organization's perspective.

In the final chapter of this part, and the concluding chapter of this book, we explore aggregate adoption decisions by reviewing telework adoption rates from different societies. These adoption rates provide some insight into the differences between societal telework adopters and non-adopters and also serve as a baseline from which the growth of the virtual workplace can be measured. Finally, we explore the future of telework in the remainder of Chapter 13.

11. Telework adoption: an employee perspective

Employees who adopt or desire to adopt telework arrangements provide the demand necessary to grow the virtual workplace. Thus, in this chapter we provide an in-depth analysis of the differences between employee telework adopters and non-adopters. Highlighting these differences, and developing models to predict telework adoption, offers insight into how best to increase future employee telework adoption.

While many of the previous chapters cited secondary data and reviews, this chapter relies on the findings from our recent survey of 284 employees from 14 different organizations. In analysing this data we assess the demographic, personality, and perceptual differences between telework adopters and non-adopters. We also analyse factors leading to increased frequency of telework among telework adopters.

METHOD AND SAMPLE

The employee-level data were collected via paper and web-based surveys. The sample of employees was drawn from 14 organizations based in Calgary, Canada. As will be described in the next chapter, these organizations ranged in size from large multinational firms to small local companies. The surveys were administered in combination with telework seminars/focus groups where employees were educated on and communicated their thoughts about telework. Employees first received a brief overview of the project, then completed the questionnaires, and concluded by participating in a focus group discussion. This order was used to ensure that survey results were not biased by hearing the impressions of other employees

The surveys were designed to capture demographic, perceptual and personality variables. The demographic variables largely referred to work history, hours worked, job satisfaction, telework frequency and other basic demographics. The perceptual variables were largely based on the pre-identified potential impacts found in the literature (which were reviewed in Chapter 2's discussion of the employee's perspective on telework impacts).

There were 45 perceptual questions that were grouped in five theory-based categories, which we will describe in our analysis of the data. For each of these potential impacts the employees were asked to rate the level of positive or negative impact they have experienced, or expect to experience, as a result of telework. Utilizing seven-point Likert scales, the survey also included seven items designed to assess job satisfaction and performance, as well as a six-item job autonomy scale. Personality characteristics were measured using sub-scales from both the Manifest Needs Questionnaire (MNQ) (Steers and Braunstein, 1976) and the HEXACO-PI (Lee and Ashton, 2004).

Our analysis of the data included running basic descriptive statistics, testing for differences in scores between adopters and non-adopters with analysis of variance (ANOVA), correlation analysis, factor analysis, and regression analysis (both Logit and ordinal least squares (OLS)).

The average age of our sample was 41, and the employees had an average of 21 years of work experience. Of the sample, 56 per cent were female, 31 per cent were managers, the average workweek was 44 hours, and the average education was between a post-secondary diploma and a bachelor's degree. Of the respondents, 70 per cent indicated telework was optional in their firm, and 43 per cent of the firms had formal telework arrangements; 56 per cent teleworked (and were thus considered 'telework adopters'), with 98 per cent of those teleworking from a home office. The average frequency of telework among the telework adopters was nine days per month.

DEMOGRAPHIC DIFFERENCES BETWEEN ADOPTERS AND NON-ADOPTERS

Using ANOVA we looked for statistically significant differences between telework adopters and non-adopters.[1] First we note that the average age of adopters is significantly higher than the average age of non-adopters (mean = 43.03 versus 38.95; $P < 0.0004$). Telework adopters have an average work experience of 23.4 years compared with non-adopters' work experience of 19.6 years ($P < 0.0012$), and telework adopters also have an average organizational tenure of 113 months compared with non-adopters' 96 months ($P < 0.0006$). There is considerable overlap between the age, work experience, and organizational tenure variables of telework adopters and non-adopters. All three are significantly correlated with each other. Not surprisingly, age has a 0.87 correlation with work experience and a correlation of 0.45 with organizational tenure. Such correlations suggest multicolinearity, and even the possibility of a single dimension factor that we could label 'experience'. Within the context of telework adoption, the key point is that employees with more 'experience' (be it age, organization tenure, or work experience) are more likely to adopt telework. One possible explanation for this finding is that people with more experience share more of the values of their supervisors, are more trusted by their supervisors, and have more of the knowledge needed to be able to work from home. Higher experience among telework adopters may also indicate that adopters are in higher-level positions that are more suited to telework.

Consistent with this last possibility, we also found that telework adopters were more likely to be supervisors than were non-adopters. Of telework adopters, 33 per cent were in some sort of supervisory role while only 24 per cent of non-adopters were in such a role ($P < 0.0086$). This is an encouraging and important finding because it provides evidence against the common misconception that managerial positions and duties are not amenable to telework (due to the perception, for example, that more FTF time is needed in managers' jobs). Managerial and supervisory roles often demand more hours of work per week; thus, unsurprisingly, we found that telework adopters worked on average 4.2 hours more per week. The average telework adopter worked 45.9 hours while the average non-adopter worked 41.6 hours ($P < 0.0001$). This finding may also be explained by the fact that teleworkers apply a portion of the time saved by not commuting to increased work hours.

Our analysis also indicates that telework adopters have significantly higher levels of education than non-adopters (mean = 2.79 versus 2.46; $P < 0.0038$). For this question education was a categorical variable with 1 = high school; 2 = post-secondary diploma; 3 = bachelor's; 4 = master's/PhD. As can be seen in Figure 11.1, telework adopters more frequently have bachelor's or master's degrees while non-adopters more frequently have high school or post-secondary diploma degrees. This finding is consistent with the literature: teleworkers tend to have higher levels of education than non-teleworkers.

The final employee demographic variable that differentiated telework adopters from non-adopters was the number of children that the employee had (both the number of children under five and the number of children 5–17 years of age). The fact that telework adopters tended to have more children under the age of five than non-adopters is not surprising, as telework offers the flexibility for employees to balance the demands of young children. Figure 11.2 displays the number of children under five for adopters and non-adopters (the average number of children for adopters is 0.30, while for non-adopters it is 0.14; $P < 0.015$).

Our survey also found that telework adopters have more children between the ages of 5 and 17 than non-adopters do: the average number for adopters is 0.67 whereas for non-adopters it is 0.38 ($P < 0.01$). While this

Level of education

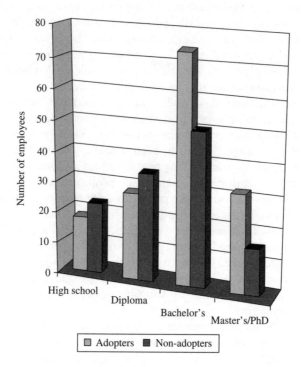

Figure 11.1   Education level for adopters and non-adopters

may also be explained by the need for flexible work arrangements, it might simply indicate that telework adopters, being older than non-adopters, are more likely to have older children.

While the use of ANOVA in the above analysis allows us to highlight areas of significant differences between adopter and non-adopter mean scores, it is also useful to look at the correlations between demographic variables and telework adoption. As expected, most of the variables that significantly differentiated adopters from non-adopters also provide statistically significant correlative values with telework adoption. Table 11.1 provides a summary of demographic variables and their correlations, all significant $P < 0.05$, with telework adoption.

These correlations are all low: no single demographic variable has a large correlation with telework adoption. The greatest correlation is between hours worked and telework adoption, with an r of 0.23. Given the nature of correlations, we cannot infer causation from this result. This finding may indicate that employees who work more hours per week will be more likely

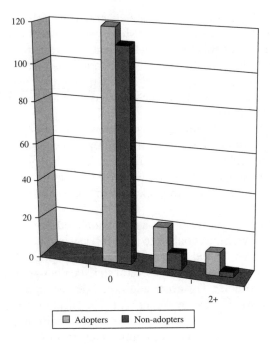

Figure 11.2   Number of children under five for adopters and non-adopters

Table 11.1   Telework adoption correlation values

Demographic variable	Correlation with telework adoption
Age	0.2159
Education	0.1739
Work experience	0.1946
Organizational tenure	0.2063
Managerial position	0.1570
Hours worked	0.2306
Children under five	0.1452
Children 5–17	0.1547

to adopt telework; alternatively, the finding may indicate that telework adopters are able to, and do, work more hours per week (presumably because they have more time to work due to the reduction in commute times).

A notable non-significant demographic variable is job tenure, which is practically uncorrelated with telework adoption (with an *r* of 0.052). This is somewhat surprising given the significant relationship that age, work experience, and organizational tenure have with telework adoption. A possible explanation for this finding is that general organizational and work experience help nurture the shared values and trust between worker and supervisor that facilitate teleworking, while specific and tacit job experience is not as important. Presumably the skills required for a specific job can be acquired while teleworking.

While the above correlations analysed in isolation are of interest, the use of logistic regression allows us to use multiple demographic variables to explain and possibly predict telework adoption. The coefficients reported in logistic regressions represent odds ratios, thus in our regression models the increase in odds of adopting telework are indicated by subtracting 1.0 from the coefficient.

Table 11.2 displays the results of a regression model that utilizes the eight significant demographic variables to predict telework adoption. This model explains 15 per cent of the variance in telework adoption decisions.

The regression model identifies several statistically significant individual demographic variables. For every additional degree attained, the odds of adopting telework increase by 47 per cent. The effect of work experience is positive, but marginally significant: with every additional year of work experience, an employee is 5 per cent more likely to adopt telework. Finally, the influence of children is quite significant, as with every child under five the odds of adopting telework increase 168 per cent, while with every additional child 5–17 the odds of adopting telework increase by 34 per cent. These findings regarding children are consistent with the notion that telework offers the flexibility to deal with the demands of children (presumably these demands are more pressing with young children than older ones). Gender, age and managerial position do not affect the odds of adopting

Table 11.2   Logistic regression model predicting telework adoption

Demographic variable	Odds ratio	Alpha ($P > z$)
Gender	1.402702	0.268
Age	1.017735	0.571
Education	1.474871	**0.024**
Work experience	1.055052	**0.091**
Managerial position	0.712150	0.295
Hours worked	1.04667	**0.009**
Children under five	2.687764	**0.001**
Children 5–17	1.346223	**0.055**

Note: Bold alphas are statistically significant.

telework in this model, although managerial position and age do have a significant correlation with telework when analysed independently.

PERCEPTION OF TELEWORK IMPACTS

As discussed in Part I of this book, telework has a multitude of potential impacts at the employee level. Employees' perceptions of the significance of these impacts are likely to affect employee propensity to adopt telework. Our survey measured perceptions of 45 potential impacts utilizing a seven-point Likert scale. The number 1 on this scale was anchored as a 'very negative impact' and 7 was a 'very positive impact'. The midway point of number 4 was anchored by 'no impact: neutral'. Thus, aggregate scores below 4 indicate an overall perceived negative impact, while those above 4 indicate an overall perceived positive impact.

Given the focus of this chapter, employee telework adoption, we are most interested in how telework adopters differ from non-adopters in their perception of telework impacts. Out of interest, however, we also analysed the dataset in its entirety, aggregating both adopter and non-adopter scores. This analysis revealed that eight items were perceived as negative impacts of telework by the overall sample. These negative impacts and their associated means are presented in Table 11.3. Most of these negative impacts relate to the organization's efficiency (training, scheduling meetings, and communicating).

The remaining 37 items were rated as overall positive telework impacts (rated above 4 on a seven-point scale). At a general level this is consistent with much of the literature and our analysis of telework impacts in Part I of this book, namely that the benefits (positive impacts) of telework outweigh the costs (negative impacts) of this work arrangement. Of the 37

Table 11.3   Employees' perceived negative impacts of telework

Impact	Mean rating
My relationships with other employees who do not telework	3.63
Informal training possibilities (e.g., mentoring)	3.74
Communication with other employees in my organization	3.83
Scheduling meetings	3.89
Promotion opportunities	3.91
My ability to separate my work and non-work life	3.95
My personal expenditures on ICT in my home office	3.96
My opportunity to give input into processes that affect me	3.99

Table 11.4   Employees' highest-rated perceived positive impacts of telework

Impact	Mean rating
Balancing my work and non-work life	5.65
My independence/autonomy	5.66
Flexibility of my employment contract	5.71
My ability to structure my workday	5.78
Overall quality of my life	5.84
My job satisfaction	5.90
Possibilities for childcare and eldercare	5.92
My capability to continue to work when working in the office isn't possible (e.g., downtown bomb scare)	6.00
Job opportunities for disabled people	6.04
Flexibility of my working hours	6.19

positively perceived impacts of telework, Table 11.4 highlights the ten most positively rated. Note that most of these positive impacts refer to the flexibility inherent in telework work arrangements, thus suggesting that work flexibility is a major driver and potential motivator for continued and future telework adoption.

Because of our effort to grow the virtual workplace, our remaining analysis in this chapter will focus on the differences between telework adopter and non-adopter perceptions of telework impacts. Assessing these differences will allow policymakers, organizations and employees to gain insights into misperceptions about the impacts of telework.

Of the 45 potential perceived impacts, there are 26 where telework adopters significantly differed in their rating from those of non-adopters. Table 11.5 presents the 26 impacts rated significantly differently by adopters and non-adopters. In all cases adopters rated the impact with a higher (more positive) score. It is worth highlighting that items with a mean score of less than 4 indicate a perceived negative telework impacts.

Interestingly, there are a number of impacts that are perceived as negative by non-adopters, but rated as slightly positive by adopters (crossing over from a rating below 4 to one above 4). The two impacts that are rated significantly differently by adopters and non-adopters, and yet are still rated as negative by both groups, are teamwork and relations with other staff members (adopters viewed these as negative, but as less negative than did non-adopters). This indicates that in practice these are valid concerns that should be regularly addressed in the implementation of a telework program.

Table 11.5   Difference in perceptions of telework impacts between adopters and non-adopters

Impact	Adopter mean	Non-adopter mean	P level
My commitment to excellence	5.8	5.1	0.0000
Productivity (my ability to get work done)	5.8	4.9	0.0000
Flexibility of my employment contract	5.8	5.2	0.0003
My manager's trust in me	4.6	4.1	0.0003
Teamwork	3.8	3.2	0.0003
My relationship with my manager	4.4	3.8	0.0006
Scheduling meetings	4.0	3.4	0.0006
Access to the information I need to work effectively	4.3	3.7	0.0007
Communication with other employees in my organization	4.0	3.4	0.0008
My manager's ability to supervise me	4.0	3.6	0.0009
My ability to structure my workday	5.9	5.4	0.0009
Communication with my manager	4.1	3.6	0.0010
Customer service (e.g., extended hours of service)	5.2	4.6	0.0021
My performance appraisal (i.e., fair assessment of my performance)	4.1	3.8	0.0024
My motivation to get work done	5.5	4.9	0.0027
Availability of and access to ICT	4.6	4.1	0.0041
My job satisfaction	6.0	5.6	0.0043
My opportunity to give input into processes that affect me	4.1	3.6	0.0051
Design and structure of my job	5.3	4.8	0.0075
Security of company data	4.2	3.8	0.0079
My staying with this organization	5.6	5.2	0.0180
My loyalty to the organization	5.4	5.1	0.0185
Knowledge sharing with other employees	4.2	3.7	0.0296
My relationships with other employees who do not telework	3.6	3.3	0.0316
Reducing absenteeism	5.6	5.3	0.0341
Flexibility of my working hours	6.2	6.0	0.0389

The fact that non-adopters, in all the statistically significant cases, perceived telework impacts more negatively than adopters will be an impediment to the growth of the virtual workplace. Non-adopters' desire to participate in telework arrangements will be diminished by perceived higher costs and lower benefits with this type of work arrangement. Thus, the potential effectiveness (benefits minus costs) of telework is reduced for the non-adopter group, and they will therefore be less likely to give telework a try.

The differences in telework impact perceptions also suggest that the perception of negative telework impacts is diminished with actual telework experience. Those who have adopted telework perceive the impacts of this work arrangement more positively than do those who have no experience with the work arrangement. In fact, as discussed above, several impacts perceived as negative by non-adopters are perceived as positive by adopters. Thus, the experience of teleworking alleviates concerns over potential negative impacts and can even transform those perceptions from negative to positive.

As previously mentioned, the 45 potential telework impacts were largely drawn from impacts identified in the literature, as reviewed in Chapter 2. As illustrated above, there is value in looking at each of these potential impacts in isolation. Combining these individual impacts into potential composite measures, however, offers the advantage of reducing the complexity of both the analysis and presentation of the results (while also providing more robust results, as composite or factor scores are better perceptual indicators than scores on individual items). Readers not interested in the statistics of such factor scores may wish to skip the rest of this chapter, as it is rather technical.

PERCEPTUAL IMPACT FACTORS AND TELEWORK ADOPTION

To create factor scores from the 45 telework impacts, we first explored the theoretical foundations from which these items were drawn. The 45 telework impacts roughly fall into five theoretical categories that we named organizational impacts of telework (OIT), impacts of telework on operational HR issues (ITOHR), impacts of telework on the organization's efficiency (ITOE), impacts of telework on external stakeholders (ITES) and other impacts of telework on my life (OITML). We used confirmatory factor analysis (CFA) to further assess the validity of these five factors. In keeping with the focus of this chapter, the reduction of 45 telework impact items to five impact factors lets us differentiate adopters and non-adopters according to more robust factor-level data. The use of factor scores also offers consolidated impacts that organizations and policymakers can focus on in their attempts to increase telework adoption. Finally, the use of factor scores will reduce the resource (time) requirements for subsequent research into the perception of telework impacts (for example, instead of a 45-item survey, employees only need to fill out a 30-item survey, because items that do not load well on a given factor can be discarded from the questionnaire).

Organizational Impacts of Telework (OIT)

Ten items formed the theoretical base for organizational impacts of telework. Principal factor analysis offered a four-factor model for these ten items, but the majority of the items loaded on a single factor. Further, a good rule of thumb for keeping a factor is to look for eigenvalues greater than 1. In the case of the ten OIT items, only one factor had an eigenvalue greater than 1, and its value was 5.27. Thus, these ten items load well both theoretically and statistically on one factor, which we label OIT. The item loadings for OIT are presented in Table 11.6 and indicate that at least seven of the ten items should be kept for future use in assessing the OIT factor (these are the seven items with factor loadings above 0.7).

Figure 11.3 offers a graphical view of the ten OIT items and their mean scores and variances. As can be seen in this figure, items 8 and 9 do not fit the overall OIT profile. In an effort to reduce survey time requirements, subsequent studies utilizing our survey could drop OIT 1, 8 and 9 because their

Table 11.6   OIT factor loadings

Item number	Item	Mean response	Factor loading on OIT
OIT 1	My joining this organization	5.33	0.61094
OIT 2	My staying with this organization	5.54	0.78804
OIT 3	Flexibility of my employment contract	5.71	0.71806
OIT 4	My commitment to excellence	5.59	0.79674
OIT 5	My feeling part of the organization's culture	4.47	0.73491
OIT 6	My loyalty to the organization	5.36	0.82757
OIT 7	Design and structure of my job	5.21	0.72874
OIT 8	Knowledge sharing with other employees	4.05	0.63923
OIT 9	My status in the organization	4.26	0.63750
OIT 10	My job satisfaction	5.90	0.74799

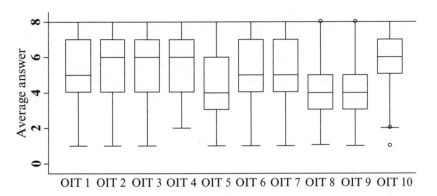

Figure 11.3   Average OIT item responses

factor loadings are below 0.7. That said, these items still have value at an individual level (for example, does telework impact an employee's decision to join an organization? (OIT 1)). Thus, while the items can be dropped from the OIT factor, they can be retained for the individual results they offer.

Impacts of Telework on Operational HR Issues (ITOHR)

The second theoretical category focused on impacts of telework on operational HR issues (ITOHR). Theoretically related to ITOHR were 18 items. Principal factor analysis on these 18 items indicated there were two with eigenvalues greater than 1. This finding suggests that ITOHR may actually be composed of two factors, and we suggest that a two-factor solution be considered for ITOHR in future research. For the purposes of this analysis, however, we maintain ITOHR as a single factor. A single factor solution is justified because the factor analysis indicated one factor with an eigenvalue of 9.12 while the second factor had an eigenvalue of only 1.35; most of the 18 items load well on a single factor; and theory suggests a single factor. The 18 items and their loadings on the single ITOHR factor are shown in Table 11.7.

As indicated by the results in the table, items 1, 11, 12, 13 and 17 do not load particularly well on the single ITOHR factor. Thus, future research could eliminate these items from the survey (reducing ITOHR from 18 items to 13) or seek a two-factor solution that better accounts for all the items and yet is still theoretically justified. As an example of a possible second factor, items 1, 11 and 12 could possibly form a second factor called work flexibility, as the items seem to relate to issues surrounding telework's impact on work flexibility.

Table 11.7   ITOHR factor loadings

Item number	Item	Mean score	ITOHR factor loading
ITOHR 1	Reducing absenteeism (# of days I cannot work; e.g., because of illness)	5.53	0.44358
ITOHR 2	Promotion opportunities	3.91	0.67618
ITOHR 3	Informal training possibilities (e.g., mentoring)	3.74	0.75033
ITOHR 4	Accessing formal training (e.g., courses, seminars)	4.26	0.72109
ITOHR 5	My performance appraisal (i.e., fair assessment of my performance)	4.10	0.83500
ITOHR 6	My manager's ability to supervise me	4.01	0.81482
ITOHR 7	My manager's trust in me	4.52	0.74160
ITOHR 8	My relationship with my manager	4.25	0.83166
ITOHR 9	My opportunity to give input into processes that affect me	3.99	0.83485
ITOHR 10	Availability and access to IT/ communication technology	4.44	0.63410
ITOHR 11	My ability to structure my workday	5.78	0.50421
ITOHR 12	Flexibility of my working hours	6.19	0.39917
ITOHR 13	My motivation to get work done	5.32	0.56030
ITOHR 14	Communication with other employees in my organization	3.83	0.84002
ITOHR 15	My relationships with other employees who do not telework	3.63	0.78349
ITOHR 16	Communication with my manager	4.02	0.87963
ITOHR 17	My independence/autonomy	5.66	0.51991
ITOHR 18	Access to the information I need to work effectively	4.06	0.76950

Impacts of Telework on Organizational Efficiency (ITOE)

The third theoretical factor has eight items that focus on the impacts of telework on organizational efficiency (ITOE). Principal component factor analysis suggests these eight items load on one factor, with a single solution eigenvalue of 3.399. As shown in Table 11.8, however, many of these items do not load well on the single factor. Items 2, 3, 4, 5 and 7 could be removed from subsequent applications of the survey. This would leave only items 1, 6 and 8 as items loading on the ITOE factor.

Table 11.8   ITOE factor loadings

Item number	Item	Mean score	Factor loading on ITOE
ITOE 1	Scheduling meetings	3.89	0.76842
ITOE 2	Productivity (my ability to get work done)	5.47	0.57905
ITOE 3	Availability of space in the office when I need it	4.59	0.65368
ITOE 4	My expenses related to coming to the office (e.g., gas, parking)	5.49	0.53047
ITOE 5	My capability to continue to work when working in the office isn't possible (e.g., downtown bomb scare)	6.00	0.45911
ITOE 6	Security of company data	4.10	0.74369
ITOE 7	My personal expenditures on ICT in my home office	3.96	0.62829
ITOE 8	Teamwork	3.58	0.77849

Impacts of Telework on External Stakeholders (ITES)

The fourth theoretical factor has four items that focus on impacts of telework on external stakeholders (ITES). Principal component analysis suggests a one-factor solution with an eigenvalue of 1.4. Unfortunately, as indicated by the results in Table 11.9, these four items do not load well on the ITES factor. While all four items do deal with external stakeholders, it is possible that the four items do not load well on a single factor because each one focuses on a different stakeholder group (namely customers, the public, the disabled, the elderly and the young). Given the theoretical rationale for these items and the marginally acceptable loadings (all above 0.5), we will maintain the ITES factor. Future research, however, should seek to enhance the items that form the ITES factor.

Other Impacts of Telework on My Life (OITML)

The final theory-derived category captures other impacts of telework on the employee's life; we called this factor other impacts of telework on my life (OITML). Principal component analysis suggested a single factor solution with an eigenvalue of 2.14. As indicated by the results in Table 11.10, three of the four items loaded well on this single OITML factor.

Only item 2 was somewhat problematic. It is interesting to note that item 1 assessed the impact of telework on balancing work and non-work

Table 11.9   ITES factor loadings

Item number	Item	Mean score	Factor loading on ITES
ITES 1	Customer service (e.g., extended hours of service)	5.11	0.52388
ITES 2	Image of my organization (e.g., environmentally responsible)	5.54	0.64206
ITES 3	Job opportunities for disabled people	6.04	0.67388
ITES 4	Possibilities for childcare and eldercare	5.92	0.50896

Table 11.10   OITML factor loadings

Item number	Item	Mean score	Factor loading on OITML
OITML 1	Balancing my work and non-work life	5.65	0.70177
OITML 2	My ability to separate my work and non-work life	3.95	0.59619
OITML 3	My job stress	5.34	0.80630
OITML 4	Overall quality of my life	5.84	0.80257

life (which was rated as a positive impact of telework) while item 2 assessed the ability to separate work and non-work life (which was rated a negative impact). Thus, the lower loading on the OITML factor for item 2 is understandable, and at a marginally acceptable 0.6 loading we recommend the continued inclusion of this item in the OITML scale.

Factor Score Differences between Telework Adopters and Non-adopters

Comparing the five factor scores outlined above, we can observe the factor-level perceptual differences between telework adopters and non-adopters. We note a statistical difference between adopters' and non-adopters' mean factor score for organizational impacts of telework (OIT) (the adopters' mean rating was 5.13 compared with the non-adopters' 4.75, $P < 0.0097$). Thus, adopters see a more positive overall impact of telework on their organization and role. This can also be seen by the significant 0.18 correlation between OIT scores and telework adoption.

An even larger difference is found in the impacts of telework on operational HR issues (ITOHR) scores. Adopters' mean rating was 4.63 while non-adopters' was 4.17 ($P < 0.0001$). Thus, adopters perceive a more positive impact of telework on operational HR issues. There is a significant 0.24 correlation between ITOHR and the adoption of telework.

Finally, we note that the impacts of telework on the organization's efficiency (ITOE) is also rated higher by adopters than non-adopters (4.72 compared with 4.33, $P < 0.0007$). Thus, adopters perceive a more positive impact of telework on organizational efficiency than do non-adopters. There is a significant 0.20 correlation between ITOE and telework adoption. It should be noted that we did not find statistical differences between adopters and non-adopters' mean factor scores for ITES (5.47 compared with 5.42, $P < 0.6889$) and OITML (5.17 compared with 5.17, $P < 0.979$).

As previously mentioned, the advantage of using these factor scores is that they allow for a more targeted approach to increasing telework adoption and growing the virtual workplace. Thus, instead of dealing with 26 items that adopters and non-adopters rate significantly differently, we now have only three factors of significant difference to focus our attention on. Given the relevance of these three particular factors (OIT, ITOE and ITOHR) to telework adoption, efforts to grow the virtual workplace should pay special attention to them. For example, by using information dissemination policies, governments and organizations could promote the positive impacts telework has on the employee's relationship to the organization, the efficiency of the organization itself, and operational HR issues. The highest return on investment among these three factors would come from promoting telework's positive impacts on operational HR issues such as scheduling flexibility, as this is the factor with the highest correlation to telework adoption. We continue to utilize the factor scores developed above in subsequent sections of this chapter.

JOB CHARACTERISTICS AND TELEWORK ADOPTION

Our survey used a six-item scale to measure self-reported overall job autonomy (for example, 'the way my job is performed is influenced a great deal by company rules, policies and procedures'). Higher scores indicate more autonomy (that is, a higher level of worker discretion when selecting appropriate work behaviours, deciding the order and pace of job tasks and coordinating those activities with others (Barrick and Mount, 1993)).

As could be expected, there was a significant difference between telework adopters and non-adopters on the aggregate job autonomy score.

Adopters' mean factor score was 4.7 while non-adopters' score was 4.3 ($P < 0.0004$). The correlation of job autonomy to telework was a significant 0.21. As stated before, such correlations are open to bidirectional interpretation. In this case, one interpretation is that those who have autonomous jobs will be more prone to telework. The alternative interpretation would be that those who telework are afforded more autonomy in their job because they telework.

Using the first interpretation one could attempt to grow the virtual workplace by focusing telework adoption efforts at those who have more autonomy in their jobs, on the grounds that these employees would be more likely to adopt telework. Using the second interpretation, one could view job autonomy as a positive impact of telework and promote telework as offering this benefit. This reasoning is in line with the perceptual findings discussed previously, wherein telework is viewed as having a positive impact on job flexibility.

PERSONALITY MEASURES AND TELEWORK ADOPTION

The first test assessed the employees' need motivations using the Manifest Needs Questionnaire (Steers and Braunstein, 1976), which contains 20 items designed to measure four different need motivations: achievement, affiliation, dominance and autonomy. Individuals high in need for achievement are typically characterized as goal seekers; they react positively to competition and consistently aspire to accomplish difficult tasks (Jackson, 1989). Individuals with a high need for affiliation tend to focus their energy on being with friends and people in general, and on maintaining emotional ties with others (Jackson, 1989). Individuals high in need for dominance tend to seek leadership opportunities. They typically desire control and authority over other people and attempt to influence others by making suggestions, giving their opinions and evaluations, and controlling the activities of others (Steers and Braunstein, 1991). Finally, individuals high in need for autonomy generally value independence of thought; they prefer self-directed work, care less about others' opinions and rules, and prefer to make decisions alone (Steers and Braunstein, 1991).

The needs scores for adopters and non-adopters are presented in Table 11.11. It is interesting to note that need for achievement was higher in non-adopters. A possible explanation for this result is that people with higher levels of need for achievement desire the FTF contact they perceive as needed to move up the corporate ladder. It is also interesting that telework adopters actually had higher levels of need for affiliation. This finding is

Table 11.11   Manifest needs scores

Personality trait	Adopters	Non-adopters
Need for achievement	5.32	5.56
Need for affiliation	3.89	3.77
Need for autonomy	4.81	4.76
Need for dominance	4.59	4.33

somewhat counterintuitive as telework adopters choose a work style that reduces interaction with colleagues, so one would expect this group to be lower in need for affiliation. Perhaps this finding indicates that telework does not isolate the worker to the extent one would expect. Alternatively, maybe working makes workers feel more isolated, thereby increasing the importance and salience of their need for affiliation. Finally, the only statistically significant difference between adopters and non-adopters was the higher need for dominance for telework adopters ($P < 0.036$). This may be explained by the fact that the telework adopters in our sample tended to be in supervisory roles; thus this group is more prone to have higher needs for dominance.

The second test used the Hexaco personality inventory (Lee and Ashton, 2004). From the broad Hexaco inventory of traits, we selected the four traits that we deemed the most relevant to telework. From the conscientiousness domain we utilized organization (corg), which assesses the tendency to seek order; diligence (cdil), which assesses the tendency to work hard; and prudence (cprud), which assesses the tendency to deliberate carefully and inhibit impulses. From the extraversion domain we used the sociability trait (xsoc), which assesses the tendency to enjoy conversations, social interactions and parties.

The scores of the four traits are shown in Table 11.12. Adopters and non-adopters did not differ significantly on these scales. It is interesting to note that non-adopters tended to be higher on the corg scale, which is somewhat counterintuitive given that telework by its nature requires the ability to remain organized (thus, teleworkers would presumably need to be even more organized than their non-teleworking peers). As evidenced by the non-significant results, we find little in terms of personality differences for telework adopters and non-adopters. This finding is nonetheless valuable to efforts to grow the virtual workplace, because it suggests that the choice to adopt telework is not determined by any of these particular personality traits. We conclude that efforts to grow the virtual workplace can focus instead on perceptions of telework impacts, demographic characteristics of the employee and job characteristics.

Table 11.12   Hexaco sub-facet scores

Personality trait	Adopters	Non-adopters
Organization (corg)	3.66	3.86
Diligence (cdil)	4.18	4.14
Sociability (xsoc)	3.03	3.00
Prudence (cprud)	3.83	3.89

PREDICTING TELEWORK ADOPTION

In an effort to grow the virtual workplace, we now bring all the factors discussed above together to develop a regression model that predicts telework adoption. Taking into account demographic, perceptual, personality, and job characteristics we can develop a series of regression models that predict telework adoption. For example, Table 11.13 shows the results from a model that explains 27 per cent of the variance in telework adoption versus non-adoption.

In this table, the odds ratio column indicates the effect that the independent variable has on the dependent variable. For example, with every unit increase in need for achievement (NeedAchieve), the odds that that person will adopt telework are 62 per cent lower ($0.38 - 1 = -0.62$). With education, on the other hand, every additional degree (for example, diploma versus bachelor's degree) increases the odds that the person will adopt telework by 84 per cent ($1.84 - 1 = 0.84$). With every additional year of work experience the odds of telework adoption increase by 8 per cent. For every additional child under the age of five the likelihood of telework increases by 197 per cent. Thus, someone with two children under the age of five would be almost three times as likely to adopt telework as someone with only one child under the age of five. Applying these results to growing the virtual workplace, targeting of potential telework adopters should focus on those with children under the age of five, those with higher education levels and those lower in need for achievement.

As indicated in Table 11.13, the regression model to predict telework adoption also includes a total perception variable. This variable is the aggregate score of all 45 perceived telework impact variables. We used this aggregate score because the five factors developed earlier in this chapter did not significantly predict telework adoption in our regression models. The total perception variable is useful as it indicates the overall perceptual attitude an employee has towards the impacts of telework. Our regression model indicates that for every one unit increase in this rating (for example,

Table 11.13   Telework adoption regression results

Variable	Odds ratio	Std. err.	Z	$P > (z)$
Education	1.844	0.404	2.80	0.005
Work experience	1.083	0.023	3.75	0.000
Hours worked	1.094	0.027	3.62	0.000
Children 0–5	2.971	1.061	3.05	0.002
Children 5–17	1.352	0.301	1.40	0.161
Need for achievement	0.381	0.106	−3.46	0.001
Job satisfaction	1.565	0.388	1.81	0.071
Aggregate telework perception	2.478	0.629	3.58	0.000

from no impact to slightly positive impact) the odds that a person will adopt telework increase by 148 per cent. In other words, for every unit increase in overall impact perception rating, the employee will be 2.48 times more likely to adopt telework. This finding seems to indicate the importance of positive perceptions of telework impacts in making the decision to telework. Alternatively, it could instead indicate the importance of adopting telework in improving the perception of telework impacts, suggesting that telework experience improves perceptions of telework impacts. The implication of these potential explanations is either that efforts to grow the virtual workplace should focus on increasing awareness of the positive impacts of telework, or else that telework should be adopted (even on a trial basis) to increase the positive perception of telework impacts.

PREDICTING THE FREQUENCY OF TELEWORK

While our analysis to this point has focused on the adoption of telework, it is also of interest to analyse the frequency of telework. Thus, for the sub-sample of telework adopters, we utilize telework frequency as the dependent variable; this variable measures the days of telework per month. The average telework frequency was 9.2 days per month, but this number is skewed by the inclusion of many full-time teleworkers who telework 20 days per month. The distribution of the frequency of telework is shown in Figure 11.4.

Looking at perceptual variables, we note that the frequency of telework is significantly correlated with OIT (0.259), ITOHR (0.324), ITOE (0.3499) and ITES (0.2451). Thus, those who telework more tend to rate the impacts of telework higher than those who telework less frequently. This finding is intuitive, as those who telework more have more buy-in to this type of work

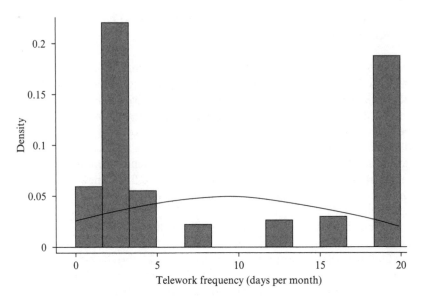

Figure 11.4   Frequency distribution of days teleworked per month

arrangement and thus are more likely to perceive the impacts of telework more positively. It should be noted that these five factors had high levels of multicolinearity, and that no significant results came out of an ordinal least squares (OLS) model that used the five perceptual variables to predict telework frequency.

In further assessing telework frequency, we utilized an OLS model that explained 18 per cent of the variance in telework frequency. This model indicated that education level has a negative impact on telework frequency. In fact, for every additional degree obtained the frequency of telework dropped by 2.1 days. This is probably due to the fact that more highly educated employees tend to fill management roles where exclusive telework is not feasible, while presumably lower educated teleworkers possess jobs that are more amenable to full-time telework (for example, at customer call centres).

Another interesting result from this model is that employees with children 5–17 years old telework more. For every additional child in this age range the teleworker will spend 1.29 days more per month teleworking. Oddly, the younger children variable (0–5 years) had no effect on telework frequency. This is the opposite of what we found with telework adoption, where it was the younger children that significantly influenced the likelihood of the parent to adopt telework.

PREDICTING JOB SATISFACTION AND PERFORMANCE

We also assessed job satisfaction and job performance using self-report measures. Employees were asked to indicate their job satisfaction and job performance for the overall job; when the employee teleworked; and in comparison with traditional office work arrangements. These variables are best suited as dependent variables, as job satisfaction and performance are likely to be influenced by other job characteristics and not the other way around (for example, with job performance influencing employee characteristics). Thus, changing the dependent variable from telework and telework frequency, we now look at predictors of job satisfaction and job performance.

Correlates with job satisfaction, all of which are statistically significant, are shown in Table 11.14. For the purpose of this book the most interesting finding is that telework frequency has a 0.1821 correlation with job satisfaction. This suggests that those who telework more will also be more satisfied with their job. While job satisfaction is not the focus of this book, it is worth noting the large correlation between job satisfaction and need for achievement (0.8254). A relationship of that magnitude could almost allow us to use need for achievement as a proxy for job satisfaction. Not surprisingly, in running regression models on the data the only variable that significantly predicted job satisfaction was need for achievement.

Finally, we also analysed correlations between job performance and the other variables from our survey. Telework adoption and telework frequency were not significantly related to job performance. Using a simple regression model of telework and telework frequency predicting job performance, we

Table 11.14   Job satisfaction correlations

Variable	Job satisfaction correlations
Gender	0.1626
Education	−0.1238
Telework frequency	0.1821
Corg (organization)	0.1853
Cdil (diligence)	0.3889
Need for achievement	0.8254
Need for autonomy	0.6784
Need for dominance	0.5023
OITML	0.1434
Job performance	0.6487

are able to explain just under 5 per cent of the variance. The model suggests that those who telework more believe that they perform better. More specifically, for every extra day of telework per month the performance rating increased by 0.297 (the performance scale is out of 7). It should be noted that most regression models we ran did not predict job performance well.

CONCLUSION

As we have argued, the telework adoption decision at the employee level (together with the employer's decision in favour of the practice) is critical to the growth of the virtual workplace. An understanding of the differences between telework adopters and non-adopters will allow policies and programs intended to grow the virtual workplace to better target employees who are more likely to adopt telework. Understanding adopter and non-adopter differences will also provide direction for programs that target the development of employee and job characteristics that are more amenable to telework. Thus, in this chapter we have provided an in-depth analysis of the differences between employee telework adopters and non-adopters.

To analyse the differences between adopters and non-adopters we utilized primary data from a survey we conducted with 284 employees. The data suggest that telework adopters have more work experience and longer organizational tenure. Adopters are also more likely to be in supervisory positions, have higher levels of education and have more young children at home. With regard to perceptions of telework impacts, adopters view these impacts more positively than non-adopters. In fact, several impacts are viewed negatively by non-adopters yet positively by adopters. One possible interpretation of these results is that, as one engages in telework, misconceptions of negative impacts diminish and sometimes even transform to a positive view of that impact. Finally, we note that adopters and non-adopters show little difference in personality measures. Given that personality traits are not easily malleable, the result that personality traits do not predict telework adoption is encouraging for the growth of the virtual workplace.

This chapter also explored the factors leading to increased telework frequency and overall job satisfaction. Telework frequency appears to increase with the number of older children at home and, interestingly, is inversely related to level of education achieved. Increased telework frequency also increases the positive perception of telework impacts and the overall rating of job satisfaction.

Finally, we applied data reduction techniques to consolidate the 45 telework impact items into five theoretically justified factors. These factors are useful for focusing policies and programs intended to grow the virtual workplace and will be useful for reducing the resource requirements of future research into telework impacts.

While the employee-level analysis of telework adoption presented in this chapter is valuable, we have purposely ignored one of the greatest predictors of employee-level telework adoption: organizational support. In the next chapter we continue our exploration of telework adoption, but now from the organizational perspective. Consistent with the EOS integrative framework, we will explore the interaction between employee-level and organizational-level telework adoption decisions.

NOTE

1. Sampling errors are an alternative explanation for significant differences in demographic variables between adopters and non-adopters, in which case the demographic differences between the adopter and non-adopter samples may be responsible for the various differences between them.

12. Telework adoption: an organizational perspective

The telework adoption decision at the organizational level can be either driven from the top down (induced) or developed from the bottom up with employee initiatives (autonomous). As illustrated by the EOS integrative telework framework, the adoption of telework at the organizational level will be heavily influenced by the perception and realization of telework impacts. This relationship is probably most salient at the organizational level, because organizational decisions are driven by performance indicators such as cost savings and increased profit, productivity and employee retention – all of which are measurable impacts of the telework arrangement.

In this chapter we explore the adoption of telework from an organizational perspective. Continuing from the last chapter, we utilize primary data collected from surveys of 284 employees, as well as surveys of the 14 organizations from which the employee sample was drawn. Our analysis seeks to assess how telework impacts are perceived from the organizational viewpoint. We also analyse the interaction effect that organizations have on the employee telework adoption decision. We end this chapter with a brief overview of secondary data that indicate potential intra-organizational telework adoption rates.

METHOD AND SAMPLE

Our organizational-level data is drawn from FTF interviews with personnel managers from 14 organizations. Empirical results were also derived from surveys filled out by these managers. The organizational-level surveys followed a similar format to those administered at the employee level. These surveys captured basic demographic information including organizational size by number of employees, years in operation, the presence of an official telework program and estimated telework penetration rates. The survey roughly paralleled the employee-level survey with regard to questions on the perceived impacts of telework. For organizations, there were 32 potential telework impacts that were theoretically grouped in four categories. These categories were impacts on strategic HR issues, impacts on operational HR

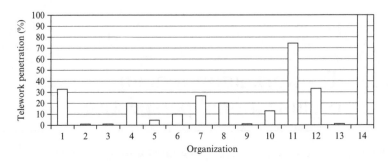

Figure 12.1   Telework penetration in 14 sample organizations

issues, impacts on the organization's efficiency, and impacts on external stakeholders. (These 32 potential impacts, the four categories and their associated theoretical support were outlined in Chapter 3.)

The FTF interviews with the personnel managers also captured information on the drivers of telework adoption and suggestions for what could be done to grow the virtual workplace. The organizational-level data were analysed using content analysis, descriptive statistics, and hierarchical linear modeling (HLM).

The 14 organizations constitute a convenience sample. Of the organizations approached, those that were willing to participate in the study and encourage their employees to complete the employee-level survey were included in the sample. We attempted to get a broad range of organizations in our sample; for example, we achieved a mix of government, privately owned, and publicly owned businesses. As shown in Figure 12.1, telework penetration rates in the organizations ranged from 1 per cent to 100 per cent.

Beyond telework penetration, we sought a broad spectrum of organizational demographic characteristics. This range of characteristics allows for better generalizations of our analyses across organizational types. As Figure 12.2 shows, organizational size ranged from small local organizations (employees <10) to large multinational organizations (employees >12 000).

We also sought a broad spectrum of employee characteristics. For example, a one-way ANOVA of the education level of employees from different organizations suggests a significant difference between organizations (Bartlett's test for equal variances was non-significant). Figure 12.3 displays this difference in education levels between organizations. It should also be noted that employee organizational and job tenure (in months) also varied across organizations, while no substantial differences in employee age or supervisory position were found between the organizations.

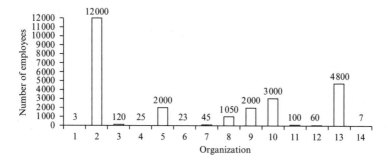

Figure 12.2 Organizational size by number of employees

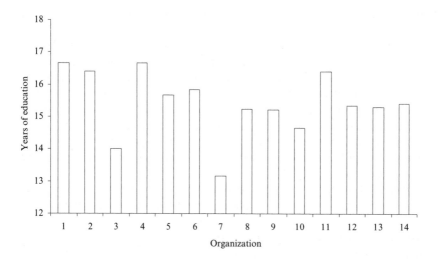

Figure 12.3 Employees' years of education by organization

ORGANIZATIONAL PERCEPTION OF TELEWORK IMPACTS

Organizations rated nine of the 32 impacts as negative; Table 12.1 details these nine impacts and their associated mean scores. As with the employee survey, we used a seven-point Likert scale, with 4 being 'no impact: neutral'. Aggregate scores below 4 indicate an overall perceived

Table 12.1   Organizations' perceived negative impacts of telework

Impact	Mean score
Social contact	3.21
Teamwork	3.21
Manager's ability to supervise employees	3.29
Scheduling meetings	3.29
Costs of ICT	3.29
Security of company data	3.71
Knowledge sharing between employees	3.79
Training possibilities (e.g., mentoring)	3.79
Appraising employee performance	3.93

negative impact, while those above 4 indicate an overall perceived positive impact.

As Table 12.1 illustrates, organizations' perceptions of negative telework impacts largely relate to organizational efficiency (teamwork, scheduling, security, ICT costs) and HR operations (supervising, training, appraising). Given the importance of organizational efficiency and HR operations to the internal functioning of the organization, it is likely that a major impediment to organizational telework adoption is a managerial belief that telework negatively influences the operational efficiency of the organization. Thus, in order to grow the virtual workplace, these perceptions, accurate or not, must be addressed.

Besides directly addressing perceived negative impacts of telework, telework adoption will increase at the organizational level if the benefits, or positive impacts, are perceived to outweigh the negative impacts. Table 12.2 lists the 12 most positively rated impacts of telework from the organizational perspective. As indicated by the three most positive impacts in the list, organizations view telework as beneficial to strategic HR issues such as employee retention, loyalty, and contract flexibility. One implication of this finding is that organizations may place a greater value on telework in times of scarce labour or in industries where labour is critical to an organization's competitive advantage (for example, high-technology industries).

As with the employee-level data, collapsing the 32 potential impacts into their respective theoretical factors allows for simpler interpretation of the data and more focused implications and recommendations. With only 14 organizational surveys, statistical factor analysis would not be feasible for the 32 impact items. Thus, we rely on the theoretical justification for forming factors for the 32 items. The four theoretically-derived factors are impacts on strategic HR issues, impacts on operational HR issues, impacts

Table 12.2   Organizations' highest-rated perceived positive impacts of telework

Impact	Mean score
Employee retention	6.36
Employee loyalty	6.21
Employment contract flexibility (e.g., move from full- to part-time status)	6.00
Adjustment capability when catastrophes occur (e.g., downtown bomb scare)	5.93
Ability to respond to environmental regulations/concerns	5.93
Relations with trade unions	5.93
Recruiting potential	5.86
Employee commitment to excellence	5.79
Image of the organization (e.g., environmentally responsible)	5.64
Organizational culture	5.57
Working time (i.e., number of work hours per day)	5.57
Job opportunities for disabled people	5.57

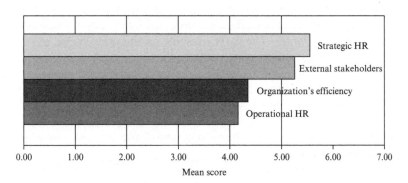

Figure 12.4   Organizational perceptions of telework impact factors

on the organization's efficiency, and impacts on external stakeholders. Figure 12.4 displays the mean rating for each of these factors, with a rating of 0 anchored by a 'very negative impact' and 7 anchored by 'a very positive impact'. As illustrated by the figure, organizations rated strategic HR factors as the most positive impact and operational HR factors as the least positive impact.

Organizations perceive that, while telework has positive impacts on retaining, developing, and attracting employees, it has neutral and even negative impacts on employees' operational functioning (as illustrated in

Table 12.1, telework is perceived to have a slight negative impact on super-vision, training, and social contact issues). If the negative perceptions are correct, then efforts to grow the virtual workplace will need to focus on better implementation of organizational telework programs. If, on the other hand, the negative perceptions are incorrect, then efforts to grow the virtual workplace should utilize information dissemination policies to provide evidence to organizations of the true impacts of telework. Our analysis of the literature in Chapter 3 suggested that most of telework's org-anizational impacts are positive, but we did identify a number of impacts where proper telework implementation could mitigate potential negative organizational impacts.

QUALITATIVE ANALYSIS OF TELEWORK IMPACTS

To complement the organizational-level surveys we utilized FTF interviews with the HR managers of the 14 organizations in our sample. These inter-views provided some useful insights into the organizational perspective on positive and negative telework impacts. It is important to note that impacts identified from the interviews were unprompted, thus indicating that these are the impacts that are immediately considered by managers when assess-ing a telework program. The survey results, on the other hand, offered a more analytical assessment of impacts, as they prompted the managers to think of the direction and magnitude of a specific telework impact on the organization. Some of the positive impacts of telework described most fre-quently by organizations are:

- Increased productivity (the most common unprompted answer given by organizations).
- Quiet time, no interruptions (leads to increased productivity).
- More creative and focused time (leads to increased productivity).
- Useful for avoiding bad weather and heavy traffic.
- Reduces wasted time commuting.
- Better work/life balance.
- Better quality of life (more time with families).
- Helpful for a 24/7 business.
- Makes us a more attractive employer.
- Risk mitigation (for example, in a snow storm, home workers can cover calls).
- Low turnover.
- Decreases politics because away from the office.
- Promotes need to respect diversity (for example, physical disabilities).

- Community as a whole benefits (for example, parents can volunteer at children's school; more general volunteering).
- Shows caring/valuing of employees; displays trust.
- Keeps team morale strong (value time together more because of less face time; therefore waste less time during meetings).

As indicated above, increased productivity was the most commonly cited positive impact. Thus, as a follow-up question, HR managers were asked to estimate the percentage increase in productivity that teleworkers have over traditional office workers in similar jobs. Two organizations indicated that productivity was about equal between teleworkers and non-teleworkers, and one suggested that teleworkers were 5–10 per cent less productive when working from home. The remaining 11 organizations, however, all indicated that teleworkers were more productive when working from home or in comparison with non-teleworking employees in similar jobs. The estimates of increased productivity ranged from 20 per cent up to 50 per cent.

The interviews also assessed the negative impacts and difficulties that organizations had with their telework arrangements. Once again, the answers to such open-ended questions are valuable because these are the 'costs' that first come to mind for managers considering telework adoption for their organizations. Examples of telework negative impacts given by the organizations included:

- Sometimes difficult for teleworkers to feel part of company (isolation).
- More advance planning needed to arrange meetings; logistics (for example, scheduling meetings).
- Leadership lack of buy-in.
- Security issues.
- Perception that you need to be seen (promotion; avoid layoff).
- Those who lack discipline may be a problem.
- Telework pilot 4 years ago – used routine jobs and found it did not work because needed more direct supervision (discontinued program).
- Technology has been biggest challenge.
- Some resentment on part of office workers about teleworkers not being there for ad hoc meetings.
- Costs of home office technology expensive (for example, accessing network).
- Ergonomic issues in home office; union trying to negotiate this as a benefit.
- When away on holidays still working (checking e-mails); can't get away from work.

An interesting aspect of the interviews was that when managers listed the difficulties with telework they would often qualify the statements with solutions to the problems. For example, to combat isolation organizations suggested managers must plan social events. Managers also volunteered that organizations need to make it socially unacceptable for office employees to comment on teleworkers who come to the office late or leave early. One of the most common solutions proposed to deal with telework difficulties was the development and implementation of clear telework policies, expectations, and guidelines (a topic covered in Chapter 9).

ROLE OF ORGANIZATIONS IN EMPLOYEE TELEWORK ADOPTION

Up to this point, we have looked at the organizational perception of telework impacts because that will drive the organizational telework adoption decision, which is perhaps the biggest single influence on the crucial employee telework adoption decision.

It is not surprising to find that telework adopters tend to belong to organizations that have formal telework plans or that offer telework as an option for all employees. Of telework adopters, 75 per cent reported that their organization had some type of formal telework plan, compared with 41 per cent of non-adopters (highly significant difference at $P<.0000$). Of telework adopters, 64 per cent stated that telework was optional for all employees, compared with 28 per cent of non-adopters (again highly significant at $P<.0000$). The importance of organizational support for telework on the adoption rates of employees is displayed graphically in Figure 12.5.

The salience of organizational telework programs' effect on employee telework adoption is further highlighted by adding these variables to the regression models developed in Chapter 11 that predict employee telework adoption. With these additions we find that the odds of employee telework adoption increase by 75 per cent in organizations with a formal telework program. In organizations where telework is an option for all employees but there is no formal program, the odds of an employee adopting telework increase by 70 per cent.

Organizations also have a significant impact on the frequency of employee telework. For example, in organizations with formal telework programs employees telework 8.66 days per month more than in organizations without formal programs. To further demonstrate the importance of organizational support we note that the addition of formal and optional organizational telework programs to the regression model that predicts

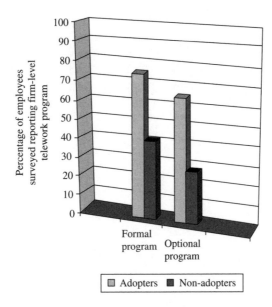

Figure 12.5   Organizational programs and employee adoption

telework frequency moved the variance explained from 23 per cent to 47 per cent.

The influence of organizational-level variables on the employee telework adoption decision can also be shown using hierarchical linear modelling (HLM) analysis. HLM incorporates data from multiple levels in an attempt to determine the impact of individual and grouping factors upon some individual-level outcome. We note that while our employee sample size of 284 is sufficient for HLM analysis, the organization sample size of 14 limits the interpretations we can draw from the analysis. Nonetheless, HLM analysis still indicates the effect that organization-level data has on employee-level data.

An example from the HLM analysis is provided in Figure 12.6. The figure illustrates that the effect of having children under the age of five on the decision to telework is more salient in some of the surveyed organizations than others. More specifically, in organizations with greater telework penetration the relationship between the number of children under five and telework adoption is stronger than in organizations with lower levels of telework penetration.

Another example of organizational influences on employee-level data is shown in Figure 12.7. This figure illustrates that the effect of ITOHR (that is, the factor score of impacts of telework on operational HR issues) on the employee decision to telework is more salient in some organizations than

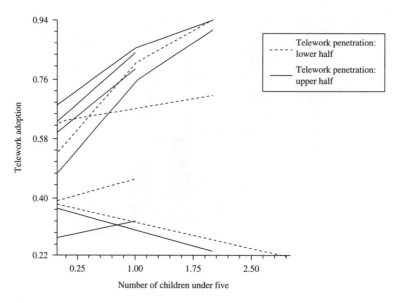

Figure 12.6   Organizational effects on the relationship between number of children under five and telework adoption

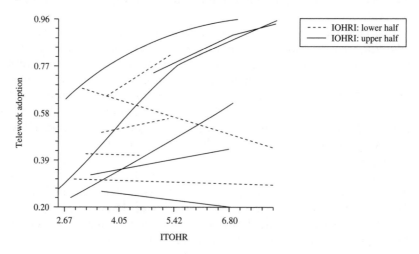

Figure 12.7   Organizational effects on the relationship between ITOHR and telework adoption

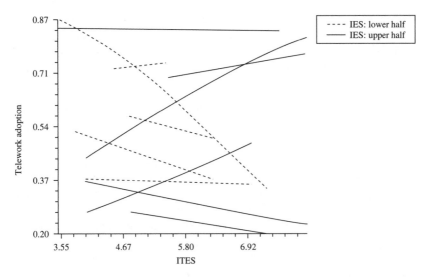

Figure 12.8   *Organizational effects on the relationship between ITES and telework adoption*

others. First, we introduce the organizational equivalent to ITOHR, which we call impacts on operational HR issues (IOHRI). It turns out that, in organizations with higher IOHRI ratings, the relationship between ITOHR and telework adoption is stronger than in organizations with lower IOHRI ratings. This is an interesting result as it suggests that the effect of employee perceptions of telework impacts on the decision to adopt telework is stronger when these perceptions are also shared by the employer.

To further support the above finding we offer a similar analysis using the ITES factor scores (and the organizational equivalent of impacts on external stakeholders: IES). These scores measure the perception of telework impacts on external stakeholders. As shown in Figure 12.8, the effect of ITES on telework adoption depends on organizational IES score. More specifically, the effect of ITES on telework adoption is stronger and positive in organizations characterized by high IES; the relationship is weaker or even negative in organizations that are in the lower half on IES scores. Thus, employees who score higher on ITES are more likely to telework in organizations with high IES scores than in organizations with low IES scores.

The above HLM results, while interesting on their own merit, are provided to illustrate the important role organizations play in employee telework adoption decisions. The interaction of multiple levels of data is also consistent with the EOS integrative telework framework, which proposes that growing the virtual workplace requires an integrative approach – an approach that acknowledges the interaction between employees, organizations, and society, as well as between telework's impacts, tracking, implementation, and adoption.

INTRA-ORGANIZATIONAL TELEWORK ADOPTION

Turning from the organization's overall decision to adopt telework, we now address the details of telework adoption within a single organization. On this issue, several findings from secondary sources are worth highlighting. Surveys indicate that a general guideline for telework penetration within organizations is between 5 per cent and 20 per cent of all employees. In order to apply this overall figure to each type of job, however, we must consider each job's interface requirements (especially in terms of how much FTF contact is required). Table 12.3 provides examples of various work groups and their potential telework penetration levels.

Another illustration of potential intra-organizational telework adoption rates is revealed in the results of a 2004 agency survey conducted by the US Office of Personnel Management (OPM and GSA, 2005). Of the 86 agencies surveyed, 85 per cent had telework policies in place and 52 per cent specified occupations that are eligible for telework. The qualifying criteria to be eligible to telework included a minimum performance rating for teleworkers (66 per cent of the agencies reported this criterion). Of the agencies, 52 per cent excluded employees with past disciplinary problems; 32 per cent of the agencies required employees to have been in their positions for

Table 12.3   Work group telework penetration potential

Work group	Telework penetration potential (%)
Average office environment	5–20
Facility	5–10
Sales (no FTF retail)	85–90
HR	5–10
Exec. management	70–73
Line management	20–30
Finance–legal	15–20
Planning	15–20
Translation	80–90

Source: based on normative information from Canadian and US corporations, GHG Registries, 2006.

a minimum amount of time. Categories of employees that were excluded from telework included:

- Support staff (40 per cent of respondents).
- Temporary employees (37 per cent of respondents).
- Executives (30 per cent of respondents).

These findings surrounding telework eligibility criteria and intra-organizational telework penetration rates can be used as a guideline to assess the potential for organizational-level telework adoption.

CONCLUSION

The analysis provided in this chapter suggests that organizations play a critical role in employee-level telework adoption. As we have argued, the adoption decision at the employee level is fundamental to the growth of the virtual workplace; employees who adopt (or desire to adopt) telework arrangements provide the demand necessary to grow the virtual workplace. For their part, organizations obviously influence the employee's decision to telework directly by making this work arrangement available (either formally or informally). Our analysis, however, – driven by our EOS integrative framework – also suggests that organizations indirectly influence employee telework adoption through congruence between organizational and employee perceptions of telework impacts, and even through existing levels of telework adoption in the organization.

Given the important role that organizations play in the telework adoption decision, it is valuable to assess organizational perceptions of telework impacts. Our analysis suggests that organizations perceive that telework may have positive impacts on retaining, developing, and attracting employees but that it can also negatively influence the operational efficiency of the organization. We contend that the negatively perceived impacts of telework must be addressed through proper telework program implementation, thus reducing negative impacts; increased information dissemination on telework, thus dispelling misconceptions of negative telework impacts; and tracking telework impacts, thus providing a mechanism to perform cost–benefit analyses that weigh the positive impacts of telework against the negative impacts.

As has been stated, organizational-level telework adoption influences employee-level adoption. The aggregation of telework adoption at these two levels translates into societal-level telework adoption. The aggregation of employee and organizational-level adoption rates suggests that it is at the societal level that one can best assess the growth of the virtual work-place. Thus, in the next and final chapter of this book we will explore current societal telework adoption rates and potential telework penetration saturation levels. These two rates respectively serve as a baseline and a theoretical target; between them growth in the virtual workplace can be measured. We will also explore the future drivers of telework adoption.

13. Telework adoption: a societal perspective

Societal-level telework adoption captures the aggregation of employee and organizational-level adoption, so it is at the societal level that one can best assess the growth of the virtual workplace. For this reason, we conclude this book with a chapter that explores societal-level telework adoption, the associated telework penetration saturation levels, and future drivers of societal-level telework.

Telework adoption at the societal level may vary by region and country, depending on economic, geographic and cultural factors. Consistent with the EOS integrative telework framework, differences in adoption will also be affected by different levels of government support and policy selection. In the first section of this chapter we assess the influence of societal work structures on telework adoption. We then utilize secondary data to present estimates and forecasts of telework adoption rates for various regions around the world.

In the final sections of this chapter we suggest what will be the future drivers of telework adoption. We have categorized these drivers as the five 'C's: climate change mitigation, continuity planning, congestion avoidance, competing for employees, and communication advances. As a complement to these telework adoption drivers, we add a sixth 'C', that of conceptualizing telework, as a catalyst to the future growth of the virtual workplace. We contend that conceptualizing telework using the EOS integrative telework framework will magnify the effects that future telework adoption drivers have on growing the virtual workplace. To this end, we conclude the chapter with a summary of the book and the findings that came from our analysis using the EOS integrative telework framework.

SOCIETAL STRUCTURES AND TELEWORK ADOPTION

Illegems and Verbeke (2003) suggest that a country's welfare system influences the penetration and characteristics of telework in that country. For example, free market regimes are characterized by lower mutual commitment between employers and employees, and thus allow for more experimentation in telework arrangements between the employees and employers. In regulated labour markets, by contrast, labour contracts are tightly regulated. In regulated societies telework adoption cannot be as informal or ad hoc and needs to be introduced with appropriate regulations. Thus, in regulated labour markets telework adoption may be slower than in free market regimes. It could be argued, however, that eventually the regulated labour markets would provide better protection of the teleworker's rights.

As outlined in Chapter 10, there are a number of societal-level policy options that will affect telework adoption rates. For example, the development of an enabling infrastructure is a necessary but insufficient condition for telework growth. In an effort to avoid repeating our assessment of policy alternatives, we simply make the broader point that societal infrastructure in general will affect telework adoption. Adequately developed ICT infrastructure is likely to increase telework adoption within societies, while highly developed transportation infrastructure (for example) may decrease telework adoption (presuming that well-developed transportation infrastructure will reduce commute times, thus partially reducing the benefit of commute time savings to the teleworker).

Societal structures such as ICT and transportation infrastructure are also somewhat related to a society's GDP: higher GDP societies can better afford to build ICT infrastructure, thus allowing for increased telework adoption. Higher GDP may also be associated with increased human resource scarcity, thus suggesting the need for higher levels of telework in order to attract employees and to increase the productivity of scarce human capital resources. Related to human resource scarcity is the type of industry concentration found within a society. Some industries are more capital- and equipment-intensive, while others are more human-resource-intensive. Societies with human-resource-intensive industry concentrations (for example, high technology) will probably have higher telework adoption rates than those with more capital-intensive industries (for example, natural resource-based industries). The above examples are provided as an illustration of the potential societal structures that may influence the variation of telework adoption rates across societies. As suggested throughout this book, however, the biggest influences on societal adoption rates are likely to be employee-level demand for telework, organizational-level support of telework, and societal-level telework policies.

SOCIETAL TELEWORK ADOPTION RATES

As suggested by the above discussion, there are many potential drivers for societal telework adoption. In this section of the chapter we simply offer estimates of telework adoption or penetration for various societies. These rates could be used in conjunction with structures specific to each society to tease out possible correlates or predictors of telework adoption. Our main intention in exploring societal adoption rates, however, is to provide a societal baseline measure from which efforts to grow the virtual workplace can be measured.

Worldwide Telework Adoption

At the global level, we note that it was estimated that by 2006 89.5 million employees worldwide will telework eight hours or more per month (Gartner Group, 2005). This equates to approximately a 3.1 per cent worldwide telework penetration level. Table 13.1 illustrates the projected worldwide growth of telework adoption.

North American Telework Adoption

Within Canada, approximately 6.4 per cent of employees were found to do paid work from home within normally scheduled work hours (Statistics Canada, 2001a). The Gartner estimates are slightly higher, with 2001 projections of one day per month telework hitting the 7.7 per cent mark and 2006 projections at the 11.7 per cent mark. While these rates are lower than the US levels, Canadians who do telework tend to do so for a greater proportion of their working week than those teleworking in the US and parts of Western Europe (Gartner, 2000).

Interestingly, while Canadian telework adoption rates lag behind those of the US, the Canadian environment is in many ways as suitable or better for telework adoption. For example, Canada has widespread accessibility to the Internet, with 7.9 million households (64 per cent) using the Internet

Table 13.1   Worldwide telework adoption rates

Year	Worldwide teleworkers ($>$ 8 hr/month)	Penetration of employee population (%)
2003	63.29	2.2
2004	73.78	2.6
2005	82.47	2.8
2006	89.46	3.2
2007	94.88	3.2
2008	100.13	3.3

Source: adapted from Gartner, 2005.

regularly (InnoVisions, 2005). Smith also points out that, with low population density per square mile, Canadians would benefit from increased telework adoption to reduce their longer than average commutes. While not influencing current adoption rates, perhaps these factors are affecting Canadian perceptions of telework. For example, a recent survey of 5000 Canadians found that over 50 per cent expressed an interest in working from home (InnoVisions Canada, 2002).

Depending on how a teleworker is defined, estimates of the number of teleworkers within the US range from 29 million (ITAC, 2004) to 30 million (Cahners In-Stat Group, 2001). The Association for Advancing Work from Anywhere found that in 2004 24.1 million US workers teleworked (from home) at least one day per month, a 2.6 per cent increase from 2003. This figure represents 18.3 per cent of employed adult Americans (ITAC, 2004). The United Kingdom's Department of Trade and Industry places US penetration at a similar level. It reports 2001 American telework penetration as having represented 21 per cent of the workforce (Hotopp, 2003). Likewise, the Gartner (2005) estimates are at 21.3 per cent in 2003 and 25.3 per cent forecast for 2006.

Nilles (1999) suggests that the United States' lead in telework adoption is due in part to the fact that there are few legal and regulatory barriers to telework in the US other than those relating to telecommunications regulation. As we have discussed, the federal and, increasingly, state governments in the US are also proactively trying to increase telework adoption. This is most apparent from legislation requiring that telework be made available to almost all government workers.

The prevalence of telework in the US can also be seen in the variety of locations from which it is being practised. For example, as part of Dieringer's 2005 American Interactive Consumer Survey, respondents were asked to check the different locations where they had conducted work from outside the main office in the last month. Results suggested that of the 135.4 million US workers:

- 45.1 million worked from home.
- 24.3 million worked at a client's or customer's place of business.
- 20.6 million worked in their car.
- 16.3 million worked while on vacation.
- 15.1 million worked while at a park or outdoor location.
- 7.8 million worked while on a train or airplane.

(ITAC, 2005)

Despite the current large adoption rates in the US, Gartner (2005) projects the dominance of US telework, in terms of its proportion of the worldwide market, to decline through to 2008. In relation to this projection, it is not surprising that awareness of telework is lower in the US (75 percent of the population) than in countries such as Finland, the Netherlands and Sweden (Nilles, 1999).

European Telework Adoption

Within Europe, ECaTT (2000) estimated that in 1999 there were approximately 9 million teleworkers across Western Europe. Gareis (2004) approximated 2002 European telework adoption rates at 13 per cent. Moreover, Gartner (2005) estimated 7.45 million teleworkers in Europe in 1999, rising to 22.2 million by 2006. This would represent a 15.3 per cent penetration level. Beyond employee levels of telework adoption, ECaTT (2000) reports that across ten European countries there is approximately a 29.7 per cent organizational telework adoption rate (that is, where at least one employee in the organization teleworks).

Within Europe it is interesting to note that there is a remarkable difference in the speed of telework adoption between the northern and southern European countries. The highest rates are found in Finland, Sweden and the Netherlands, although the United Kingdom and Germany have the highest populations of teleworkers (Gartner, 2005). ECaTT (2000) suggests that better prerequisites for telework exist in the Scandinavian countries and the Netherlands, as these countries have a greater openness toward technological and organizational innovations and possess sufficient and appropriate technical infrastructure for teleworking.

Asian Telework Adoption

In Asia, Gartner (2005) forecasts Japan's 2006 telework adoption rate at 19.2 per cent. The Japanese work environment is a conservative one with many structural and market rigidities built in that would slow the progression of telework adoption (Spinks et al., 1999). The Japanese government, however, views telework positively and would like to see a rapid increase in teleworker penetration in the next six years. The Japanese government has an IT Strategy Committee, which is responsible for driving the use of IT in employment and labour as part of its e-Japan Strategy (Gartner, 2005). The drivers of Japanese telework are similar to ones discussed throughout this book. These include:

- Promoting flexible work styles.
- Productivity gains.
- Fostering empowerment/creativity.

- Making management styles more autonomous/results-oriented.
- Creating customer-oriented business styles.
- Improving work/life balance.

(Spinks et al., 1999)

Data on the rest of the Asia Pacific region are difficult to find, although Gartner (2005) forecasts an overall 0.8 per cent penetration level for telework in the Asia Pacific region. These forecasts are significantly lower than for Europe or North America owing to the large proportion of farmers and blue-collar workers in India and China. Gartner notes that these projections have a high level of uncertainty, largely due to the unavailability of data on telework rates in China and India.

TELEWORK ADOPTION SATURATION LEVELS

When looking at the current societal telework penetration rates, it is important to weigh these rates against the maximum potential for telework in a given society. In Chapter 7 we provided a series of templates that assist regions in calculating potential telework penetration levels. Estimations of the maximum telework penetration for a given population will depend on the distribution of job types, societal attitudes toward telework, and access to required infrastructure.

ECaTT (2000) surveyed employees to assess their suitability for telework. The survey asked whether the employee spent at least six hours per week on office work, such as work that could be done at an office desk or on a computer. On this basis the survey found that two-thirds of the jobs were technically feasible for telework (at least on a part-time basis). Thus, assuming a similar distribution of job types in the total European sample, one could use a generous estimation of a 66 per cent maximum telework penetration rate.

An approximately two-thirds telework saturation level is in line with a number of other analyses. For example, as mentioned in Chapter 1, the US Employment Policy Foundation, a non-profit public policy research foundation that focuses on workplace trends and policies, reported that roughly 65 per cent of jobs are thought to be amenable to teleworking, at least on a part-time basis (EPF, 2001).

The above estimates provide a target for growing the virtual workplace. Depending on the region, we know that most developed countries' current telework adoption rates are in the 15–20 per cent range. We also have an estimation of the theoretical maximum telework penetration rate of 66 per cent. Thus, in growing the virtual workplace, we can ask: what future drivers of telework will shift adoption rates from the 15–20 per cent range up into the 60–65 per cent range?[1] The following section explores some of the future telework drivers that may have such an effect.

FUTURE TELEWORK ADOPTION DRIVERS

While there are many current and potential drivers of telework adoption, we identify five factors that will play a significant role in encouraging future telework adoption. We categorize these factors as the five 'C's: climate change mitigation, continuity planning, congestion reduction, competing for employees, and communication advances. These five drivers are displayed graphically in Figure 13.1.

Note that the bottom three drivers (climate change mitigation, congestion reduction, and communication advances) are external to the organization. Thus, organizations and employees will increase telework adoption in reaction to these drivers. By contrast, the middle two drivers shown in Figure 13.1 (continuity planning and competing for employees) are internal to the organization. These internal organizational drivers will increase telework adoption for strategic reasons such as maintaining or increasing organizational core capabilities. In the following paragraphs we briefly describe each of these future telework adoption drivers.

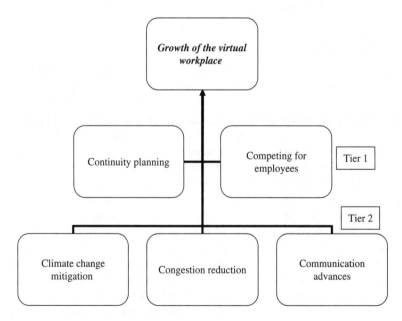

Figure 13.1   Future telework drivers

Climate Change Mitigation

Climate change mitigation is a current driver for telework adoption, as telework offers a mechanism for reducing GHG emissions, which are partly responsible for climate change. As the realities of climate change increase, and as GHG reduction policies become more stringent, we will see an associated push to move to telework to help meet GHG reduction quotas.

Climate change mitigation will work on all three stakeholder levels of the EOS integrative framework to increase telework adoption. At the societal level, policymakers will be pressured to develop policies that will help minimize climate change. As mentioned, many of these policies will focus on GHG reductions, and telework will be seen as a policy tool to accomplish such reductions. At the organizational level, there are a range of political, regulatory, and market responses emerging to address global warming and emission reductions (Kolk and Pinkse, 2005). Telework offers one such option to assist organizations in responding to climate change. Thus, for organizations, climate change mitigation will make telework more desirable from a cost–benefit perspective. Finally, at the employee level, climate change mitigation will increase telework adoption as employees desire to do their part for the environment. Of course, the organizational adoption of telework for climate change reasons will also highly impact the employee telework adoption decision.

Continuity Planning

Continuity planning for business operations will play an increasing role, given the realities of disruptions in our increasingly globalized work environment. Pandemics, terrorist attacks and severe weather are increasing threats to operational or business continuity. These threats to operational continuity can be mitigated by the adoption of telework, which can geographically diffuse HR assets and increase levels of operational continuity in the face of traditional office disruptions.

Business continuity planning (BCP), also called continuity of operations planning (COOP), enables organizations to take a proactive approach in protecting the enterprise against threats to facilities, employees, and other assets. BCP helps organizations respond to events so that critical business functions continue with minimum interruption (WorldatWork, 2005). A recent KPMG study indicated that 80 per cent of companies with more than 500 employees had BCP in place; the number fell to 42 per cent for organizations with less than 500 employees (KPMG, 2003). The motivation for BCP is apparent when considering that the average loss per hour of downtime is $78 000 for Fortune 1000 companies (WorldatWork, 2005).

Telework is a valid BCP solution. Not only does telework allow for the geographical dispersion of HR assets, but it does so cost-effectively. For example, one-off setup costs for telework range from $500 to $1500 per worker, with annual ongoing support costs ranging from $300 to $700 per worker. These costs are considerably lower than setting up a dedicated seat at a workplace recovery centre (which is kept empty until a disaster strikes) (WorldatWork, 2005). As an illustration of telework's role in BCP we note that the US Federal Emergency Management Agency (FEMA) requires that all federal agencies designate alternate operating facilities, and FEMA encourages agencies to consider telecommuting locations, including work at home, as viable alternative facilities (ITAC, 2005).

While terrorism and severe weather are increasing threats, for illustrative purposes we will focus on business continuity through telework in the face of a flu pandemic. Experts agree it is a question not of if, but when, the next flu pandemic will strike. An influenza pandemic could last for a year or more, infecting up to one-third of the population, and infecting 15–35 per cent of an organization's workforce at any one time (Health Canada, 2006). Telework, as a key component of BCP, offers organizations a mechanism to maintain operations during such a pandemic. The ability to have employees work from home not only allows employees to look after ill family, and work while sick, but also reduces the spread of the virus by limiting human-to-human contact.

Congestion Reduction

Congestion on roadways will continue to increase as the world's rural communities consolidate into urban environments. Congestion will be further compounded by increases in wealth and affordability of motor vehicles. Telework, especially at high penetration levels, will offer relief to increasing roadway congestion. Telework also offers the ability to peak shift, which does not decrease the number of commuters, but does reduce congestion by diffusing the timing of commute trips away from peak travel times.

Competing for Employees

Competing for employees will increase in importance, particularly in Europe and North America, as we see a shift in the workforce with baby boomers reaching retirement age. Organizations can use telework as an incentive to attract and retain employees as the pool of qualified HR assets diminishes. Telework also allows organizations to leverage existing HR assets, as individuals with specialized skills are not locked in by a remote geographic location.

A dramatic example of leveraging existing HR assets is provided by recent advances in surgical robotics. NeuroArm, developed at the University of Calgary, is capable of performing the most technically challenging surgical procedures. The robot has two manipulators that mimic human hands while the surgeon guides the robot using hand controllers at a workstation. The workstation recreates the sight, sound, and sensation of surgery. Currently this technology allows surgeons to operate remotely but in close proximity to the patient; it is easy to imagine, however, that NeuroArm could allow surgeons to operate (telework) from locations far removed from the operating room. Thus, surgical assets would not be geographically bound to the patient's physical location.

Communication Advances

Communication advances will also continue to drive telework adoption. Advances in ICT, particularly the accessibility and affordability of broadband, will facilitate telework implementation. Radical advances in communication technology will also increase the types of jobs suited to telework. The above description of the potential of surgical robotics is one example of the development of a new teleworkable job. Beyond surgical advances, development of GPS and robotics will open up many resource-sector jobs, including agriculture, forestry, and mining, to the telework option.

While current ICT in North America and Europe is sufficient to allow for telework, it will be the spread of ICT to developing economies that will influence telework adoption rates there. Advances in mobile technology will also shift the focus of virtual work from the home office to the mobile office, thus allowing people to work from anywhere. Advances in ICT will also smooth telework implementation by allowing for virtual replacements of FTF meetings (for example, more affordable videoconferencing).

In addition to increasing the types of jobs open to telework and facilitating the implementation of telework in developing countries, technological advances will assist in telework tracking. For example, the proliferation of affordable GPS tracking devices will allow employees and employers to track the location where work is performed. Such technology will also allow societal-level policy administrators to track the impact of their policies and better specify the design and implementation of their telework policies.

Conceptualizing Telework: the Sixth 'C'

We suggest that the five 'C's described above will be the future drivers of telework. All five drivers will be significant factors in the future environment. Societies, organizations and employees will face climate change, congestion, and advances in ICT, and organizations will need to compete for employees while dealing with business continuity in the face of multiple disruptive threats. One of the most significant future drivers of telework, however, will be the way in which this work arrangement is conceptualized. We separate this driver as a sixth 'C' because, while it is potentially significant to growing the virtual workplace, its development remains uncertain.

Conceptualizing telework encompasses two key elements that, if realized, will increase telework adoption. The first focuses on the way managers, employees, and society at large conceive of telework. For virtual work arrangements to increase, telework will need to be conceived as a mainstream form of work (either full- or part-time), not as an alternative work arrangement as it is so often described. Implicit to this new conception of work is the need to shed nineteenth-century management practices. For example, evaluating work performance based on processes should be replaced by evaluations based on results (what is produced, not how). This shift will also dispense with the traditional notion that managers can only supervise what they can see.

While the first element of conceptualizing telework focuses on re-conceiving work, the second element focuses on re-conceiving the telework process. This re-conceptualization of telework has been addressed throughout this book in our development of the EOS integrative telework framework. This framework adjusts the traditional telework model, and moves the focus from telework impacts to telework adoption. This shift includes an assessment of how each of the constructs within the process model (impacts, tracking, and implementation) influences the telework adoption decision. The new framework also integrates the telework process with the perspectives of the key telework stakeholders (employee, organization, and society). It is this shift in focus to the adoption of telework and the incorporation of all the key telework stakeholders' perspectives that will drive its future adoption. Thus, it is our position that the adoption of the EOS integrative telework framework, in combination with the re-conception of traditional work to include telework, will produce significant future growth within the virtual workplace. To this end, we conclude with a summary of the EOS integrative telework framework analysis that has been presented throughout this volume.

CONCLUSION

Throughout this book, the EOS integrative telework framework has served as a useful structure for discussing the telework phenomenon. This framework has allowed for concentrated discussion of each of the four telework process constructs from the perspectives of the employee, the organization, and society. We wish to emphasize, however, that for telework research and practice to progress, the 12 components of the EOS integrative framework should not be considered in isolation, as there is a great deal of interdependency among them.

The EOS integrative telework framework highlights a number of key findings from our primary and secondary research. For example, there are numerous potential telework impacts that are specific to the employee, organizational and societal perspectives. These impacts can be divided into five employee-level factors, four organizational-level factors, and two very broad societal-level factors.

Telework tracking is the linchpin in our integrative framework, as it links all the constructs in our model together through its feedback function. Our research indicates that, while tracking is increasingly important to the future development of telework, this process is generally overlooked and underutilized at the employee, organizational, and societal levels. Preferred tracking tools require minimal resources to administer and use, and will also provide the ability to aggregate tracking data from employees to organizations and organizations to society. Tracking efforts must focus on utilization rates, as tracking tools are usually limited by the lack of database population. In the absence of real-time tracking data, a series of templates built on research-based assumptions provide a mechanism to calculate societal-level telework penetration and its impacts.

Factors determining the optimal implementation of telework become progressively more complex as one moves from the employee to the organizational and ultimately to the societal level. At the employee level, there are a series of straightforward recommendations that will assist employees in implementing telework. These recommendations include self-assessment, setting up home office space, and developing telework procedures. At the organizational level, suggestions for telework implementation become more complex as the number of stakeholders and intervening variables increase. This complexity is evident in the decisions organizations make regarding the selection of teleworkers, telework policies, and the management of virtual teams. At the societal level, telework implementation is largely composed of policy analysis, including the generation of policy options and evaluating the potential and procedural effectiveness of these policies. Six telework policy focal points are providing moral support, disseminating information, leading by example, creating an enabling infrastructure, instituting tax and regulatory policies, and creating incentives and disincentives. Our analysis suggests none of these in isolation is sufficient to grow the virtual workplace, but a combination or portfolio of the six policy categories could produce the desired results.

We found that a variety of demographic, perceptual, and job character-istics influence the telework adoption decision at the employee level. Employees who are older, are more experienced, and have more young chil-dren are more likely to adopt telework. Telework adopters can also be differentiated by their perception of telework impacts, as adopters tend to perceive impacts more positively than non-adopters. Organizations also play an important role in employee telework adoption decisions, as the presence of formal or optional telework programs is a significant predictor of employee telework adoption. We also found that organizations perceive telework as a positive influence for retaining, developing, and attracting employees but as a neutral or negative influence on the operational func-tioning of employees. At the societal level, telework adoption varies across cultures and countries. The estimated worldwide telework adoption rate is 3.1 per cent, with the US leading the way with estimated penetration rates of about 25 per cent. Telework adoption saturation is generously estimated at about 65 per cent.

In closing the gap between the current baseline telework adoption rates and the theoretical saturation level, the future growth of the virtual work-place will be driven by five main factors: climate change mitigation, conti-nuity planning, congestion reduction, competing for employees, and communication advances. If realized, a sixth driver for growing the virtual workplace will be conceptualizing telework. This driver consists of both re-conceiving traditional work to include the realities of telework and reconceptualizing telework to align with the EOS integrative telework framework and its related value proposition.

NOTE

1. In this case the focus is on increased telework adoption; efforts to grow the virtual work-place can also focus on increasing the frequency of telework for current telework adopters.

References

Allenby, B. and J. Roitz (2006), 'Telework technology and policy', AT&T Knowledge Ventures, http://www.att.com/telework/article_library/tech_policy.html.

Arnfalk, P. (1999), *Information Technology in Pollution Prevention: Teleconferencing and Telework Used as Tools in the Reduction of Work Related Travel*, Lund: IIIEE, Lund University.

Arnison, L. and P. Miller (2002), 'Virtual teams: a virtue for the conventional team', *Journal of Workplace Learning*, **14** (4), 166–73.

AT&T (2003), 'Creating a network-centric future: summary of 2003 AT&T employee telework research', retrieved 1 September 2005 from http://www.att.com/telework/article_library/survey_results_2004.html.

Avolio, B.J., S. Kahai and G.E. Dodge (2000), 'E-leadership – implications for theory, research, and practice', *The Leadership Quarterly*, **11** (4), 615–68.

Avolio, B.J., S. Kahai, R. Dumdum and N. Sivasubramaniam (2001), 'Virtual teams: implications for e-leadership and team development', in L. Manuel (ed.), *How People Evaluate Others in Organizations*, Mahwah, NJ: Lawrence Erlbaum, pp. 337–58.

Bailey, D.E. and N.B. Kurland (2002), 'A review of telework research: findings, new directions, and lessons for the study of modern work', *Journal of Organizational Behavior*, **23**, 383–400.

Balepur, P., K. Varma and P. Mokhtarian (1998), 'Transportation impacts of center-based telecommuting: interim findings from the Neighborhood Telecenters Project', *Transportation*, **25**, 287–306.

Baltes, B.B., M.W. Dickson, M.P. Sherman, C.C. Bauer and J.S. LaGanke (2002), 'Computer-mediated communication and group decision making: a meta-analysis', *Organizational Behavior and Human Decision Processes*, **87** (1), 156–79.

Barrick, M.R. and M.K. Mount (1993), 'Autonomy as a moderator of the relationships between the big five personality dimensions and job performance', *Journal of Applied Psychology*, **78** (1), 111–18.

Bass, B.M. and B.J. Avolio (1993), 'Transformational leadership: a response to critiques', in M.M. Chemmers and R. Ayman (eds), *Leadership Theory and Research: Perspectives and Directions*, San Diego, CA: Academic Press, pp. 49–88.

Bednarz, A. (2005), 'Finding telework opportunities', retrieved 2 September 2005 from http://www.networkworld.com/net.worker/columnists/2005/0725bednarz.html.

Belanger, F. (1999), 'Communication patterns in distributed work groups: a network analysis', *IEEE Transactions on Professional Communication*, **42** (4), 261–75.

Belanger, F., R. Webb Collins and P.H. Cheney (2001), 'Technology requirements and work group communication for telecommuters', *Information Systems Research*, **12** (2), 155–76.

Bell, B.S. and S.W.J. Kozlowski (2002), 'A typology of virtual teams: implications for effective leadership', *Group and Organization Management*, **27** (1), 14–49.

B.I.M. (1996), *De Luchtkwaliteit in het Brussels Hoofdstedelijk Gewest, Immissiemetingen 1994–1995–1996*, B.I.M. Rapporten 1–2.

Brown, H.J. (1976), 'De Betekenis van het Veranderen van Baan voor het Verhuisgedrag', *Bouwen en Wonen*, 7.

Cahners In-Stat Group (2001), 'Entering the Access Era: US telecommuter demographics and the impact of fragmentation on IT platforms', retrieved 29 August 2006 from http://www.instat.com/.

Carroll, J. (2004), 'Courting the Net generation', *CA Magazine*, **137** (14), October.

Cascio, W.F. and S. Shurygailo (2003), 'E-leadership and virtual teams', *Organizational Dynamics*, **31** (4), 362–76.

Ceridian, E.S. (1999), 'Companies with virtual environments find success in retaining workers', *Wall Street Journal*, 5 October.

Choo, S., P. Mokhtarian and I. Salomon (2005), 'Does telecommuting reduce vehicle-miles traveled? An aggregate time series analysis for the U.S.', *Transportation*, **32**, 37–64.

Chu, C.-P. and J.-F. Tsai (2004), 'Road pricing models with maintenance costs', *Transportation*, **31**, 457–77.

Churchman-Davies, J. (2002), 'Just a WEEE problem . . .', *IEE Review*, **48** (6), 38–40.

Cooper, C.D. and N.B. Kurland (2002), 'Telecommuting, professional isolation, and employee development in public and private organizations', *Journal of Organizational Behavior*, **23**, 511–32.

Crockett, D. (2004), 'Government Reform Committee to examine telecommuting within Federal workforce: has 9/11 made it more than just a human capital tool? What's the hold up?', retrieved 1 September 2005 from http://www.telcoa.org/id175.htm.

Daniels, K., D. Lamond and P. Standen (2001), 'Teleworking: frameworks for organizational research', *Journal of Management Studies*, **38** (8), 1151–85.

Davis, D. (2006), 'Are your staff members ready for telecommuting?', Tech Republic, retrieved 29 August 2006 from http://techrepublic.com.com/5100-10878_11-1059332.html.

DeSanctis, G. and P. Monge (1999), 'Introduction to the special issue: communication processes for virtual organizations', *Organization Science*, **10** (6), 693–703.

Dickerson, A., J. Peirson and R. Vickerman (2000), 'Road accidents and traffic flows: an econometric investigation', *Economica*, **67**, 101–21.

Dinnocenzo, D.A. (1999), *101 Tips for Telecommuters*, San Francisco, CA: Berrett-Koehler Publishers.

Duarte, D.L. and N.T. Snyder (1999), *Mastering Virtual Teams*, San Francisco, CA: Jossey-Bass.

ECaTT (2000), 'Benchmarking progress on new ways of working and new forms of business across Europe', ECaTT Final Report, retrieved 28 August 2006 from http://www.ecatt.com/.

Ellison, N.B. (1999), 'New perspectives on telework', *Social Science Computer Review*, **17** (3), 338, retrieved 28 August 2006 from http://ssc.sagepub.com.ezproxy.lib.ucalgary.ca/ cgi/reprint/17/3/338.

Ellison, N.B. (2004), *Telework and Social Change: How Telework is Reshaping the Boundaries between Home and Work*, Westport, CT: Praeger Publishers.

Energy Information Administration (2006), *Annual Energy Review 2005*, Washington, DC: US Department of Energy, retrieved 1 July 2006 from http://www.eia.doe.gov/emeu/aer/consump.html.

EPF (2001), 'Computer ownership and internet access: opportunities for workforce development and job flexibility', Washington, DC: Employment Policy Foundation.

European Commission (1998), 'Status report on European telework 1998', retrieved 2 February 2007 from http://www.eto.org.uk/twork/tw98/.

Federal Bureau of Investigation (2006), 'Crime in the United States 2004', retrieved 28 August 2006 from http://www.fbi.gov/ucr/cius_04/.

Froggatt, C.C. (2001), *Work Naked: Eight Essential Principles for Peak Performance in the Virtual Workplace*, San Francisco, CA: Jossey-Bass.

Gareis, K. (2002), 'The intensity of telework in 2002 in the EU, Switzerland and the USA', presentation held at the New York 2002 – Annual International Telework Forum Congress in Badajoz, Spain, 3–5 September.

Gareis, K. (2004), 'What drives eWork? An exploration into the determinants of e-work uptake in Europe', paper presented at the 9th International Telework Workshop, Heraklion, Greece, 6–9 September.

Garrison, W. and E. Deakin (1988), 'Travel, work and telecommunications: a view of the electronic revolution and its potential impacts', *Transportation Research*, **22A** (4), 239–45.

Gartner (2000), 'What is the future of telework?', *HR Focus*, **78** (3), 5–6.

Gartner (2005), *Dataquest Recommendations*, 14 September.

GHG Registries (2006), 'Products and services', Canadian Standards Association, Climate Change, retrieved 2 February 2007 from http://www.ghgregistries.ca/index_e.cfm.

Gibson, C.B. and S.G. Cohen (2003), *Virtual Teams That Work*, San Francisco, CA: Jossey-Bass.

Gillespie, A. (1998), 'Telework and the sustainable city', paper presented at the NECTAR EuroConference on Sustainable Transport: Europe and its Surroundings, Israel, 19–25 April.

Gillespie, A., R. Richardson and J. Cornford (1995), 'Review of telework in Britain: implications for public policy', paper prepared for Parliamentary Office of Science and Technology, Centre for Urban and Regional Development Studies, University of Newcastle upon Tyne, UK.

Goodman, J. (2004), 'Climate change issues and initiatives in the ICT industry', Forum for the Future, retrieved 28 August 2006 from http://www.gesi.org/events/docs/Climate%20change/3-Goodman-FFF-Climate%20change%20workshop.pdf.

Gordon, P., H. Richardson and M.J. Jun (1991), 'The commuting paradox: evidence from the top twenty', *Journal of the American Planning Association*, **57** (4), 416–20.

Gray, M., N. Hodson and G. Gordon (1994), *Teleworking Explained*, New York: John Wiley.

Guria, J. (1999), 'An economic evaluation of incremental resources to road safety programmes in New Zealand', *Accident Analysis and Prevention*, **31**, 91–9.

Hambley, L., T. O'Neill and T. Kline (2007), 'Virtual team leadership: perspectives from the field', *International Journal of e-Collaboration*, **3** (1), 40–64.

Hamer, R., E. Kroes and H. Van Ooststroom (1991), 'Teleworking in the Netherlands: an evaluation of changes in travel behaviour', *Transportation*, **18**, 365–82.

Hamer, R., E. Kroes and H. Van Ooststroom (1992), 'Teleworking in the Netherlands: an evaluation of changes in travel behaviour – further results', *Transportation Research Record*, **1357**, 82–9.

Handy, S. and P. Mokhtarian (1994), *Present Status and Future Directions of Telecommuting in California*, Sacramento, CA: California Energy Commission.

Handy, S. and P. Mokhtarian (1995), 'Planning for telecommuting: measurement and policy issues', *Journal of the American Planning Association*, **61** (1), 99–111.

Handy, S. and P. Mokhtarian (1996), 'Forecasting telecommuting: an exploration of methodologies and research needs', *Transportation*, **23**, 163–90.

Harpaz, I. (2002), 'Advantages and disadvantages of telecommuting for the individual, organization and society', *Work Study*, **51** (2), 74–80.

Harrington, S.J. and C.P. Ruppel (1999), 'Telecommuting: a test of trust, competing values, and relative advantage', *IEEE Transactions on Professional Communication*, **42**, 223–39.

Hart, R.K. and P.L. McLeod (2003), 'Rethinking team building in geographically dispersed teams: one message at a time', *Organizational Dynamics*, **31** (4), 352–61.

Health Canada (2006), 'What you need to know about pandemic influenza', retrieved 29 August 2006 from http://www.phac-aspc.gc.ca/influenza/pikf_e.html#h.

Helms, M.M. and F.M.E. Raiszadeh (2002), 'Virtual offices: understanding and managing what you cannot see', *Work Study*, **51** (5), 240–47.

Henderson, D., B. Koenig and P. Mokhtarian (1994), 'Travel diary-based emissions analysis of telecommuting for the Puget Sound Telecommuting Demonstration Project', Research Report UCD-ITS-RR-94-26, Davis, CA: Institute of Transportation Studies, University of California at Davis.

Henderson, D., B. Koenig and P. Mokhtarian (1996), 'Using travel diary data to estimate the emissions impacts of transportation strategies: the Puget Sound Telecommuting Demonstration Project', *Journal of Air and Waste Management Association*, **46**, 47–57.

Hill, J.E., B.C. Miller, S.P. Weiner and J. Colihan (1998), 'Influences of the virtual office on aspects of work and work/life balance', *Personnel Psychology*, **51** (3), 667–83.

Hopkinson, P., P. James and T. Maruyama (2002), 'Teleworking at BT: the economic, environmental and social impacts of its Workabout scheme', retrieved from http://www.sustel.org.

Hotopp, U. (2003), *Teleworking in the UK*, London: Department of Trade and Industry.

Huws, U., N. Jagger and S. O'Regan (1999), *Teleworking and Globalisation*, IES Report 358, Brighton: Institute for Employment Studies, retrieved 2 February 2007 from http://www.employment-studies.co.uk/summary/summary.php?id=358.

Illegems, V. and A. Verbeke (2003), *Moving Towards the Virtual Workplace: Managerial and Societal Perspectives on Telework*, Cheltenham, UK and Northampton, MA, USA: Edward Elgar.

Illegems, V. and A. Verbeke (2004), 'Telework: what does it mean for management?', *Long Range Planning*, **37** (4), 319–34.

InnoVisions (2004), 'About telework', retrieved 15 December 2004 from http://www.ivc.ca/.

InnoVisions (2005), 'Canadian studies on telework', retrieved 31 August 2005 from http://www.ivc.ca/.

InnoVisions Canada (2002), 'Royal Bank of Canada survey – Jan 2002', retrieved June 2005 from http://www.ivc.ca/studies/RoyalBank.htm.

IPTS (2004), 'The future impact of ICTs on environmental sustainability', Foresight on Information Technologies in Europe (FISTE), available at http://fiste.jrc.es/pages/detail.cfm?prs=1208.

Irwin, F. (2004), 'Gaining the air quality and climate benefit from telework', produced for US Environmental Protection Agency and the AT&T Foundation, retrieved 2 February 2007 from http://www.safeclimate.net/business/solutions/teleworkguide.pdf.

ITAC (2000), *Telework America 2000*, Washington, DC: International Telework Association Council.

ITAC (2004), 'Work at home grows in past year by 7.5% in U.S.', press release by the International Telework Association and Council, retrieved 2 February 2007 from http://benefitslink.com/pr/detail.php?id=38300.

ITAC (2005), 'Exploring telework as a business continuity strategy: a guide to getting started', World at Work, retrieved July 2006 from http://www.workingfromanywhere.org/.

Jackson, D.N. (1989), *Personality Research Form Manual*, 3rd edn, Port Huron, MI: Research Psychologists Press.

Jarvenpaa, S.L. and D.E. Leidner (1999), 'Communication and trust in global virtual teams', *Organizational Science*, **10** (6), 791–815.

Jarvenpaa, S.L. and H. Tanriverdi (2002), 'Leading virtual knowledge networks', *Organizational Dynamics*, **31**, 403–12.

Kimball, L. and A. Eunice (1999), 'The virtual team: strategies to optimize performance', *Health Forum Journal*, **42** (3), 58–62.

Kirkman, B.L., B. Rosen, C.B. Gibson, P.E. Tesluk and S.O. McPherson (2002), 'Five challenges to virtual team success: lessons from Sabre, Inc.', *Academy of Management Executive*, **16** (3), 67–79.

Kistner, T. (2002), 'Beware the virtual sweatshop', *Network World*, retrieved 2 September 2005 from http://www.networkworld.com/net.worker/columnists/2002/1209kistner.html.

Kitamura, R., J. Nilles, P. Conroy and D. Fleming (1990), 'Telecommuting as a transportation planning measure: initial results of California Pilot Project', *Transportation Research Record*, **1285**, 98–104.

Kolk, A. (2000), *Economics of Environmental Management*, Harlow, Essex, UK: Prentice Hall.

Kolk, A. and J. Pinkse (2005), 'Business responses to climate change: identifying emergent strategies', *California Management Review*, **47** (3), 6–20.

Konradt, U., G. Hertel and R. Schmook (2003), 'Quality of management by objectives, task-related stressors, and non-task-related stressors as predictors of stress and job satisfaction among teleworkers', *European Journal of Work and Organizational Psychology*, **12** (1), 61–79.

KPMG (2003), 'The current state of business continuity', Continuity Insights/KPMG Benchmark Study, http://continuityinsights.com.

Kraemer, K. (1982), 'Telecommunications/transportation substitution and energy conservation: Part 1', *Telecommunications Policy*, **6** (1), 39–59.

Kraemer, K. and J. King (1982), 'Telecommunications/transportation substitution and energy conservation: Part 2', *Telecommunications Policy*, **6** (2), 87–99.

Kurland, N.B. and D.E. Bailey (1999), 'The advantages and challenges of working here, there, anywhere, and anytime', *Organization Dynamics*, **28** (2), 53–68.

Kurland, N.B. and T.D. Egan (1999), 'Telecommuting: justice and control in the virtual organization', *Organization Science*, **10** (4), 500–513.

La Bella, A., A. Morini and M. Silvestrelli (1990), 'Telematics and business travel', *Telematics*, April, 107–32.

La Gioia, P. (2004), 'Truths about teleworking and ten traits you need before you dare to work from home', InnoVisions Canada, retrieved 2 February 2007 from http://www.ivc.ca/teleworkertruths.html.

Lee, K. and M. Ashton (2004), 'Psychometric properties of the HEXACO Personality Inventory', *Multivariate Behavioral Research*, **39** (2), 329–58.

Lie, C. and B. Yttri (1999), 'AO/DI – the future communication solutions for teleworkers?', in *Proceedings of the Fourth International Telework Workshop: Telework Strategies for the New Workforce*, Tokyo, 31 August–3 September, pp. 252–62.

Lund, J. and P. Mokhtarian (1994), 'Telecommuting and residential location: theory and implications for commute travel in monocentric metropolis', *Transportation Research Record*, **1463**, 10–14.

Lyons, G., A. Hickford and J. Smith (1998), 'The nature and scale of teleworking's travel demand impacts: insights', in R. Suomi, P. Jackson, L. Hollmén and M. Aspnäs (eds), *Telework Environments: Proceedings of the Third International Workshop on Telework*, Turku Centre for Computer Science General Publications no. 8, 1–4 September, pp. 312–30.

Madsen, S. (2003), 'The effects of home-based teleworking on work–family conflict', *Human Resource Development Quarterly*, **14** (1), 35–58.

Majchrzak, A., A. Malhotra, J. Stamps and J. Lipnack (2004), 'Can absence make a team grow stronger?', *Harvard Business Review*, **82** (5), 131–7.

Mannering, J. and P. Mokhtarian (1995), 'Modeling the choice of telecommuting frequency in California: an exploratory analysis', *Technological Forecasting and Social Change*, **49**, 49–73.

Manoochehri, G. and T. Pinkerton (2003), 'Managing telecommuters: opportunities and challenges', *American Business Review*, **21** (1), 9–16.

Mayeres, I., S. Ochelen and S. Proost (1996), 'The marginal external costs of urban transport', *Public Economics Research Paper*, no. 51.

Mayeres I., S. Proost and K. Van Dender (1997), 'Marginale externe kosten van transport: beschrijving, waardering en meeting', in B. De Borger and S. Proost (eds), *Mobiliteit: De juiste prijs*, Leuven, Apeldoorn: Garant, pp. 43–80.

Michelson, W., L.K. Palm and T. Wikström (1999), 'Forward to the past? Home-based work and the meaning, use, and design of residential space', *Research in Community Sociology*, **9**, 155–84.

MIRTI (1998), 'Self-assessment tool – your telework quotient', retrieved 29 August 2006 from http://www.telework-mirti.org/handbook/inglese/2checkee.htm.

Mitomo, H. and T. Jitsuzumi (1999), 'Impact of telecommuting on mass transit congestion: the Tokyo case', *Telecommunications Policy*, **23**, 741–51.

Mokhtarian, P. (1990), 'A typology of relationships between telecommunications and transport', *Transportation Research A*, **24** (3), 231–42.

Mokhtarian, P. (1991), 'Telecommuting and travel: state of the practice, state of the art', *Transportation*, **18**, 319–42.

Mokhtarian, P. (1998), 'A synthetic approach to estimating the impacts of telecommuting on travel', *Urban Studies*, **35** (2), 215–41.

Mokhtarian, P. and K. Sato (1994), 'A comparison of the policy, social, and cultural contexts for telecommuting in Japan and the United States', *Social Science Review*, **12** (4), 641–58.

Mokhtarian, P., G. Collantes and C. Gertz (2004), 'Telecommuting, residential location, and commute distance traveled: evidence from State of California employees', *Environment and Planning A*, **36** (10), 1877–98.

Mokhtarian, P., S. Handy and I. Salomon (1995), 'Methodological issues in the estimation of the travel, energy, and air quality impacts of telecommuting', *Transportation Research A*, **29A** (4), 283–302.

NCPC (National Crime Prevention Council) (1995), 'Strategy: Before- and After-School Programs', retrieved 29 August 2006 from http://www.ncpc.org/Topics/School_Safety/Strategy_Before-_and_After-School_Programs.php.

Nelson, P. (2004), 'Emissions trading with telecommuting credits: regulatory background and institutional barriers', Resources for the Future, Discussion Paper 04-45.

Netilla Networks (2004), 'Ability to telework would boost productivity, relieve stress and improve relationships, according to survey of commuters at New York City and London hubs', retrieved 28 August 2006 from http://www.netilla.com/pressRelease/release_83.htm.

Newman, S.A., J.A. Fox, E.A. Flynn and W. Christeson (2000), 'America's after-school choice: the prime time for juvenile crime, or youth enrichment and achievement', Fight Crime: Invest in Kids, Washington, DC, retrieved 1 October 2005 from http://www.fightcrime.org/reports/ as 2000.pdf

Nilles, J. (1977), 'Telecommunications and urban structure', in *Proceedings of the IEEE 77 International Communications Conference*, II, pp. 257–60.

Nilles, J. (1988), 'Traffic reduction by telecommuting: a status review and selected bibliography', *Transportation Research A*, **22** (4), 301–17.

Nilles, J. (1991), 'Telecommuting and urban sprawl: mitigator or inciter?', *Transportation*, **18**, 411–32.

Nilles, J. (1998), *Managing Telework: Strategies for Managing the Virtual Workforce*, New York: John Wiley & Sons.

Nilles, J. (1999), *Electronic Commerce and New Ways of Working: Penetration, Practice and Future Development in the USA*, Los Angeles, CA: JALA International.

Nilles, J., J.F. Carlson, P. Gray and G. Hanneman (1976), *The Telecommunications–Transportation Tradeoff: Options for Tomorrow*, New York: John Wiley & Sons.

Nonaka, I. (1994), 'A dynamic theory of organizational knowledge creation', *Organization Science*, **5**, 14–37.

Nortel (2004), 'Teleworking to mobility: over 10 years of evolution at Nortel', retrieved 2 September 2005 from http://www.nortel.com/ corporate/success/ss_stories/collateral/nn110521-122004.pdf.

Olszewski, P. and S.H. Lam (1996), 'Assessment of potential effect on travel of telecommuting in Singapore', *Transportation Research Record*, **1552**, 154–60.

OPM (Office of Personnel Management) and GSA (General Services Administration) Interagency Telework Site, retrieved 28 August 2006 from http://www.telework.gov/index.asp.

OPM (Office of Personnel Management) and GSA (General Services Administration) (2005), 'The status of telework in the Federal Government 2005', retrieved 2 February 2007 from http://www. telework.gov/documents/tw_rpt05/.

Pendyala, R., K. Goulias and R. Kitamura (1991), 'Impact of telecommuting on spatial and temporal patterns of household travel', *Transportation*, **18**, 383–409.

Perez, M.P., A.M. Sanchez and M.P. Carnicer (2002), 'Benefits and barriers of telework: perception differences of human resource managers according to company's operation strategy', *Technovation*, **22**, 775–83.

Potter, E.E. (2003), 'Telecommuting: the future of work, corporate culture, and American society', *Journal of Labor Research*, **24** (1), 73–84.

Potter, R.E., P.A. Balthazard and R.A. Cooke (2000), 'Virtual team inter-action: assessment, consequences, and management', *Team Performance Management: An International Journal*, **6** (7/8), 131–7.

Pratt, J.H. (1999), 'Cost/benefits of teleworking to manage work/life responsibilities', in *1999 Telework America National Telework Survey for the International Telework Association & Council*, retrieved 23 August 2005 from http://www.joannepratt.com/publications.htm#4.1.

Pratt, J.H. (2002), 'Teleworkers, trips and telecommunications: technology drives telework – but does it reduce trips?', *Transportation Research Record*, **1817**, 58–66.

Pulliam, D. (2005), 'House advances spending bill with telework require-ments', 10 November 2005, GovExec.com, retrieved 29 August 2006 from http://www.govexec.com/.

PWGSC (Public Works and Government Services Canada) (2003), 'Facility – accommodation manager's guide to virtual work environments', retrieved 28 August 2006 from http://www.ghgregistries.ca/index_e.cfm.

PWGSC (Public Works and Government Services Canada) (2006), 'Flexible working arrangements – telework guide (2006)', Government of Canada's Human Resources Bureau (HRB), retrieved from http://source.pwgsc.gc.ca/hrb/fwa/text/telework-e.html.

Raghuram, S. and B. Wiesenfeld (2004), 'Work–nonwork conflict and job stress among virtual workers', *Human Resource Management*, **43** (2–3), 259–77.

Raghuram, S., B. Wiesenfeld and R. Garud (2003), 'Technology enabled work: the role of self-efficacy in determining telecommuter adjustment and structuring behavior', *Journal of Vocational Behavior*, **63**, 180–98.

Rangarajan, N. and J. Rohrbaugh (2003), 'Multiple roles of online facili-tation: an example in any-time, any-place meetings', *Group Facilitation: A Research and Applications Journal*, **5**, 26–36.

Rathbone, D. (1992), 'Telecommuting in the United States', *ITE Journal*, December, 40–44.

Ritter, G. and S. Thompson (1994), 'The rise of telecommuting and virtual transportation', *Transportation Quarterly*, **48** (3), 235–48.

Roitz, J. (2006), 'Telework measurement systems', retrieved 3 February 2002 from http://www.att.com/telework/article_library/measurement_sys.html.

Roitz, J., B. Nanavati and G. Levy (2004), 'Lessons learned from the network-centric organization: 2004 AT&T employee telework results', AT&T Telework White Paper, Bedminster, NJ: AT&T.

Romilly, P. (2004), 'Welfare evaluation with a road capacity constraint', *Transportation Research Part A: Policy and Practice*, **38** (4), 287–303.

Salomon, I. (1984), 'Man and his transport behaviour: Part 1a Telecommuting – promises and reality', *Transport Reviews*, **4** (1), 103–13.

Salomon, I. (1985), 'Telecommunications and travel: substitution or modified mobility?', *Journal of Transport Economics and Policy*, **19** (3), 219–35.

Salomon, I. (1986), 'Telecommunications and travel relationships: a review', *Transportation Research A*, **20** (3), 223–38.

Salomon, I. (1990), 'Telematics and personal travel behaviour with special emphasis on telecommuting and teleshopping', in H.M. Soekkha, P.H.L. Bovy, P. Drewe and G.R.M. Jansen (eds), *Telematics – Transportation and Spatial Development*, Utrecht, the Netherlands: VSP, pp. 67–89.

Salomon, I., H. Schneider and J. Schofer (1991), 'Is telecommuting cheaper than travel? An examination of interaction costs in a business setting', *Transportation*, **18** (4), 291–318.

Sampath, S., S. Saxena and P. Mokhtarian (1991), 'The effectiveness of telecommuting as a transportation control measure', in *Proceedings of the ASCE Urban Transportation Division National Conference on Transportation Planning and Air Quality*, UC Davis Institute of Transportation Studies, pp. 347–62.

Sato, K. and W.A. Spinks (1998), *Teleworking: International Perspectives*, New York: Routledge.

Schrank, D. and T. Lomax (2005), 'The 2005 Urban Mobility Report', Texas Transportation Institute, The Texas A&M University System, retrieved 28 August 2006 from http://mobility.tamu.edu/ums/report/.

Shafizadeh, K., D. Niemeier and D.S. Eisinger (2004), 'Gross emitting vehicles: a review of literature', paper prepared for the California Department of Transportation Task Order No. 27.

Simmins, I. (1997), 'What is the difference between a "telecottage" and a "telecentre"?', ETO, retrieved 28 August 2006 from www.eto.org.uk/faq/faqtcvtc.htm.

Skåmedal, J. (2000), 'Telecommuting's implications on transportation – results from a Swedish study', in *Proceedings of the 5th International Telework Workshop*, Stockholm, Sweden, http://www.ida.liu.se/labs/eis/telework2000/.

Smith, C.S., L.M. Sulsky and W.E. Ormond (2003), 'Work arrangements: the effects of shiftwork, telework, and other arrangements', in D.A. Hoffman and L.E. Tetrick (eds), *Health and Safety in Organizations*, Toronto: Wiley.

Southworth F., D. Vogt and T. Curlee (2004), 'Estimation of statewide urban public transit benefits in Tennessee', *Transportation Research Record*, **1887**, 83–91.

Spinks, W.A., S.K. Steffensen, Y. Shouzugawa and Y. Yoshizawa (1999), 'Electronic commerce and new ways of working penetration, practice and future development in Japan', Empirica, November, available at http://www.ecatt.com/country/Japan/inhalt.htm.

Standen, P. (2000), 'Organizational culture and telework', in K. Daniels, D. Lamond and P. Standen (eds), *Managing Telework*, London: Business Press.

Staples, S. and J. Webster (2003), 'A review and classification of research on virtual teams and an identification of research opportunities', paper presented at the 18th Annual Meeting of the Society for Industrial and Organizational Psychology, Orlando, FL, April.

Staples, D.S., I.K. Wong and A.F. Cameron (2004), 'Best practices for virtual team effectiveness', in D. Pauleen (ed.), *Virtual Teams: Projects, Protocols and Processes*, Hershey, PA: Idea Group Publishing, Chapter VII, pp. 160–85.

Statistics Canada (2001a), *Employed Labour Force by Place of Work Status, 2001 Counts, for Census Metropolitan Areas and Census Agglomerations – 20%*, retrieved 29 August 2006 from http://www12.statcan.ca/english/census01/products/highlight/PlaceWork/Index.cfm?Lang=ESample.

Statistics Canada (2001b), *Workplace and Employee Survey Compendium* (Catalogue no. 71-585-XIE), Ottawa, Canada.

Steers, R.M. and D.N. Braunstein (1976), 'A behaviorally-based measure of manifest needs in work settings', *Journal of Vocational Behavior*, **9**, 251–66.

Sustel (2004), 'Is teleworking sustainable? An analysis of its economic, environmental and social impacts', European Commission's Information Society Technologies Initiative, available at http://www.sustel.org.

Susskind, L., R. Jain and A. Martyniuk (2001), *Better Environmental Policy Studies*, Washington, DC: Island Press.

TCI (Telecommuting Consultants International Inc.) (2003), 'Self Assessment Tool – Your Telework Quotient', http://www.telecommute.ca.

TelCoa (Telework Coalition) (2006), 'Federal legislation, news, & programs addressing telework and telecommuting', retrieved 28 August 2006 from http://www.telcoa.org/.

Transport Canada (2006), 'Commuter options: the complete guide for the Canadian worker', retrieved March 2000 from http://www.tc.gc.ca/programs/Environment/Commuter/downloadguide.htm.

US Department of Labor (2001), 'Work at home in 2001', Washington, DC: Bureau of Labor Statistics, retrieved 29 August 2006 from http://www.bls.gov/news.release/homey.nr0.htm.

Van Reisen, A. (1997), *Ruim baan door telewerken? Effecten van flexibele werkvormen op ruimtelijke ordening en mobiliteit als gevolg van veranderend tijd-ruimtegedrag*, TU Delft: Publikatiebureau Bouwkunde.

VIACK (2006), 'Implementing and managing a telework program', Telework Consortium, retrieved 29 August 2006 from http://www.teleworkconsortium.org/viack_teleworking_mgnt_60.pdf.

Wakertin, M.E., L. Sayeed and R. Hightower (1997), 'Virtual teams versus face-to-face teams: an exploratory study of a web-based conference system', *Decision Sciences*, **28** (4), 975–96.

Webster, J. and W.K.P. Wong (2003), 'Comparing traditional and virtual group forms: identity, communication and trust in naturally occurring project teams', paper presented at the 18th Annual Meeting of the Society for Industrial and Organizational Psychology, Orlando, Florida, April.

Weisband, S. and L. Atwater (1999), 'Evaluating self and others in electronic and face-to-face groups', *Journal of Applied Psychology*, **84** (4), 632–9.

Wells, K., F. Douma, H. Loimer, L. Olson and C. Pansing (2001), 'Telecommuting implications for travel behavior: case studies from Minnesota', *Transportation Research Record*, **1752**, 148–56.

Whitehouse, G., C. Diamond and G. Lafferty (2002), 'Assessing the benefits of telework: Australian case study evidence', *New Zealand Journal of Industrial Relations*, **27** (3), 257–68.

Wiggins, B. and Z.N.J. Horn (2005), 'Explaining effects of task complexity in computer-mediated communication: a meta-analysis', paper presented at the 20th Annual Meeting of the Society for Industrial and Organizational Psychology, Los Angeles, CA, April.

Williams, E., R. Ayres and M. Heller (2002), 'The 1.7 kilogram microchip: energy and material use in the production of semiconductor devices', *Environmental Science and Technology*, **36**, 5504–10.

Wirthlin Worldwide (1999), 'Americans on the Job Part 2: Rebuilding the Employer/Employee Relationship', The Wirthlin Report, retrieved January 1999 from http://www.ebri.org.

Wolf, F. (2005), 'Wolf encourages administration to make telework a priority to ensure continuity of operations in case of emergency', retrieved 11 January 2007 from http://www.house.gov/wolf/news/2005/09-16-telework.html.

WorldatWork (2005), 'Flexible work schedules', October, retrieved 29 August 2006 from http://www.worldatwork.org/.

Yap, C. and H. Tng (1990), 'Factors associated with attitudes towards telecommuting', *Information & Management*, **19** (4), 227–35.

Zaccaro, S.J. and R. Klimoski (2002), 'The interface of leadership and team processes', *Group and Organization Management*, **27**, 4–13.

Zbar, J.D. (2002), *Teleworking and Telecommuting*, Deerfield Beach, FL: Made E-Z Products.

Ziegler, M. (2006), 'Planning for the next disaster', *Federal Times*, 27 March, retrieved 28 August 2006 from http://federaltimes.com/index.php?S=1642122.

Index

absent from work, 40
absenteeism, 21, 22, 40, 41, 68, 199, 203
accessing non-electronic information, 27
adoption rates, 11, 74, 102, 150, 177, 190, 215, 222, 226, 227, 228, 229, 230, 231, 232, 233, 234, 238, 241
air pollution, 5, 10, 14, 53, 96, 112, 133, 159, 179
air quality, 65, 79, 95, 103, 114, 115, 116, 122, 130, 247, 249, 252
alliances, 47
American, 17, 18, 33, 38, 46, 182, 231, 232, 245, 249, 250, 254
ANOVA, 192, 194, 216
appraising employee, 41, 43, 218
Arizona, 57, 122, 179
Association for Advancing Work from Anywhere, 3, 232
AT&T, 18, 19, 27, 31, 45, 46, 51, 57, 93, 122, 242, 247, 251
Australian, 45, 254
autonomy, 5, 21, 22, 139, 140, 141, 192, 198, 203, 206, 207, 208, 212, 242

Baseline Emissions, 80
Belgium, 57, 59
benefits of telework, 5, 15, 32, 50, 51, 78, 101, 133, 140, 251, 254
bounded rationality, 171, 174, 178, 180, 181, 183, 184, 186
broadband, 156, 173, 180, 238
Brussels, 42, 44, 48, 57, 59, 62, 111, 243
BT, 18, 24, 28, 33, 34

Calgary, 79, 191, 238, 244
California, 57, 59, 60, 61, 62, 63, 65, 70, 96, 115, 116, 122, 123, 124, 179, 245, 246, 247, 248, 249, 252
call centres, 49, 211

Canada, 3, 50, 70, 91, 94, 138, 144, 154, 155, 157, 161, 177, 182, 187, 191, 231, 232, 237, 246, 247, 248, 251, 253
Canadian, 4, 17, 94, 102, 154, 174, 177, 226, 231, 232, 245, 247, 253
carpool, 60, 81, 83, 88, 99, 100
carpooling, 111
catastrophes, 27, 28, 29, 44, 46, 219
childcare, 31, 32, 61, 138, 141, 149, 198, 205
children, 11, 22, 32, 33, 34, 37, 40, 60, 64, 69, 72, 113, 138, 142, 147, 149, 193, 194, 195, 196, 209, 210, 211, 213, 221, 223, 224, 241
China, 234
city councillors, 12
Clean Air Act, 50
Clean Air Incentives, 103
climate change mitigation, 11, 229, 235, 236, 241
cold starts, 65, 114, 115, 116
collaboration software, 47, 156, 157
community development, 10, 14, 53, 68, 69, 71
commute hours, 103
commute logs, 83, 85
commute miles, 88, 99, 103
commute time, 2, 27, 33, 41, 44, 45, 66, 83, 99, 154, 155, 179, 195, 230
commute trip reductions, 10, 14, 53, 54, 68, 70, 71, 85, 86, 90
commuter distance, 110, 111, 112
commuter routes, 104
commuter trip reductions, 14
commutes, 56, 58, 63, 72, 74, 89, 98, 99, 100, 101, 155, 182, 232
competencies, 36, 49, 68, 156, 161
competing for employees, 12, 229, 235, 237, 241
competitive advantage, 162, 218
computers, 34, 51, 123, 138, 181

conceptualizing telework, 229, 238, 239, 241
congestion, 10, 11, 14, 46, 53, 54, 55, 56, 61, 63, 66, 67, 103, 104, 112, 113, 127, 128, 129, 130, 131, 133, 155, 159, 184, 229, 235, 237, 238, 241, 249
congestion avoidance, 11, 229
Congress, 46, 176, 244
continuity, 10, 11, 14, 29, 46, 53, 54, 68, 70, 71, 104, 112, 126, 127, 128, 133, 229, 235, 236, 237, 239, 241, 247, 248, 254
continuity of operations planning, 70, 236
continuity planning, 11, 70, 229, 235, 236, 241
core capabilities, 235
cost savings, 3, 28, 37, 38, 45, 46, 92, 162, 215
co-workers, 24, 25, 26, 40, 149
crime, 69, 244, 249, 250
CSA, 94
culture, 11, 16, 18, 37, 38, 39, 201, 219, 241, 250, 253
customer service, 49, 199, 205

definition of telework, 1, 2, 103
Deloitte & Touche, 29
Denmark, 68, 101
Department of Energy, 94, 244
Department of Labor, 3, 253
Department of Transportation, 178, 252
design, 3, 10, 11, 16, 19, 37, 39, 103, 143, 147, 151, 154, 161, 199, 201, 238, 249
disabilities, 17, 37, 69, 182, 220
disseminating information, 8, 168, 173, 177, 186, 240
distractions, 23, 45, 139, 140
document sharing programs, 30
drawbacks of telework, 24
Dutch, 56

economic models, 10, 102
education, 192, 193, 194, 195, 196, 209, 210, 212, 213, 216, 217
elasticity of demand, 62
eldercare, 31, 32, 198, 205

electronic waste, 185, 187
e-mail, 2, 23, 24, 26, 48, 58, 81, 83, 84, 86, 96, 148, 149, 156, 157, 161, 165, 221
emission reductions, 10, 14, 53, 68, 83, 95, 97, 116, 236
emissions, 5, 50, 54, 65, 66, 70, 71, 74, 78, 80, 83, 85, 94, 95, 96, 97, 98, 99, 100, 103, 114, 115, 116, 117, 118, 170, 184, 236, 246, 249
emissions trading, 80, 96, 103, 249
employee morale, 151, 159
employee recruitment, 5
employee retention, 37, 38, 215, 218, 219
employee selection, 11, 151, 153
employees, 1, 3, 4, 5, 9, 10, 11, 12, 14, 15, 16, 17, 18, 19, 20, 21, 22, 23, 24, 25, 26, 27, 28, 29, 30, 31, 32, 33, 34, 35, 36, 37, 38, 39, 40, 41, 42, 43, 44, 45, 46, 47, 48, 49, 50, 51, 52, 53, 54, 58, 59, 60, 62, 66, 67, 71, 74, 77, 78, 80, 81, 83, 85, 86, 88, 90, 91, 92, 94, 96, 97, 98, 99, 100, 102, 103, 104, 105, 106, 107, 108, 116, 122, 126, 127, 137, 138, 139, 140, 141, 142, 145, 147, 148, 149, 150, 151, 152, 153, 154, 157, 158, 160, 161, 163, 166, 168, 177, 178, 180, 181, 182, 184, 187, 190, 191, 192, 193, 194, 197, 198, 199, 201, 203, 207, 211, 212, 213, 215, 216, 217, 218, 219, 221, 222, 223, 225, 226, 227, 229, 230, 231, 234, 235, 236, 237, 238, 240, 241, 249
employees' commitment, 15, 17, 38
encryption, 152, 156, 157
energy conservation, 66, 120, 248
energy consumption, 10, 14, 53, 66, 67, 70, 79, 103, 121, 133
energy savings, 56, 67, 90, 91, 95, 112, 123, 124
ENTRANCE, 56, 57, 58
environmental management, 50, 247
environmental regulations, 49, 50, 219
environmentally friendly, 31, 32, 50
EOS integrative framework, 8, 9, 12, 189, 214, 227, 236, 240

Ericsson, 58, 60, 61, 62, 63, 71
EU, 111, 123, 124, 125, 176, 177, 181, 185
Europe, 3, 18, 20, 50, 56, 152, 154, 231, 233, 234, 237, 238, 244, 245, 248
externalities, 14, 75, 104, 105, 185, 186
extreme weather, 27, 28, 46

face-to-face, 2, 254
factor analysis, 192, 200, 201, 202, 203, 218
factor scores, 200, 201, 205, 206, 225
families, 3, 4, 31, 49, 149, 220
Federal Deposit Insurance Corporation, 94
Federal Emergency Management Agency, 237
feedback, 6, 7, 10, 24, 43, 73, 74, 77, 83, 86, 88, 89, 136, 137, 153, 158, 240
feedback loop, 7
Finland, 233
firewalls, 30
flexibility, 5, 6, 15, 16, 18, 19, 21, 22, 27, 29, 31, 32, 35, 37, 45, 61, 62, 142, 161, 193, 196, 198, 199, 201, 202, 203, 206, 207, 218, 219, 244
formal program, 59, 222, 223
free market, 229, 230
frequency of telework, 105, 108, 109, 113, 117, 119, 120, 121, 123, 124, 125, 126, 127, 128, 132, 191, 192, 210, 211, 241
fuel efficiency, 120, 121, 122
fuel saving, 121

Gartner Group, 3, 231
GDP, 230
gender, 39, 196, 212
geographically dispersed, 1, 161, 246
Germany, 68, 233
GHG, 5, 74, 80, 89, 94, 95, 96, 100, 168, 177, 184, 226, 236, 245
GHG Registries, 94, 95, 226, 245
government, 3, 4, 10, 46, 47, 50, 57, 70, 73, 91, 92, 96, 99, 102, 103, 138, 144, 146, 168, 169, 170, 172, 173, 176, 177, 178, 179, 180, 181, 183, 184, 185, 186, 187, 190, 206, 216, 229, 232, 233, 243, 250, 251

GPS, 78, 238
green commute, 86, 88, 98, 99, 100, 101, 104
greenhouse gas, 5, 74
growing the virtual workplace, 2, 4, 6, 8, 10, 11, 12, 35, 74, 135, 167, 168, 169, 171, 173, 174, 176, 178, 179, 180, 181, 184, 185, 186, 206, 209, 226, 229, 234, 239, 241

heating costs, 67, 90, 121
HEXACO-PI, 192
hierarchical linear modeling, 216
home office, 10, 28, 31, 41, 43, 48, 49, 50, 51, 93, 137, 141, 143, 144, 145, 147, 149, 150, 154, 156, 173, 181, 182, 192, 197, 204, 221, 238, 240
home office equipment, 31, 143, 182
hotelling, 29, 31, 91
HP, 93
HR operations, 218
human resource, 9, 177, 230, 248, 250, 251

IBM, 37, 44, 45, 47, 93
ICT, 2, 3, 11, 21, 26, 27, 28, 30, 31, 40, 44, 47, 48, 53, 55, 68, 152, 161, 180, 197, 199, 204, 218, 230, 238, 239, 245, 247
illness, 32, 40, 105, 106, 146, 203
incentives and disincentives, 11, 168, 170, 172, 173, 183, 186, 240
India, 234
information workers, 59, 130
infrastructure, 11, 69, 80, 103, 154, 160, 168, 169, 170, 172, 173, 175, 180, 181, 186, 230, 233, 234, 240
InnoVisions, 2, 4, 17, 33, 70, 187, 232, 247, 248
insurance, 49, 50, 94, 107, 138, 146, 147, 156, 160
integrative value proposition, 5, 15, 22, 31, 36, 45, 55, 66, 69, 71
Intel, 93
Internet, 4, 26, 30, 144, 146, 156, 180, 231, 244
interruptions, 23, 27, 41, 44, 142, 148, 149, 220
intranets, 70, 144
isolated, 18, 41, 140, 149, 162, 208

isolation, 16, 19, 24, 25, 41, 42, 139,
    140, 149, 150, 156, 161, 167, 170,
    174, 179, 185, 196, 200, 221, 222,
    240, 243

Japan, 233, 249, 252
job design, 19, 39
job flexibility, 6, 207, 244
job opportunities, 10, 14, 53, 68, 69,
    71, 113, 198, 205, 219
job satisfaction, 15, 16, 18, 23, 43, 68,
    191, 192, 198, 199, 201, 210, 212,
    213, 248
job stress, 32, 33, 35, 139, 205, 251
job tenure, 195, 216

KPMG, 236, 248
Kyoto, 50, 96, 168

labour laws, 51, 181
labour legislation, 49, 50
latchkey, 69, 72
latent demand, 53, 54, 56, 59, 62, 63,
    64, 66, 67, 71, 108, 111, 112, 121
leading by example, 11, 168, 170, 172,
    173, 178, 179, 186, 240
legal framework, 181
life balance, 10, 32, 33, 34, 35, 45, 100,
    148, 149, 155, 170, 220, 234, 246
London, 5, 246, 249, 253
Los Angeles, 46, 56, 72, 117, 250, 254

management by objectives, 24, 43, 248
managers, 11, 12, 23, 24, 41, 42, 43, 44,
    45, 47, 48, 74, 91, 108, 142, 149,
    151, 152, 153, 155, 156, 158, 161,
    166, 177, 184, 192, 193, 215, 216,
    220, 221, 222, 239, 250
Manifest Needs Questionnaire, 192,
    207
mass transit, 10, 14, 53, 54, 55, 67, 71,
    99, 100, 104, 112, 127, 128, 129,
    130, 131, 132, 133, 155, 180, 249
mayors, 12
mentoring, 20, 21, 25, 40, 42, 197, 203,
    218
MERCs, 19, 95, 96, 99, 100
Minnesota, 60, 61, 254
modal splits, 53, 71
monetary savings, 113, 117, 119, 120,

    121, 124, 125, 126, 128, 130, 131,
    133
moral support, 11, 168, 170, 172, 186,
    240
Motorola, 93

need for achievement, 139, 207, 208,
    209, 210, 212
need for dominance, 207, 208, 212
negative telework impacts, 20, 25, 30,
    39, 41, 47, 50, 198, 200, 218, 220,
    227
Netherlands, 57, 61, 62, 68, 108, 181,
    233, 245, 252
neutral telework impacts, 18, 22, 29,
    34, 38, 47,
New York, 5, 70, 182, 244, 245, 249,
    250, 252
noise pollution, 10, 14, 53, 112, 120,
    133
non-commuting trips, 61, 62
Nortel, 47, 93, 250

Occupational Safety and Health
    Administration, 51
office environments, 24, 29, 226, 250
office equipment, 31, 70, 91, 143, 182
office network, 40
Office of Personnel Management, 146,
    179, 226, 250
office space, 27, 29, 31, 37, 44, 45, 46,
    90, 91, 92, 93, 101, 106, 142, 159,
    240
Olympic Games, 56
operational continuity, 10, 14, 29, 53,
    68, 70, 71, 236
operational HR issues, 9, 11, 14, 20,
    21, 36, 40, 41, 200, 202, 206, 218,
    223, 225
operational resilience, 70
opportunism, 171, 172, 174, 175, 180,
    181, 183, 184, 185, 186
organization's efficiency, 14, 27, 197,
    200, 206, 216, 219
organizational efficiency, 9, 14, 15, 27,
    28, 36, 44, 203, 206, 218
organizational impacts of telework,
    200, 201, 205
organizational tenure, 192, 195, 196,
    213

out of sight, 21, 24, 42, 43, 44, 156
output-oriented, 16, 19
overhead expenses, 45

part-time, 2, 5, 18, 20, 29, 31, 37, 39,
    42, 45, 51, 61, 63, 64, 92, 93, 108,
    144, 146, 152, 219, 234, 239
peak hours, 56, 57, 61, 62, 63, 67, 128,
    129, 130, 131
peak shift, 237
peak shifting, 2, 68
peak times, 45, 56
penetration level, 56, 65, 66, 71, 102,
    113, 117, 119, 120, 121, 124, 144,
    181, 226, 231, 233, 234, 237
perceived telework impact, 11, 137,
    198, 199, 208, 210, 213, 219, 225,
    227, 232
perceptions of telework, 11, 137, 198,
    199, 208, 210, 213, 219, 225, 227,
    232
performance, 5, 6, 7, 13, 18, 20, 21, 22,
    24, 25, 26, 38, 40, 41, 42, 43, 44,
    46, 68, 101, 139, 140, 142, 146,
    148, 151, 158, 159, 162, 163, 178,
    192, 199, 203, 212, 213, 215, 218,
    226, 239, 242, 244, 247, 251
policy analysis, 168, 169, 170, 171, 172,
    173, 240
policymakers, 10, 12, 73, 74, 170, 171,
    172, 174, 176, 181, 183, 185, 186,
    190, 198, 201, 236
pollutants, 99, 100, 114, 116
pollution reduction, 102
Portuguese, 141
positive telework impacts, 16, 22, 27,
    31, 33, 35, 37, 40, 44, 49, 190, 197
potential effectiveness, 104, 171, 172,
    174, 176, 178, 180, 181, 183, 184,
    186, 200
primary data, 11, 12, 213, 215
privacy, 51, 78, 90
procedural effectiveness, 171, 172, 174,
    175 176, 178, 179, 180, 181, 183,
    184, 186, 240
productivity, 3, 5, 6, 14, 26, 27, 28, 29,
    36, 38, 40, 41, 44, 45, 46, 68, 71,
    102, 113, 126, 127, 128, 140, 148,
    151, 159, 162, 164, 170, 180, 199,
    204, 215, 220, 221, 230, 233, 249

promotion, 16, 19, 20, 40, 41, 42, 80,
    176, 197, 203, 221
promotional opportunities, 16, 19
public policies, 102, 136, 168
public policy, 4, 11, 53, 168, 234,
    245
public transport, 59, 60, 61, 111
Puget Sound, 57, 61, 65, 115, 116, 117,
    122, 123, 124, 246
PWGSC, 91, 92, 138, 144, 145, 147,
    149, 152, 153, 154, 155, 156, 177,
    251

quality of life, 32, 34, 67, 69, 71, 79,
    130, 220
quality work, 68

real effectiveness, 171, 174, 176, 178,
    179, 185
recruit, 37
recruiting, 16, 37, 219
recruitment, 5, 68, 159
regression analysis, 192
regulatory, 96, 173, 175, 181, 183, 232,
    236, 240, 249
relocation, 17
residential relocation, 53, 54, 63, 71,
    108, 111, 112
retention, 5, 37, 38, 41, 68, 151, 154,
    155, 159, 215, 218, 219
risk mitigation, 220
road accidents, 10, 14, 53, 66, 112, 119,
    120, 133, 244
road congestion, 10, 14, 53, 54, 56, 66,
    67, 112, 113, 133, 155, 184
road construction, 10, 14, 53, 54, 67,
    71, 112, 124, 125, 126, 127, 133
road maintenance, 14, 53, 54, 67, 104,
    112, 133
road pricing, 184, 243
robotics, 238
rush hour, 33, 66

San Diego, 57, 60, 63, 242
satellite office, 2, 42, 56, 72, 154, 155
satellite offices, 72, 111, 154, 155
saturation levels, 228, 229, 234
schedule, 2, 24, 25, 27, 30, 43, 44, 48,
    61, 139, 141, 147, 149, 158, 231,
    254

scheduling meetings, 27, 28, 30, 44, 47, 48, 197, 204, 218, 221
security, 18, 27, 28 30, 43, 44, 48, 96, 97, 147, 152, 154, 156, 157, 166, 183, 199, 204, 218, 221
self-assessment, 10, 137, 138, 141, 143, 145, 147, 151, 153, 249
self-employed, 105
share knowledge, 16
shared values, 29, 39, 142, 153, 162, 165, 196
skill development, 25
SmartSpace, 29
social contact, 40, 41, 218, 220
social responsibility, 6
socialization, 10, 39, 148, 149
societal structures, 229, 230
society, 3, 5, 11, 36, 41, 45, 50, 52, 77, 101, 168, 174, 226, 230, 231, 234, 239, 240, 246, 250, 253, 254
Southampton, 56, 57, 58
Spain, 45, 244
spillover effects, 10, 102
stakeholder, 5, 8, 9, 31, 71, 204, 236
stakeholders, 3, 4, 5, 6, 7, 8, 9, 11, 12, 13, 14, 15, 22, 31, 32, 36, 49, 136, 173, 178, 186, 200, 204, 216, 219, 225, 239
statistics, 59, 69, 105, 106, 192, 200, 216, 231, 253
strategic HR factors, 11, 219
strategic HR issues, 14, 36, 37, 215, 218
strategic management, 6, 7
suburban, 55, 91
subway, 59
Sun Microsystems, 46
supervision, 24, 72, 78, 139, 140, 141, 220, 221
support for telework, 11, 168, 170, 186, 222
support staff, 227
survey results, 11, 177, 187, 191, 220, 242
Sweden, 60, 154, 181, 233, 252
swing office space, 91, 92

tacit, 20, 196
tacit knowledge, 16, 20, 39, 40
tangible benefits of telework, 5
tax, 11, 47, 138, 147, 156, 161, 168,

170, 172, 173, 175, 181, 182, 183, 186, 240
taxation, 50, 181, 182
teamwork, 17, 27, 28, 29, 30, 38, 44, 47, 159, 162, 163, 164, 165, 167, 198, 199, 204, 218
technical support, 26, 30, 48
technology, 1, 2, 4, 12, 31, 48, 69, 78, 90, 152, 154, 156, 157, 159, 160, 162, 174, 203, 218, 221, 230, 238, 242, 243, 245, 251, 254
telecommuter, 12, 115, 182, 243, 244, 251
telecottages, 154
telephone, 3, 4, 20, 23, 24, 58, 59, 138, 140, 143, 144, 145, 147, 148, 152, 156, 161, 165, 166
TeleProfiler, 153
teleTRAC, 94, 95, 102
Teletrips, 10, 74, 77, 79, 80, 81, 83, 85, 86, 88, 89, 95, 96, 97, 98, 99, 100, 101, 102, 103, 104
telework benefits, 22, 45, 53, 101
telework centre, 2, 29, 42, 56, 72, 86, 111, 121, 154
Telework Coalition, 181, 182, 253
telework committee, 158
Telework Consultants International, 149
telework consulting, 79, 145
telework drivers, 235
telework frequency, 81, 108, 133, 191, 210, 211, 212, 213, 223
Telework Impact Estimation Tool, 79
telework penetration, 10, 56, 73, 89, 102, 121, 177, 181, 215, 216, 223, 224, 226, 227, 228, 229, 231, 232, 234, 240
telework policies, 48, 89, 136, 148, 157, 158, 166, 170, 178, 179, 222, 226, 230, 238, 240
telework procedures, 145, 146, 148, 158, 240
temporary employees, 227
terrorist, 46, 70, 236
time-management, 148
traffic congestion, 46, 61, 66, 159
training, 21, 25, 40, 41, 42, 43, 142, 147, 158, 161, 164, 166, 181, 197, 203, 218, 220

training opportunities, 21, 25, 42
Transport Canada, 154, 157, 161, 177, 253
transport economists, 12
transportation policy, 53
trust, 29, 39, 90, 142, 153, 162, 165, 196, 199, 203, 221, 246, 247, 254

UK, 57, 68, 108, 154, 176, 244, 245, 246, 252, 253
unions, 38, 49, 51, 219
United States, 50, 56, 58, 66, 108, 111, 121, 177, 178, 232, 244, 249, 251
University of Calgary, 238
US, 3, 4, 17, 38, 47, 50, 51, 57, 60, 72, 94, 99, 103, 116, 130, 147, 178, 179, 180, 181, 182, 183, 184, 231, 232, 233, 234, 237, 241, 243, 244, 246, 247, 250

vehicle trips, 54, 55, 56, 63, 64, 65, 71, 105
vehicle-kilometres, 54, 56, 57, 59, 63, 64, 65, 71, 72, 108, 110, 111, 112, 113, 114, 115, 116, 119, 120, 121, 124, 125, 126, 127

videoconference, 20, 30
videoconferencing, 2, 58, 59, 144, 152, 161, 165, 238
virtual leadership, 159, 163, 164, 167
virtual meetings, 30, 90, 164, 167
virtual organizations, 1, 244, 248
virtual teams, 11, 29, 47, 48, 136, 151, 159, 161, 162, 163, 164, 165, 166, 167, 240, 242, 243, 244, 245, 247, 253, 254
virtual work, 1, 2, 3, 20, 21, 30, 137, 164, 166, 238, 251
virtual workplace growth, 170, 181, 187
voice mail, 26
volatile organic compounds, 65, 114

Washington, 4, 70, 117, 244, 247, 250, 253
work experience, 11, 192, 193, 195, 196, 209, 210, 213
workaholic, 143
working from home, 22, 23, 138, 142, 149, 180, 221, 232